The Campus History Series

IDAHO STATE UNIVERSITY

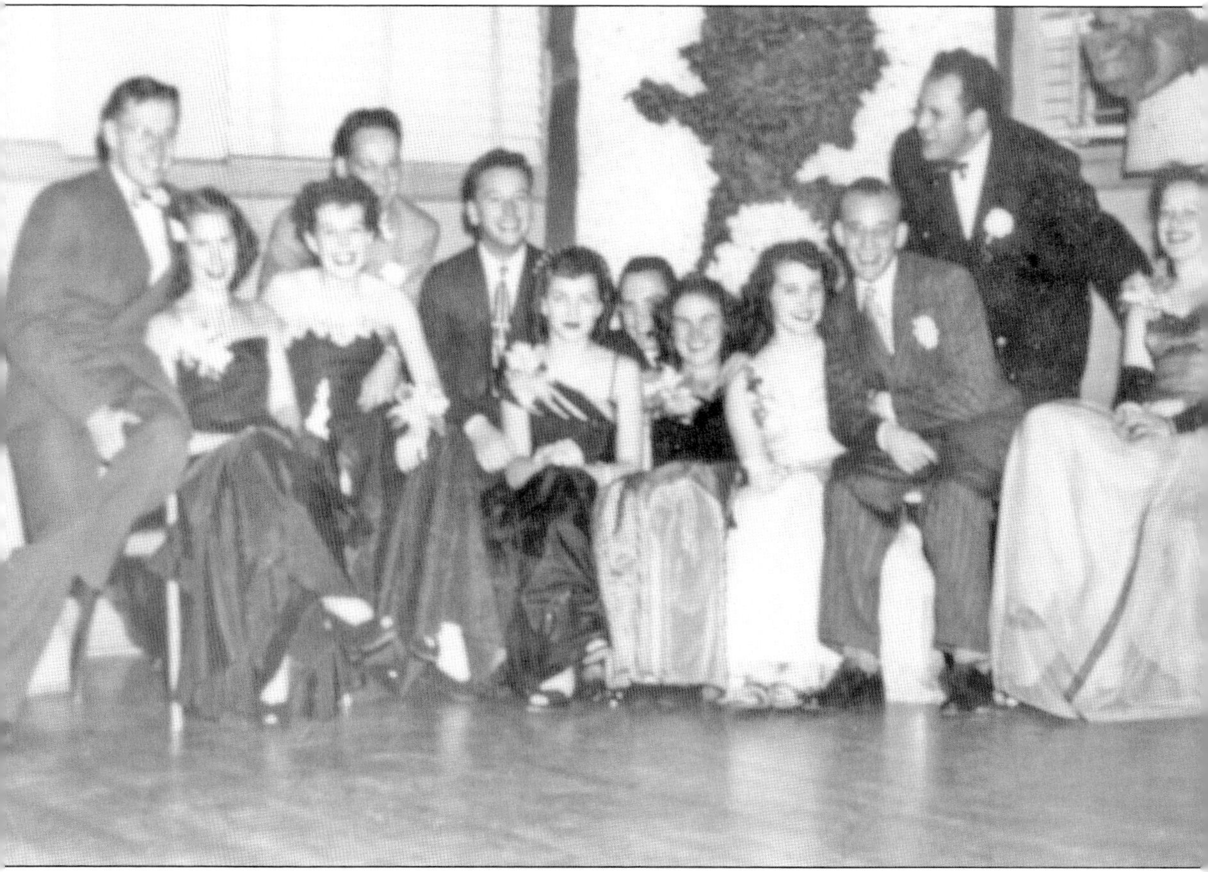

TWIRP Week, when "The Woman Is Required to Pay," was a fun annual tradition that continued at Idaho State University (ISU) into the 1960s and 1970s. Sponsored by the Associated Women Students, for the entire week, the female students were required to carry the men's books and buy them drinks in the student union building. At the end of the week, they would invite one of the men to the Sweetheart formal (pictured here). Louis Armstrong even performed at the annual affair in 1964. The night concluded with the annual Dream Man contest. The sororities and various women's floors would nominate several guys, and one lucky winner would be awarded the crown and title at the Sweetheart formal. (Courtesy of the Historic Photographs Collection in the Department of Special Collections at Eli M. Oboler Library, Idaho State University.)

On the Cover: In 1963, after strong advocacy from students, faculty, staff, legislators, and community members, the state legislature officially granted Idaho State College the status of a full university. Students celebrated the occasion by hanging up the new name over the "Idaho State College" sign on the campus library. Idaho State had officially grown up, and it was students who led the charge. (Courtesy of the Historic Photographs Collection in the Department of Special Collections at Eli M. Oboler Library, Idaho State University.)

The Campus History Series

IDAHO STATE UNIVERSITY

ISU MANAGEMENT 4499/5599 HONORS CLASS

KAITLYN BARKLEY, KITANNA BELNAP, MARIA KELLER,
JENNA LARSON, KIRK LONG, KRISTINE MCCARTY,
MELISSA MYERS, AND JORDAN WITHERS

ARCADIA PUBLISHING

ISBN 978-1-4671-2551-2

Published by Arcadia Publishing
Charleston, South Carolina

Printed in the United States of America

Library of Congress Control Number: Applied for

For all general information, please contact Arcadia Publishing:
Telephone 843-853-2070
Fax 843-853-0044
E-mail sales@arcadiapublishing.com
For customer service and orders:
Toll-Free 1-888-313-2665

Visit us on the Internet at www.arcadiapublishing.com

This book is dedicated to the students, current and alumni, over the 115 years of Idaho State University's history. Idaho State University could not have existed without the support of legislators, community leaders, faculty and staff, and the citizens of Idaho. However, it was (and remains) the students who give ISU its heart and soul. This is their story.

CONTENTS

ACKNOWLEDGMENTS

We wish to thank Bruce Nelson and the College of Business Leadership Board at Idaho State University for sponsoring and providing ongoing encouragement to this project. We are deeply indebted to Keith Smith, Dr. Ron Hatzenbuehler, Patty Bolinger, Lincoln Yamashita, Scott Turner, and many other alumni, current and former faculty, and friends who shared their experiences from Idaho State University. Thank you to K.C. Felt and Ryan Sargent of the ISU Alumni Association for meeting with us and sharing great stories. Thanks also go out to Dean Tom Ottaway, Mark Arstein, Debra Gerber, Michele O'Brien-Rose, Heidi Wadsworth, John Ney, and many others for their encouragement and great ideas. Many thanks to Dr. Sherri Dienstfrey-Swanson and Dr. Jamie Romine-Gabardi of the University Honors Program, as well as Ellen M. Ryan of Special Collections at Oboler Library, who gave up many (or most) of her Wednesday afternoons to open Special Collections for our research and scanned innumerable photographs from ISU's enormous collection. We also thank Gail Hunt for organizing the end-of-semester celebration (a "book signing before the books") and Kelsey West for creating the publicity materials for that event.

Thank you to Chris Gabettas in marketing and publicity at Idaho State University for helping to publicize this class and our activities, as well as Eric Gordon, who took photographs of our class. Special thanks go out to our editors, Jeff Ruetsche and Mike Kinsella at Arcadia Publishing, for their help and support. To those not named here who supported this project in ways big and small, direct and indirect, we thank you—this book would not have been possible without you.

Unless otherwise noted, all photographs are courtesy of the Historic Photographs Collection in the Department of Special Collections at Eli M. Oboler Library on the campus of Idaho State University.

INTRODUCTION

What is now Idaho State University began with a humble vision to satisfy the need for post-secondary education in a sparsely populated, blue-collar railroad town in a remote corner of the sprawling frontier of the United States' Intermountain West. The first miracle of ISU's existence was that the Idaho state legislature would grant a charter to a new college in a state with little population and one already-existing land-grant institution: the University of Idaho. As you will learn in the following pages, ISU underwent a rocky first six decades that included at least two "near-death" experiences (as students exited en masse to enlist in the military during World Wars I and II) and a spirited fight led by students to expand the institution into a four-year school and, eventually, a university.

The backstory of how this book came to be is almost as unlikely as the story of ISU itself. In early 2016, I received permission to teach a unique class that combined graduate and undergraduate students from a variety of majors, backgrounds, and ages. In honor of the 115th anniversary of Idaho State University's founding, I drafted a proposal for a class that would meet two goals. The first goal was to research and write about the history of ISU with particular attention from the perspective of its students. The second goal was to provide a hands-on, real-life opportunity for students to grasp the challenges of working in teams on an intensive, creative project. In addition to writing the book, our class studied Pixar Animation (per Ed Catmull's recent best-selling book, *Creativity, Inc.*) as an exemplar of managing the tensions of collaborative creativity. We talked about what it means to build a climate where individuals feel safe and invested enough to take creative risks and to be held accountable for completing their work and speaking candidly to make the project better.

This class could not have happened without the substantial commitment of Ellen Ryan and the Special Collections department at Oboler Library at ISU. Ryan provided expert guidance, access to over 100,000 photographs, documents, and other artifacts of ISU's history, and innumerable hours scanning images from the archives. Our class also benefited enormously from the sponsorship of the College of Business's administrative team and Leadership Board. I am grateful to work for a program that supports opportunities for ISU students to develop their skills with working in teams and productively managing conflict—so-called "soft skills" that employers are looking for and set employees up for success in the workplace.

Arcadia Publishing took a risk by signing on to a project with not one or a few, but eight student authors. And those eight students, in turn, signed up for an elective class that was a departure from almost any other they have taken in their educational careers. This entire project has been an act of faith for everyone involved, and I cannot thank them enough for their openness to taking on the challenge. Finally, taking on a project as ambitious as asking a class to write a book in one semester requires outside support and encouragement. My parents, Ron and Patty Bolinger, believed in this idea from the beginning and provided financial backing and invaluable encouragement.

We wish to emphasize that the scope of this book precludes us from exhaustively cataloguing every aspect of ISU's history. Instead, the purpose of this book is to give the reader a taste, from the perspective of current students, for how ISU began, how it has changed, and how it has become the institution it is today. With that in mind, the structure of this book captures a sampling of various facets of the student experience at ISU. Chapter one establishes the framework of the book by describing the early years of ISU's history, from its first class in 1901 as the Academy of Idaho until it attained full university status in 1963. The chapters that follow then describe various themes around the student experience at ISU. Chapter two discusses academics, Chapter three describes the many dimensions of the university's student life, Chapter four describes ISU's athletic history, and Chapter five chronicles the campus's buildings, old and new. Chapter six concludes the book with a look at ISU since 1980 and what the campus looks like today.

I hope that you enjoy this sampling from the vast pictorial archives of Idaho State University and that you find inspiration for what is possible from this university's unlikely story.

—Alex Bolinger
Associate Professor of Management
Idaho State University, Pocatello

One

Early Years

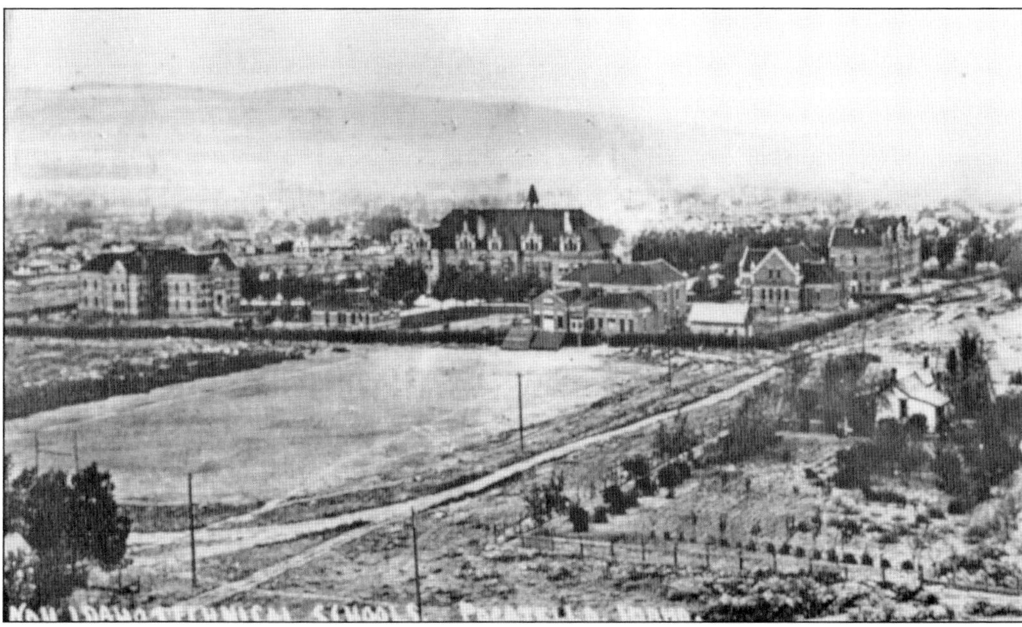

A public university founded 115 years ago in 1901 as the Academy of Idaho, Idaho State University started as a "working man and women's college." Faced with adversity from its earliest years, Idaho State University has endured four name changes, two world wars, and the fluctuating economic fortunes of its community. Yet, Idaho State University has persevered through hardships and successes as the spirit of its students, faculty, staff, and community fought with determination and dedication to make access to higher education a reality as a beacon of opportunity and a cornerstone of Eastern Idaho.

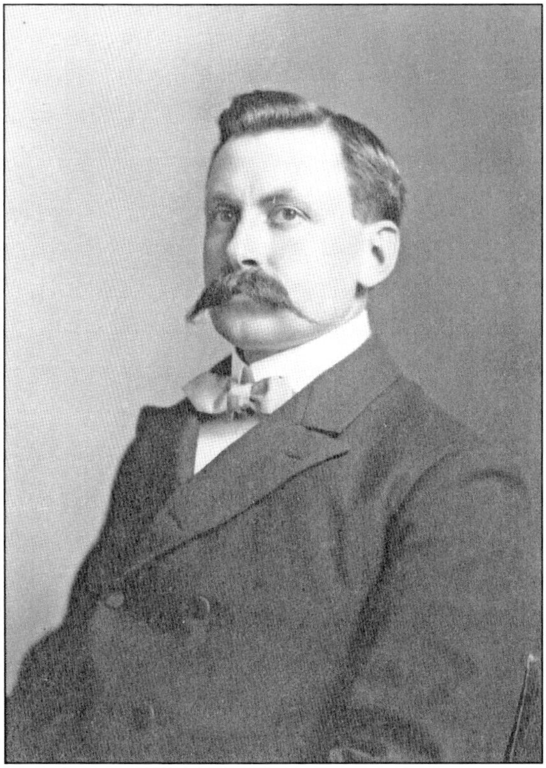

Idaho state senator and Pocatello mayor Theodore F. Turner, "Father of Idaho State University," proposed to establish a people's school after pondering the educational needs of Southeast Idaho. Mayor Turner drafted Senate Bill No. 53, forming the Academy of Idaho, with college preparatory education and vocational training in business and mechanical arts to give all elements of society an opportunity at higher learning in Pocatello.

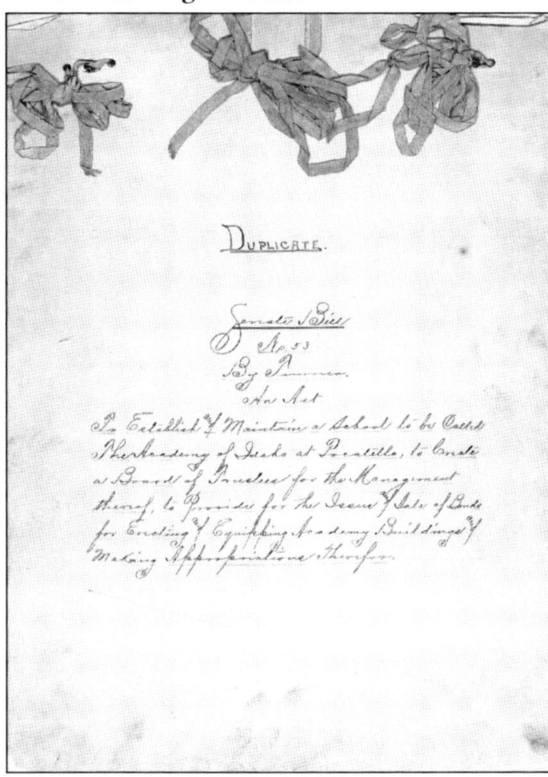

DUPLICATE.

Senate Bill
No. 53
By Turner.
An Act
To Establish & Maintain a School to be Called The Academy of Idaho at Pocatello, to Create a Board of Trustees for the Management thereof, to Provide for the Issue & Sale of Bonds for Erecting & Equipping Academy Buildings & Making Appropriations Therefor.

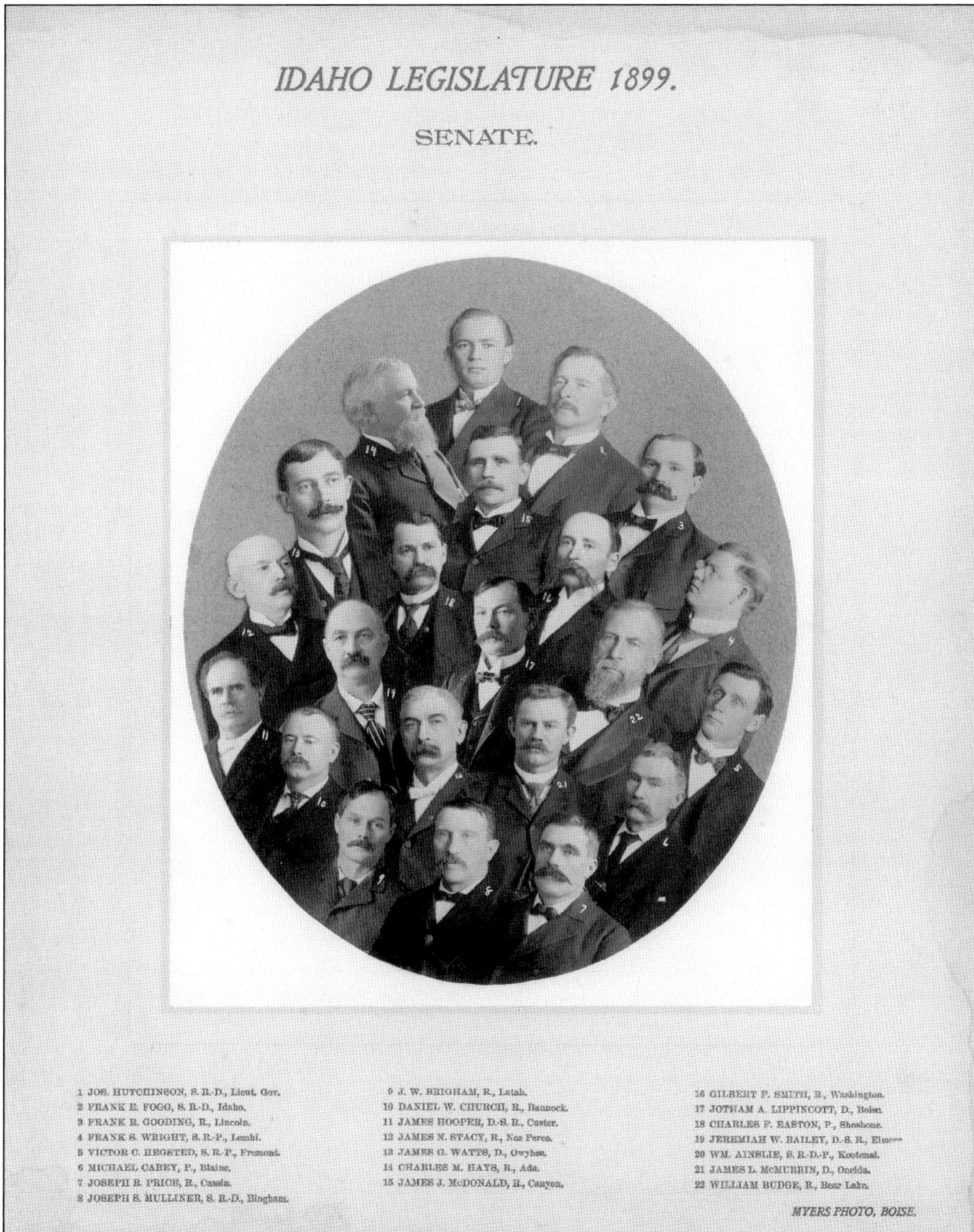

On February 25, 1901, Senate Bill No. 53 was passed unanimously by the Idaho legislature and signed by Gov. Frank W. Hunt on March 11, 1901. Shortly after, a six member, nonpartisan board of trustees was appointed for the management and control of the Academy of Idaho. The establishment of the academy was contingent upon private land donations by the citizens of Pocatello but allowed the appropriation from sale of bonds to erect and equip buildings. According to Merrill Beal's 1952 *History of Idaho State College*, "this was one of the easiest legislative victories the school was destined to experience in its first 50 years."

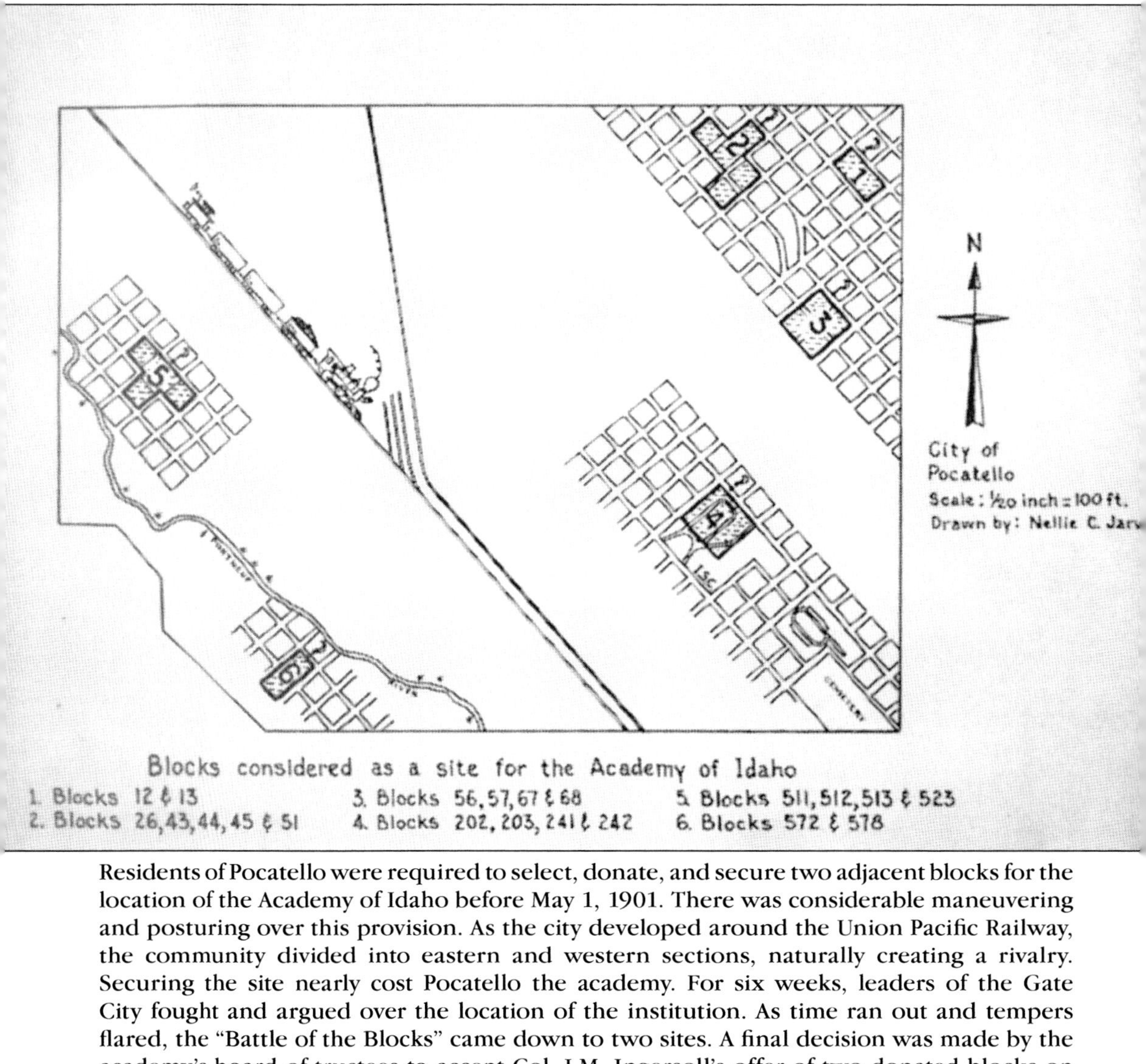

Residents of Pocatello were required to select, donate, and secure two adjacent blocks for the location of the Academy of Idaho before May 1, 1901. There was considerable maneuvering and posturing over this provision. As the city developed around the Union Pacific Railway, the community divided into eastern and western sections, naturally creating a rivalry. Securing the site nearly cost Pocatello the academy. For six weeks, leaders of the Gate City fought and argued over the location of the institution. As time ran out and tempers flared, the "Battle of the Blocks" came down to two sites. A final decision was made by the academy's board of trustees to accept Col. J.M. Ingersoll's offer of two donated blocks on the east side and to purchase two additional adjacent blocks, an 8.5-acre tract, for $1,200.

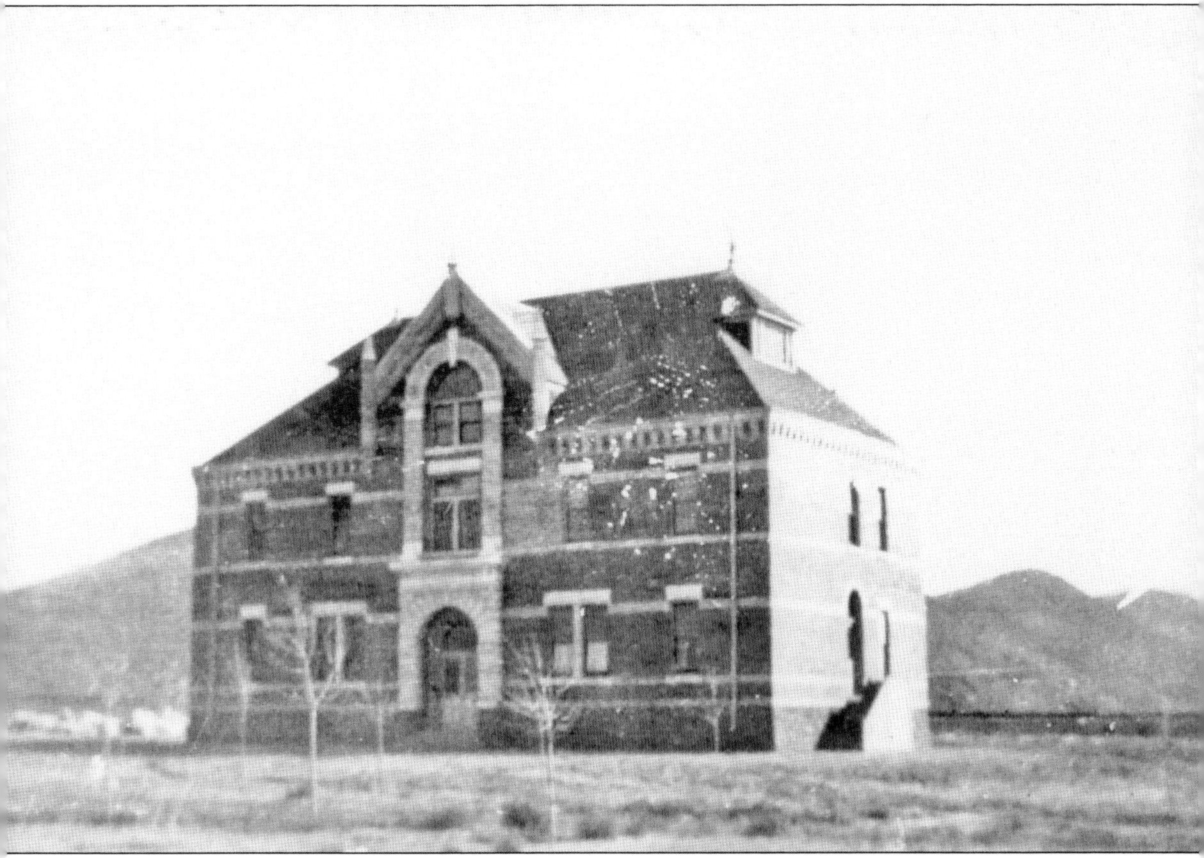

Following the contentious Battle of the Blocks, the Academy of Idaho Board of Trustees commenced operations to build a three-story Main Building, later called Swanson Hall, and a boys' dormitory (Faris Hall). On September 22, 1902, at the opening bell, there were 40 students and four teachers. A total of 70 students were enrolled during the term. There was no charge for in-state tuition, though out-of-state students paid $5 per term and $3.50 to $5 a week for room and board.

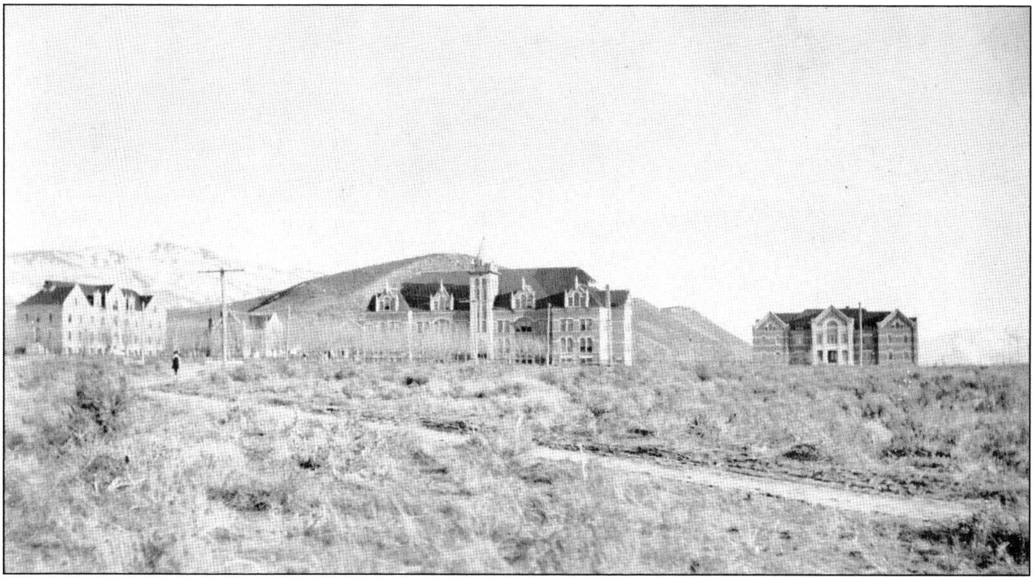

The city council secured streets and alleys belonging to the Academy of Idaho, making a 10-acre tract. The location housing the academy was within easy walking distance from the townsite. Dirt paths cut through the thick sagebrush, but the isolated campus was remote from business and residential areas west of the railroad tracks.

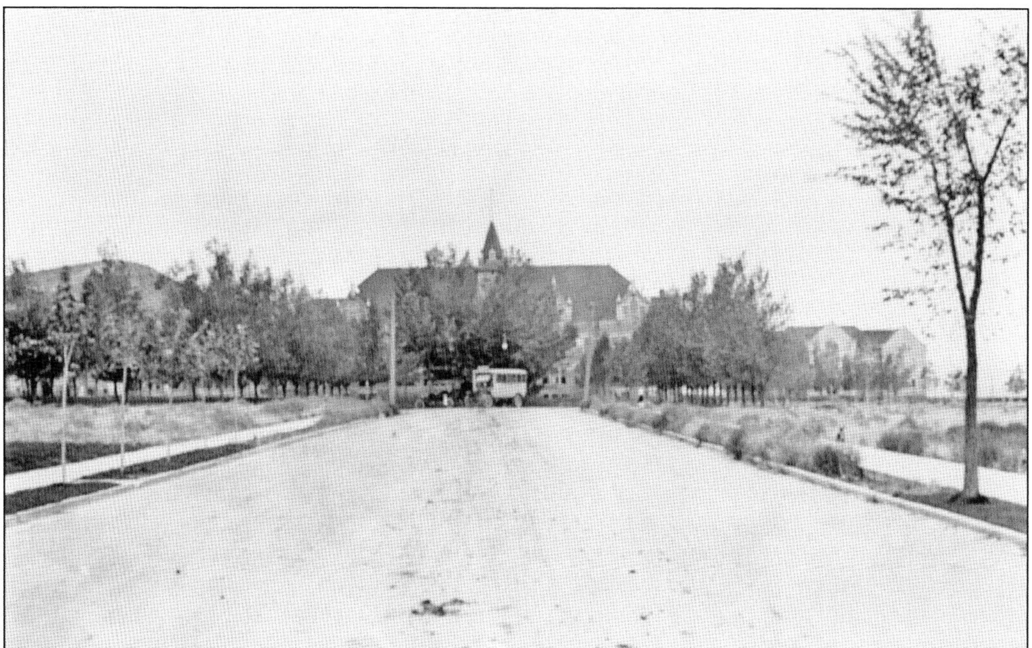

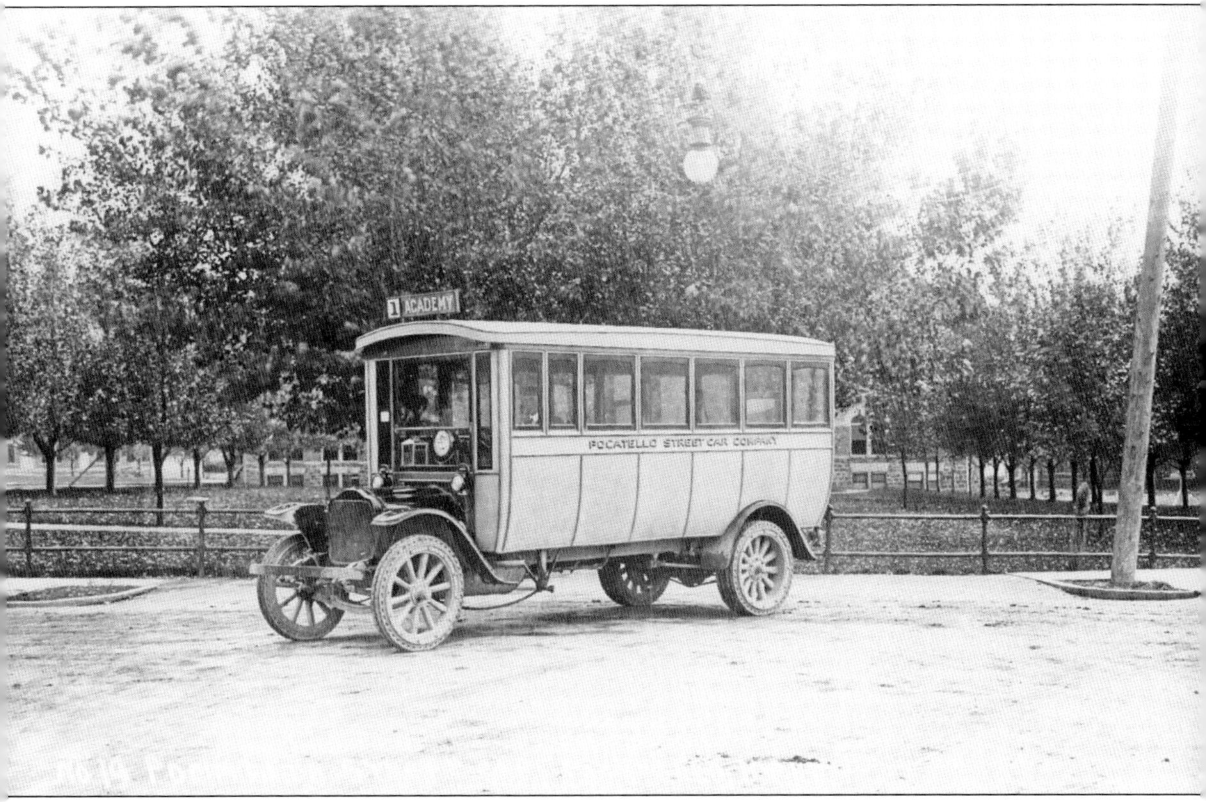

The Pocatello Street Car Company provided a rare motorized transportation option for students, stopping at the Academy of Idaho to pick up and deliver students from the train station and around the city.

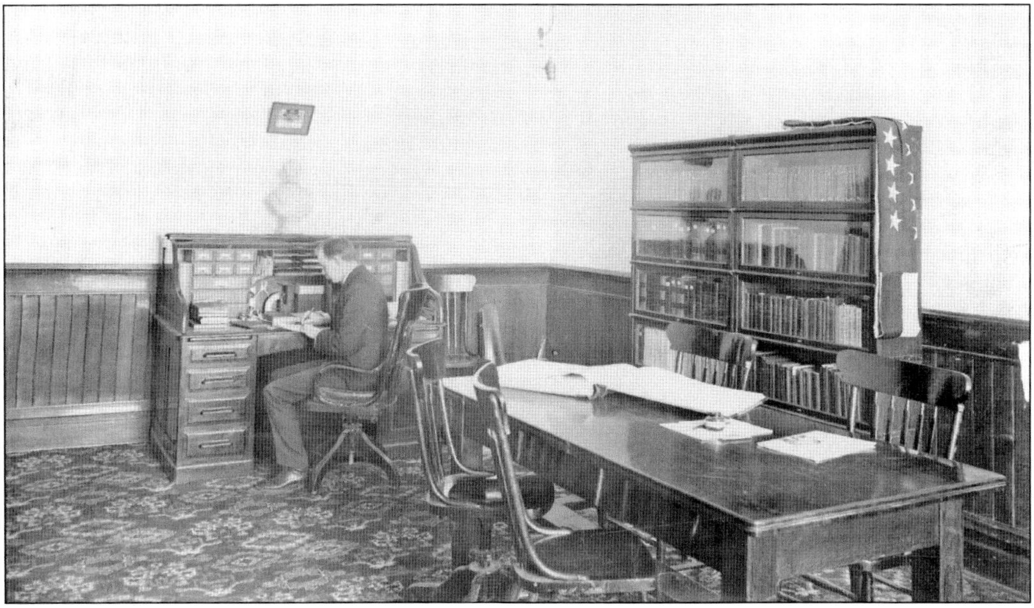

Theodore Swanson, one of the most notable members of the Academy of Idaho Board of Trustees, secured the services of John W. Faris, seen above sitting at the desk, as the first administrator, termed "principal." Admission was restricted to students who had completed the eighth grade or could show ability to do the work. Principal Faris worked aggressively to improve the curriculum and expand preparatory programs to encourage enrollment of "special students" who were deserving of the opportunity by offering nontraditional short, night, and summer courses. Below is the academy's class of 1903–1904.

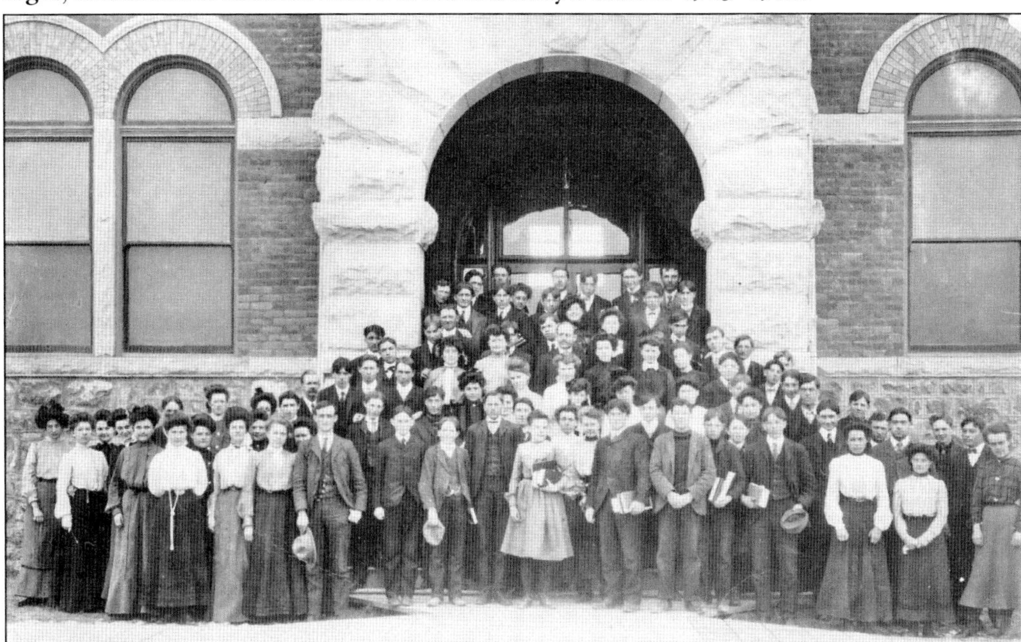

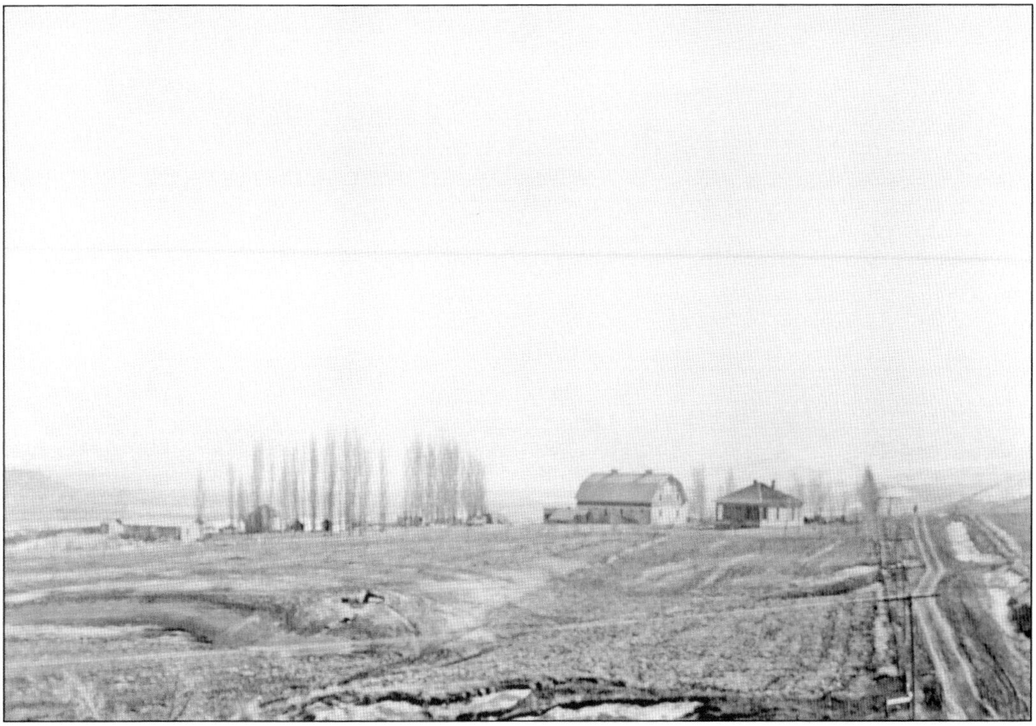

Mayor Theodore Turner, the Academy of Idaho's lifelong associate, gifted a 160-acre farm and barn to the school in 1909, named the Tech Farm. This created the school's Department of Agriculture and allowed students the opportunity to work on the farm and receive basic tractor training. Today, the land is situated south of Pocatello off of Bannock Highway as part of the Riverside Golf Course, with the clubhouse as part of the former barn. By 1910, enrollment reached almost 300 students, and the academy acquired four additional city blocks in Pocatello to help meet the growing demand.

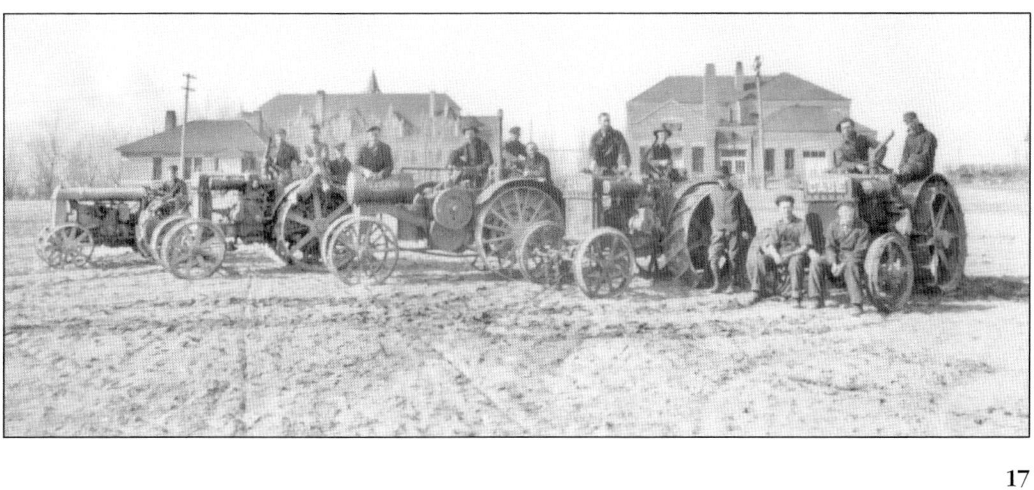

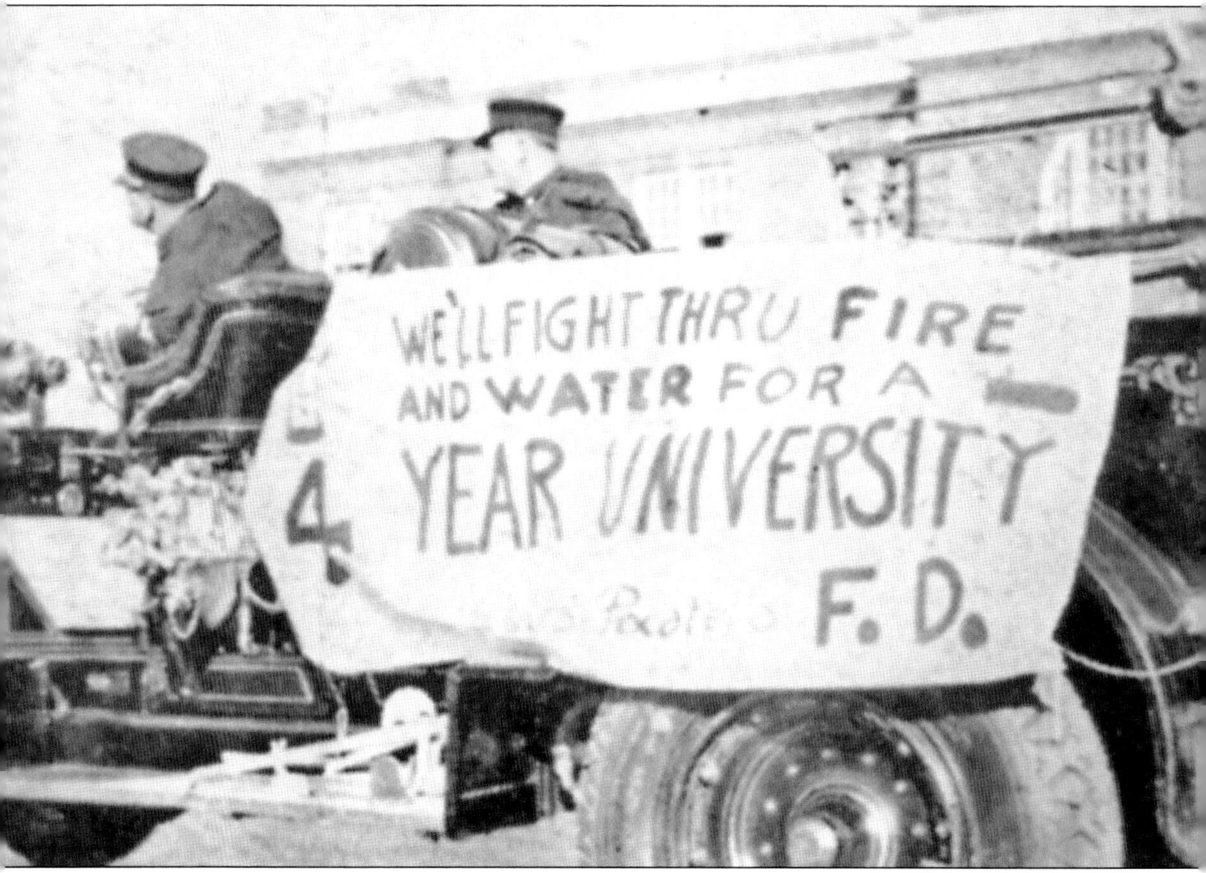

When Miles F. Reed assumed the position of principal—later named president in 1915—he was eager and ambitious to grow the school. Spirited citizens of Pocatello began to campaign to make the Academy of Idaho a four-year college and overcome the stigma of a glorified high school. In 1915, President Reed reported to the Idaho State Board of Education the need for a name change and greater resources for the academy's development and ability to fulfill educational demands. On March 16, 1915, the Idaho legislature partially responded to President Reed's appeal by allowing the name to change to Idaho Technical Institute. The two-year vocational collegiate institute was divided into two schools, the Technical School and the College Preparatory School, or junior college.

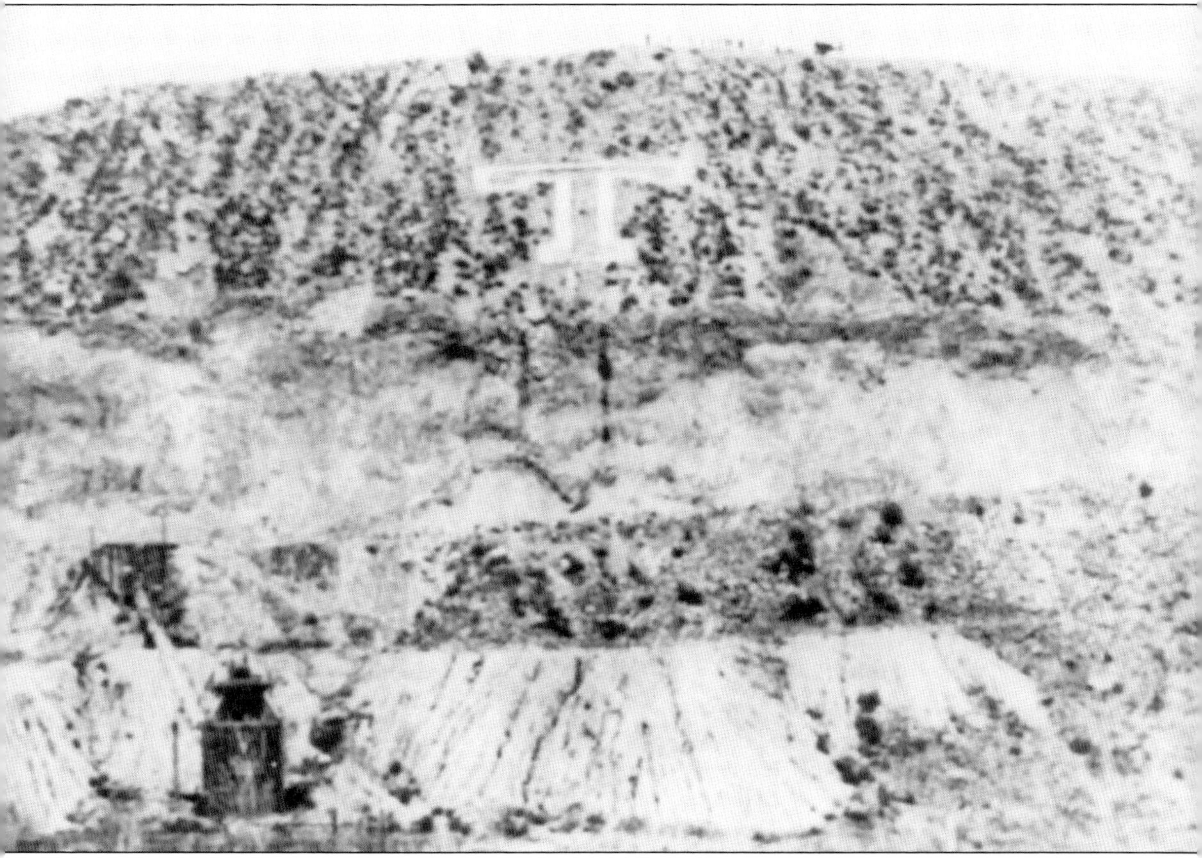

Students set forth to place an everlasting symbol to mark the great Idaho Technical Institute. In 1916, student body president Roy J. Logan held a special student assembly, and in less than 20 minutes, enough funds were collected to construct the letter "T" on the side of Red Hill by the entire student body and faculty later that afternoon. On August 6, 1919, President Reed issued a letter to the mayor and city council petitioning for the preservation of Red Hill, claiming it as "one of the finest landmarks of this community." In 1936, Mayor Turner, whose landholdings in and around the city were numerous, donated Red Hill to Idaho Tech.

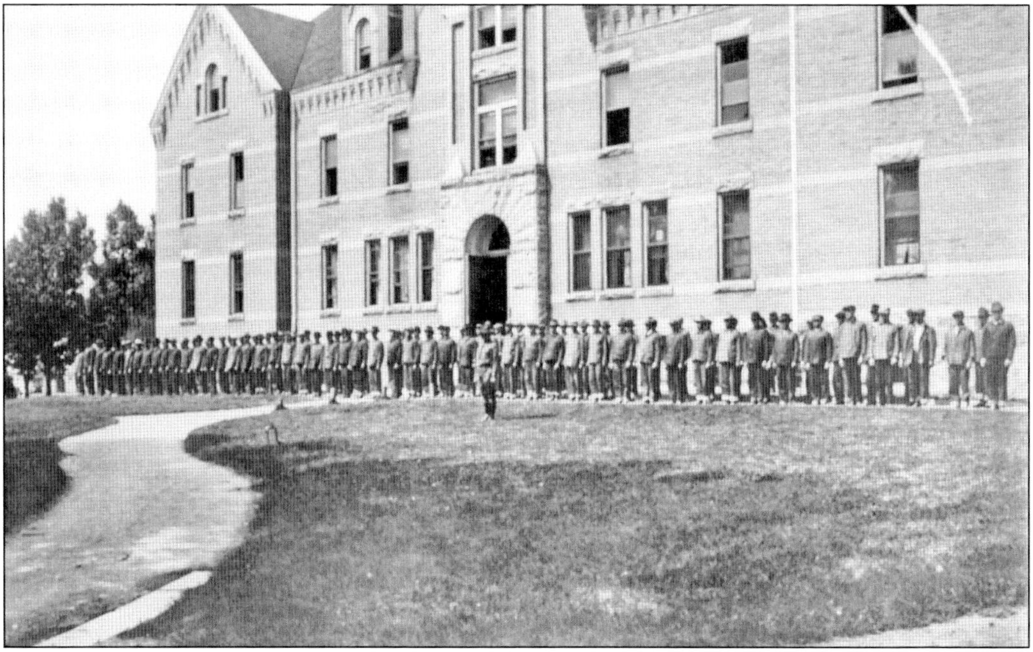

Within a few months of the United States' entry into World War I, student enrollment at the Idaho Technical Institute dropped nearly 50 percent. Without any additional appropriation from the Idaho state legislature and with the sudden, radical loss of students, the young institution struggled to keep its doors open. Idaho Tech was saved by contracting with the federal government to establish a Student Army Training Corps. Summer classes were eliminated, and financial support was reallocated to prepare and train students for the war. Four Idaho Tech students were killed in combat. Years later, a sundial was constructed by the American Legion to stand as a memorial to those who served in World War I, and the cavalry's stable was donated to Idaho Tech.

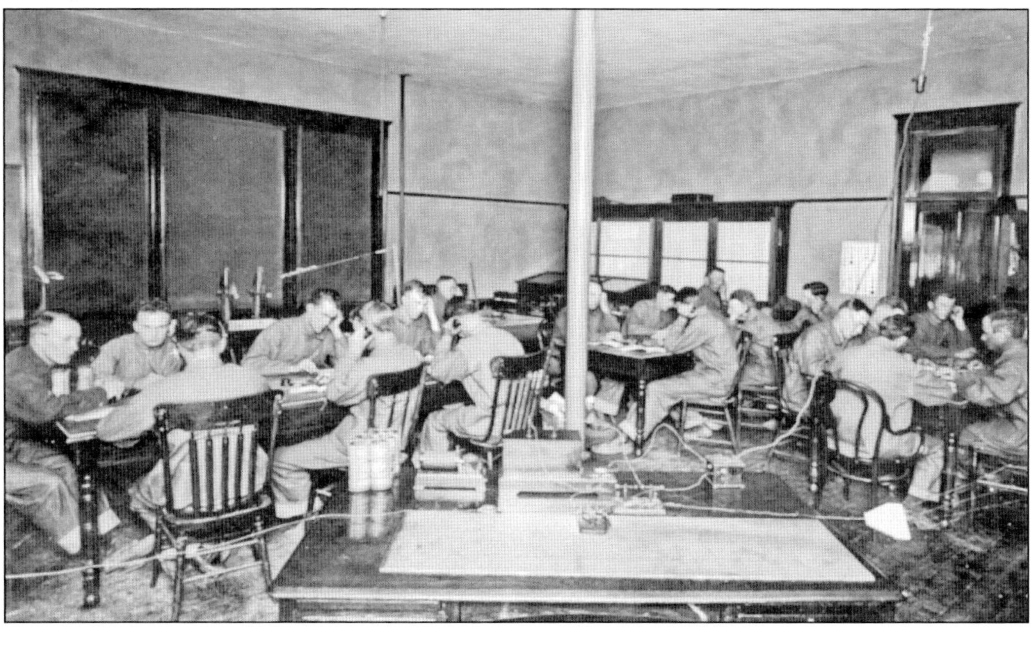

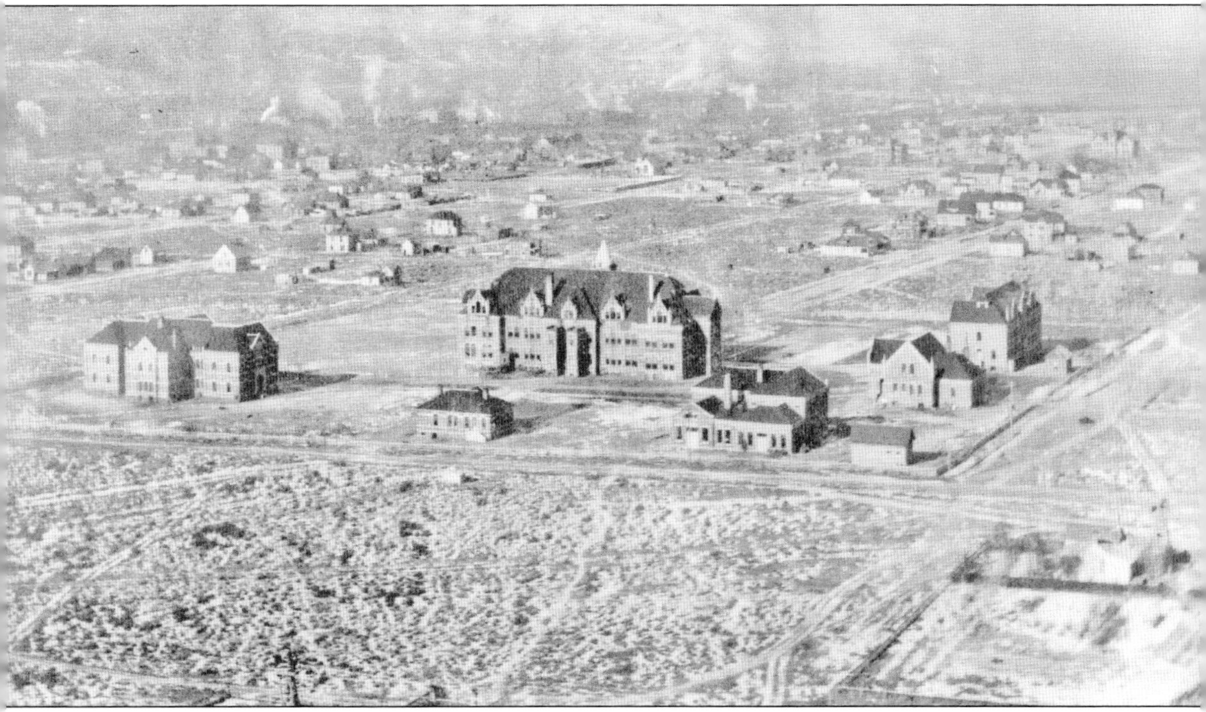

October 1918 proved to be a fateful but prophetic year. The institute closed for several months due to the Spanish flu epidemic. During this time, President Reed suffered a fatal heart attack, placing the Idaho Technical Institute's long-term plans on hold. Shortly after reopening, the institute was affected by dropping commodity prices, which caused banks to close and farms to be repossessed. All nonessential operations and activities were cancelled for the rest of the school year.

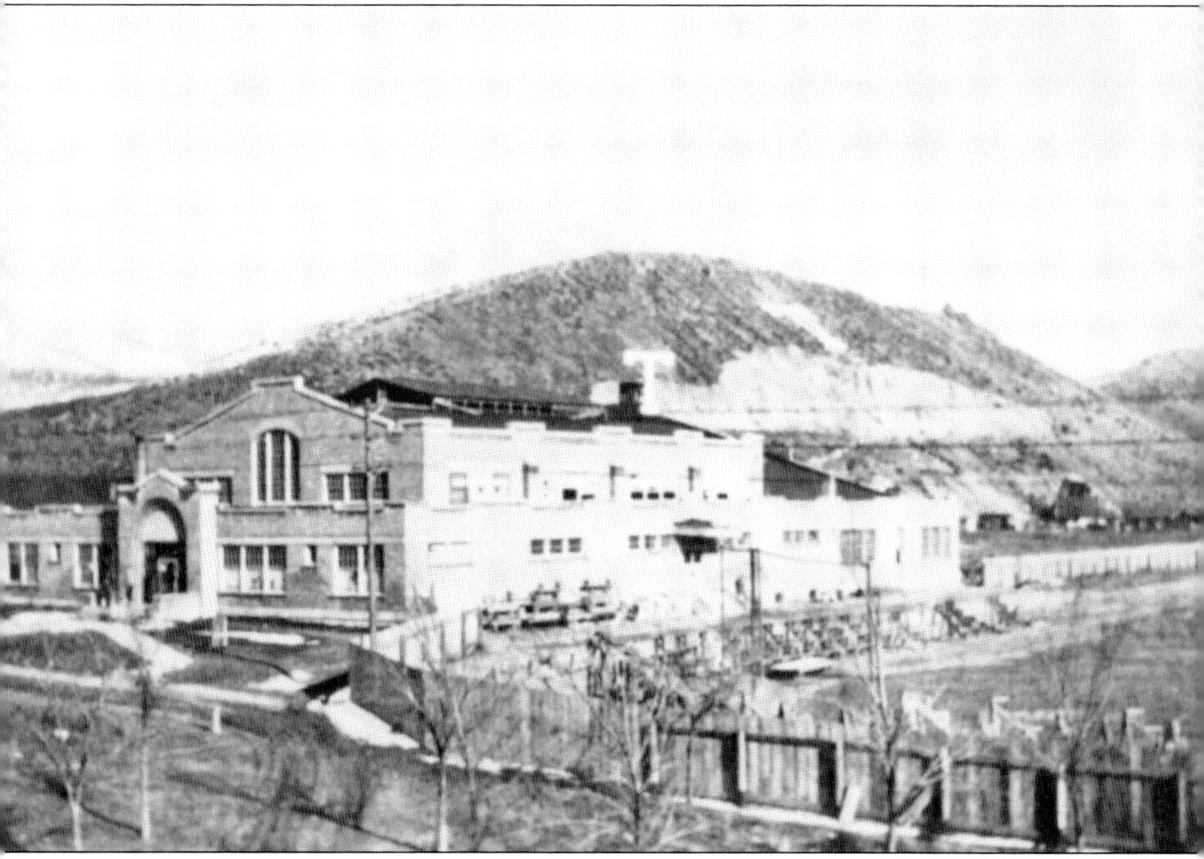

The end of World War I brought an influx of students to Idaho Technical Institute, growing enrollment to more than 1,000. The institute started encountering deteriorating roads, a severe housing shortage, and the beginnings of competition within intercollegiate athletics. The city of Pocatello filled potholes using gravel from Red Hill, initiating the scars and erosion visible on its side. In 1927, Ralph "Hutch" Hutchinson, athletic director, personally labored to improve the athletic programs and Reed Hall (pictured here), later renamed Reed Gym, by selling advertisements and establishing the Bengal mascot and orange and black colors. The "T" on Red Hill is visible above Reed Hall.

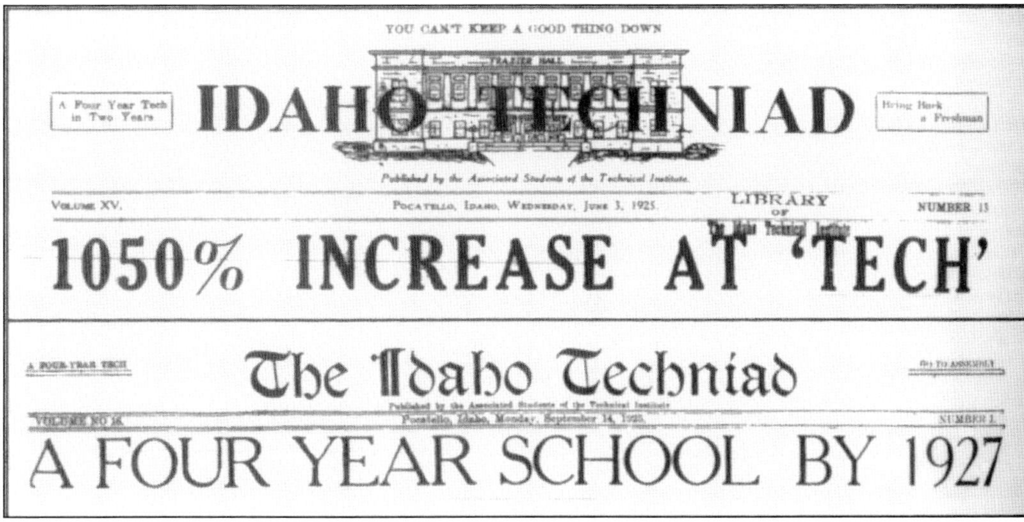
YOU CAN'T KEEP A GOOD THING DOWN

A Four Year Tech in Two Years

IDAHO TECHNIAD

Bring Back a Freshman

Published by the Associated Students of the Technical Institute

VOLUME XV. POCATELLO, IDAHO, WEDNESDAY, JUNE 3, 1925 NUMBER 13

LIBRARY OF The Idaho Technical Institute

1050% INCREASE AT 'TECH'

A FOUR YEAR TECH

The Idaho Techniad

Published by the Associated Students of the Technical Institute

Pocatello, Idaho, Monday, September 14, 1920

A FOUR YEAR SCHOOL BY 1927

Student enrollment grew 1,050 percent from 1919 to 1925. This rapid growth once again led students and faculty to push to turn the institute into a four-year college. The Pocatello community took notice that 70 percent of the Idaho population lived in southern Idaho and paid taxes, but only 30 percent of the higher education funding went to Idaho Technical Institute. Fueled by community outrage, the Bannock County delegation faced the Idaho legislature and defiantly protested, "South Idaho Demands a Four-Year School."

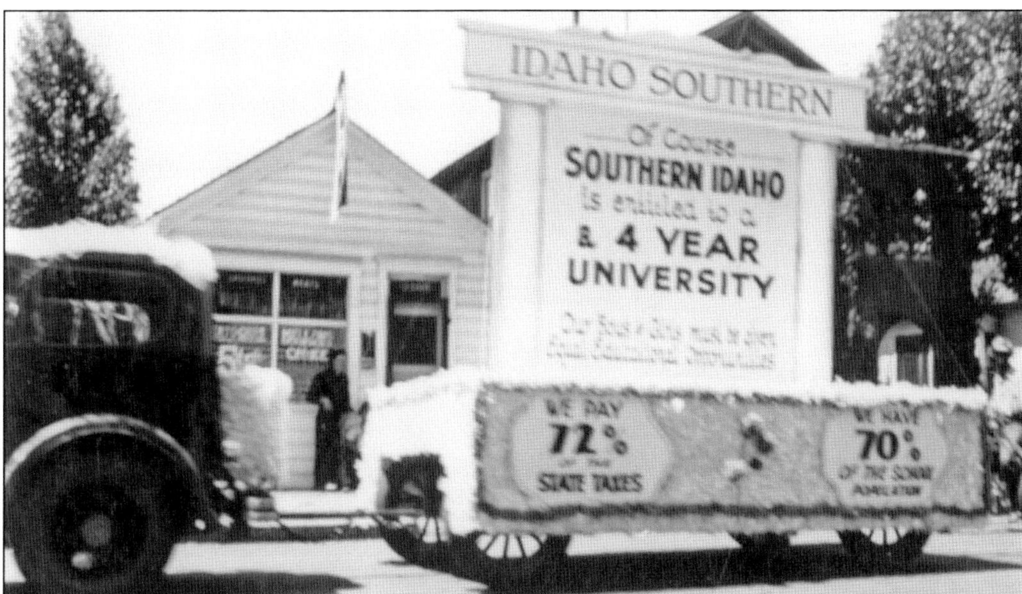

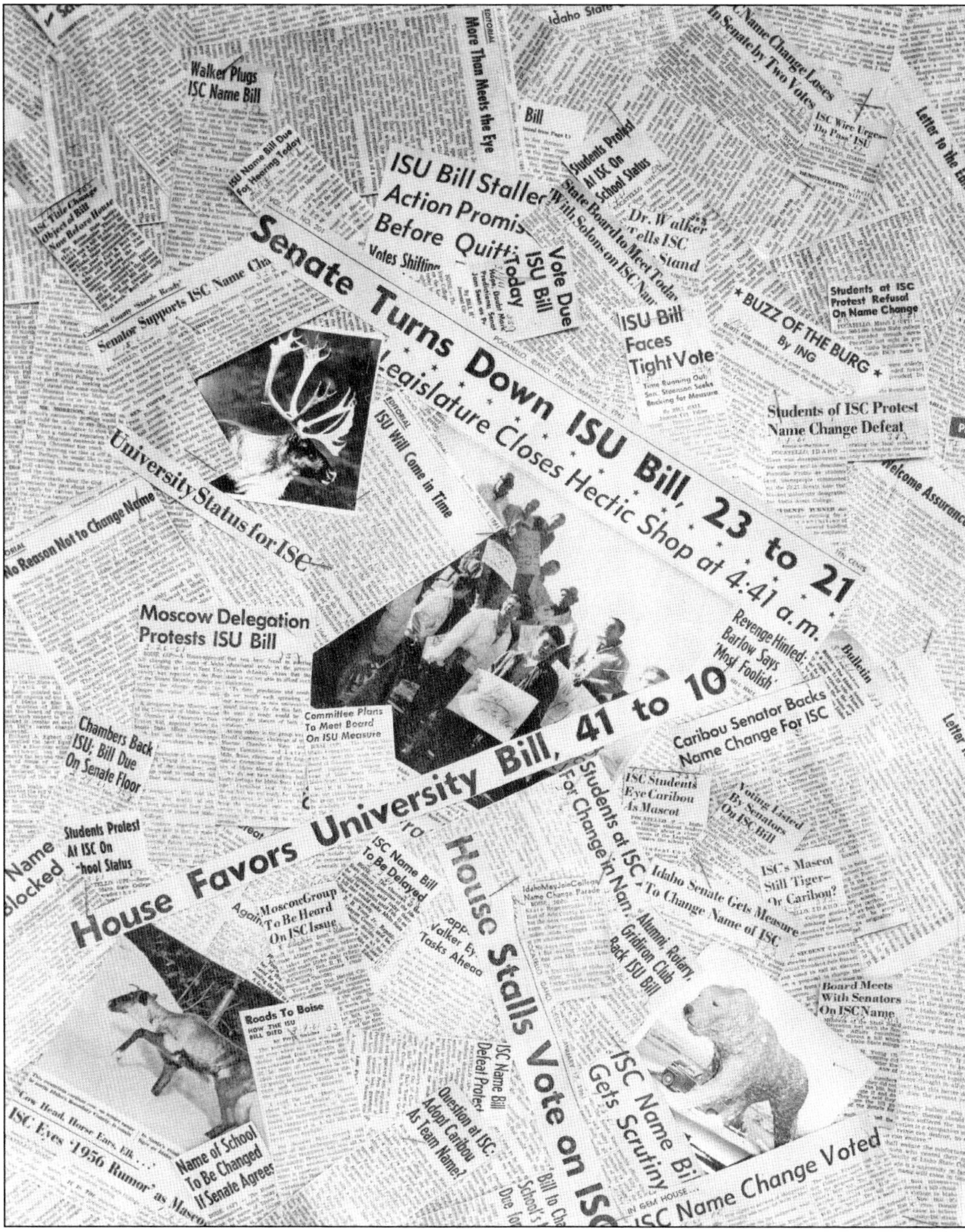

As the Idaho State Board of Education's decisions became inflexible, a cease-and-desist statement was issued to the public over the threatened conflict in Pocatello. The board continued to emphasize the vocational curriculum offered at the institute, but many students wanted more traditional academic courses in liberal arts. As students and citizens in Southeast Idaho persisted in their efforts to convert Idaho Technical Institute (also known as Idaho Tech) into a four-year collegiate institute, legislative bills and campaigns were strongly opposed on grounds that its expansion was incompatible with Idaho State Board of Education policy.

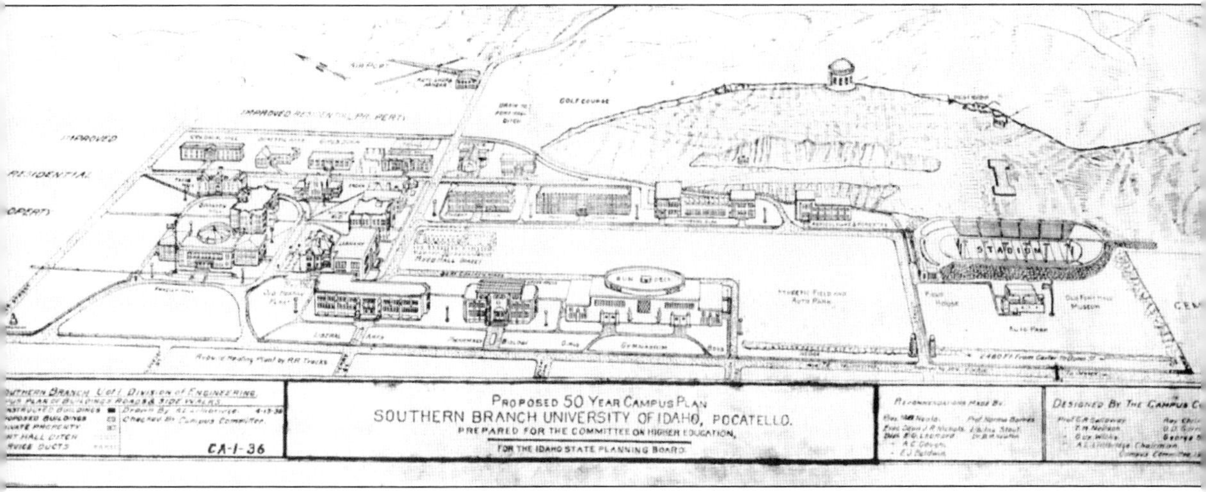

When the Idaho Technical Institute's programs became more affiliated with University of Idaho, the Idaho legislature determined that Idaho Tech's name was confusing and did not align with modern times. On February 14, 1927, Idaho Tech was renamed as the University of Idaho Southern Branch, referred to as "the Branch" or "the Twig," but remained as a two-year institute. Executive Dean John R. Nichols was innovative and persistent, and developed a 50-year plan to expand the university to add cultural and social life to the campus community.

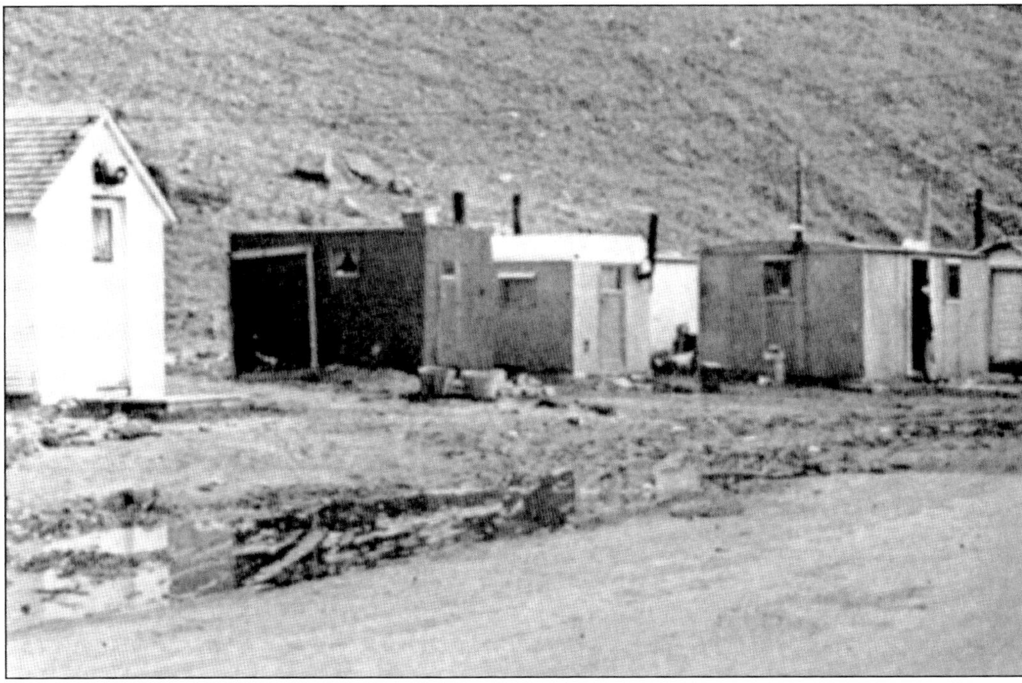

Amazingly, during the Great Depression, the University of Idaho Southern Branch's academic offerings expanded, but the institute struggled to maintain student enrollment and keep programs viable. As budgets were slashed and dormitories closed, students were strongly encouraged to stay in school. As students struggled to find work, they began to settle in a remote area at the base of Red Hill in makeshift homes called "Hooverville," or "Shanty Town." They even elected their own mayor.

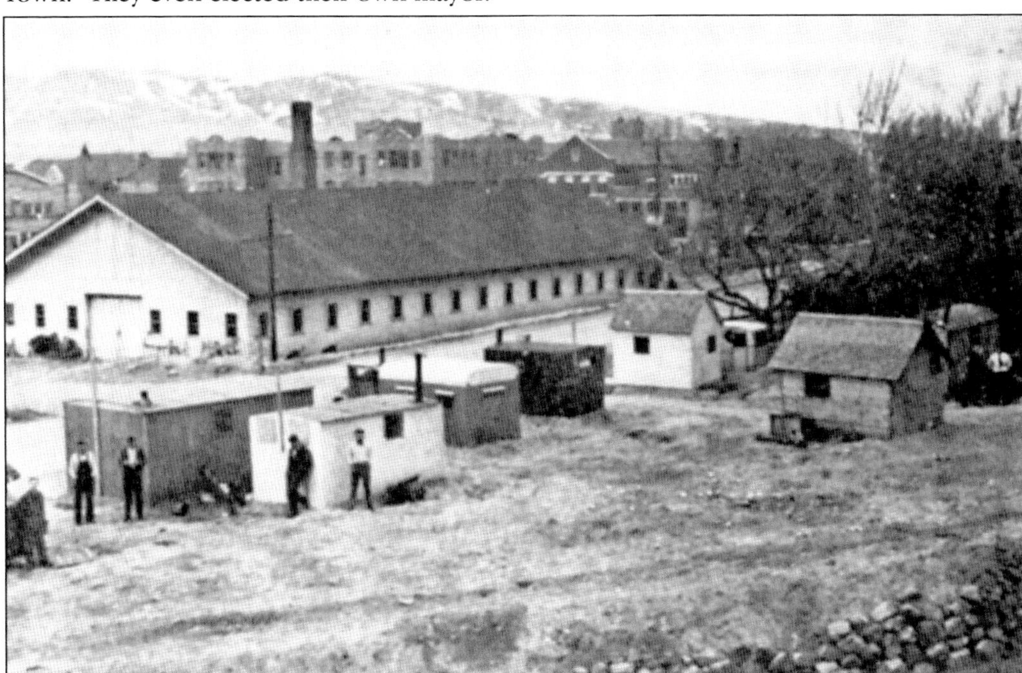

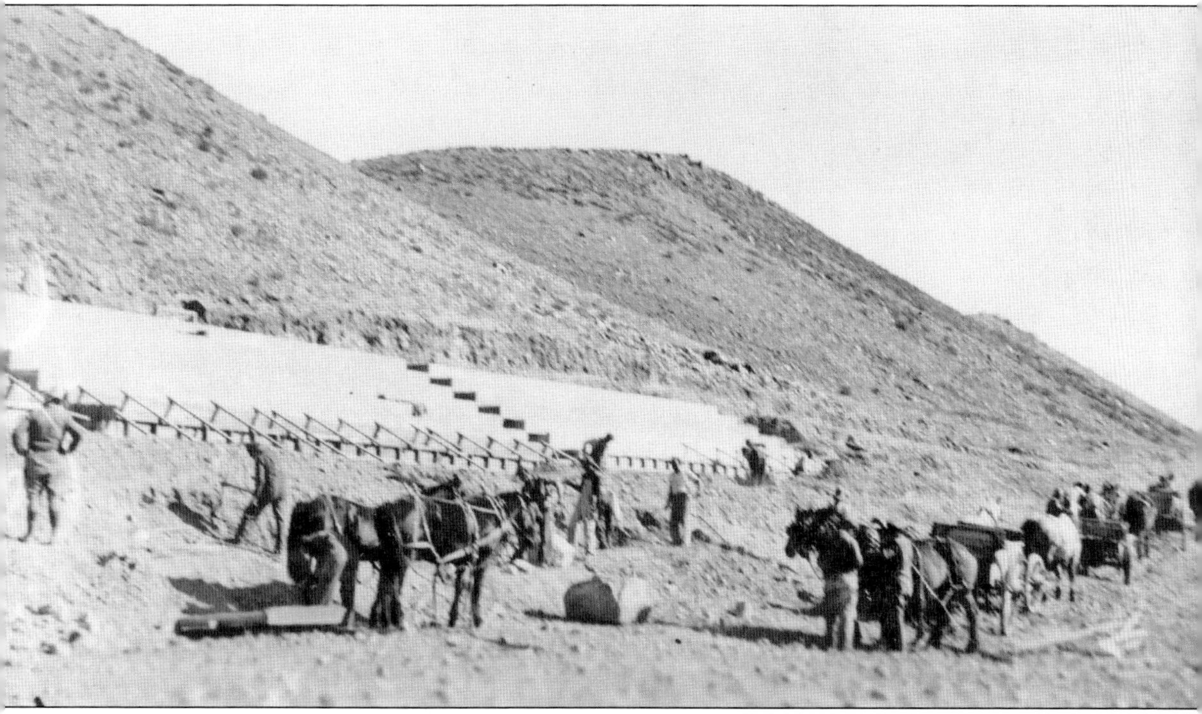

In 1933, Felix Plastino proposed the idea of building a football stadium. A team of men and horses began construction on one of the first federally funded projects, called the Spud Bowl, later named Davis Field. When the project exceeded cost estimates, the Works Progress Administration put unemployed citizens and students to work at 55¢ per hour to complete the project. On November 11, 1936, the first football game was played against Montana State with over 6,000 in attendance.

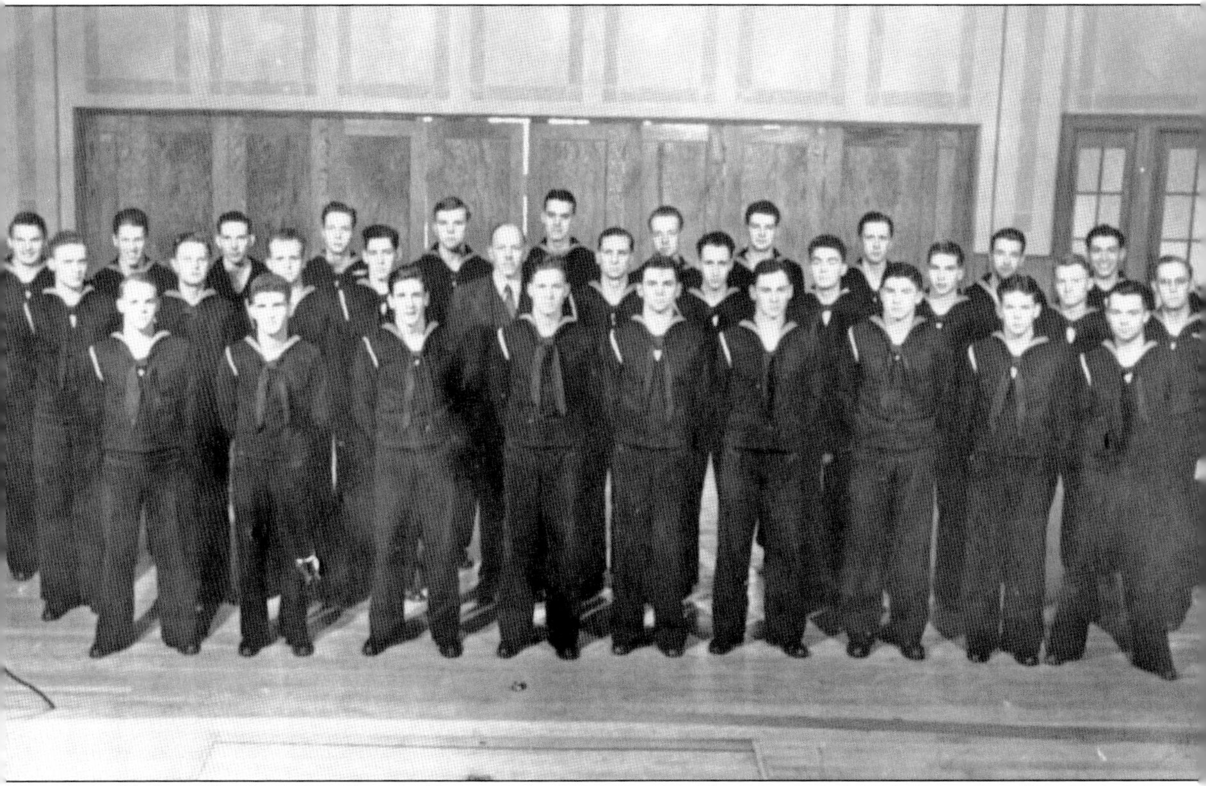

The arrival of World War II had a fortunate effect on the University of Idaho Southern Branch. In July 1943, the Southern Branch became one of 150 schools in the United States offering the US Navy training programs V-12 and V-5, for officers and aviation specialists. The "V" stood for victory, and the digit represented the number of months in the program. The program was offered to 450 cadets, who earned a commission in the Navy. An airstrip for aircraft mechanics and pilots was built across from the vocational hangar by the Works Progress Administration.

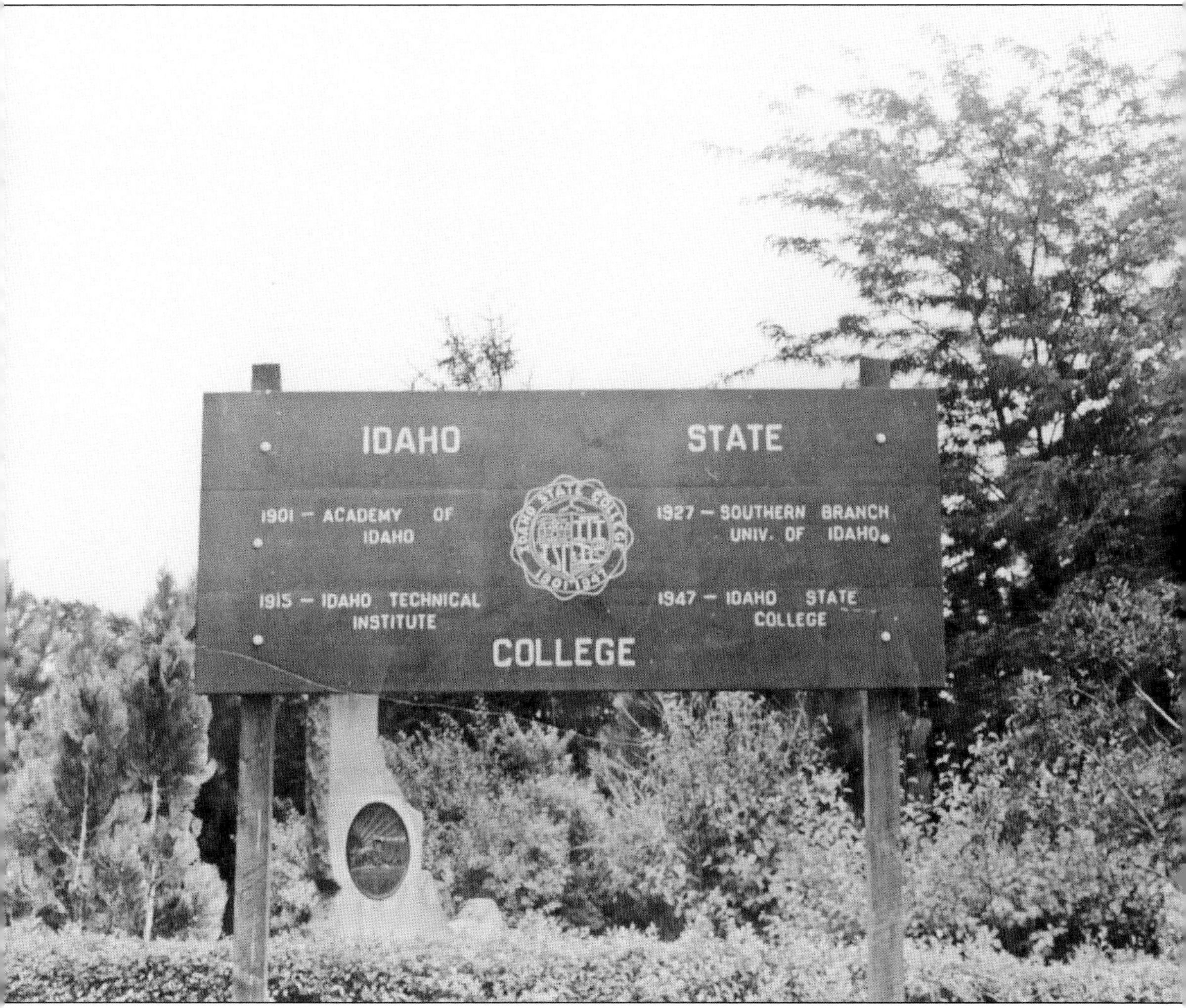

After the GI Bill passed, the University of Idaho Southern Branch registered 1,089 students, of which 1,036 were returning veterans. Gov. Arnold Williams urged the Idaho legislature to allow civilians to receive credit comparable to the cadets, but the request was defeated. The Idaho Education Survey Commission granted permission for the Peabody Commission to evaluate the state's situation. The survey concluded that the educational needs were not adequately being served in Southeastern Idaho and recommended a four-year degree college separate from the University of Idaho. On March 3, 1947, the Southern Branch became Idaho State College, ending a 30-year battle. Not wasting any time, the Idaho State College applied for and was awarded accreditation with the Northwest Association of Secondary and Higher schools on December 10, 1948.

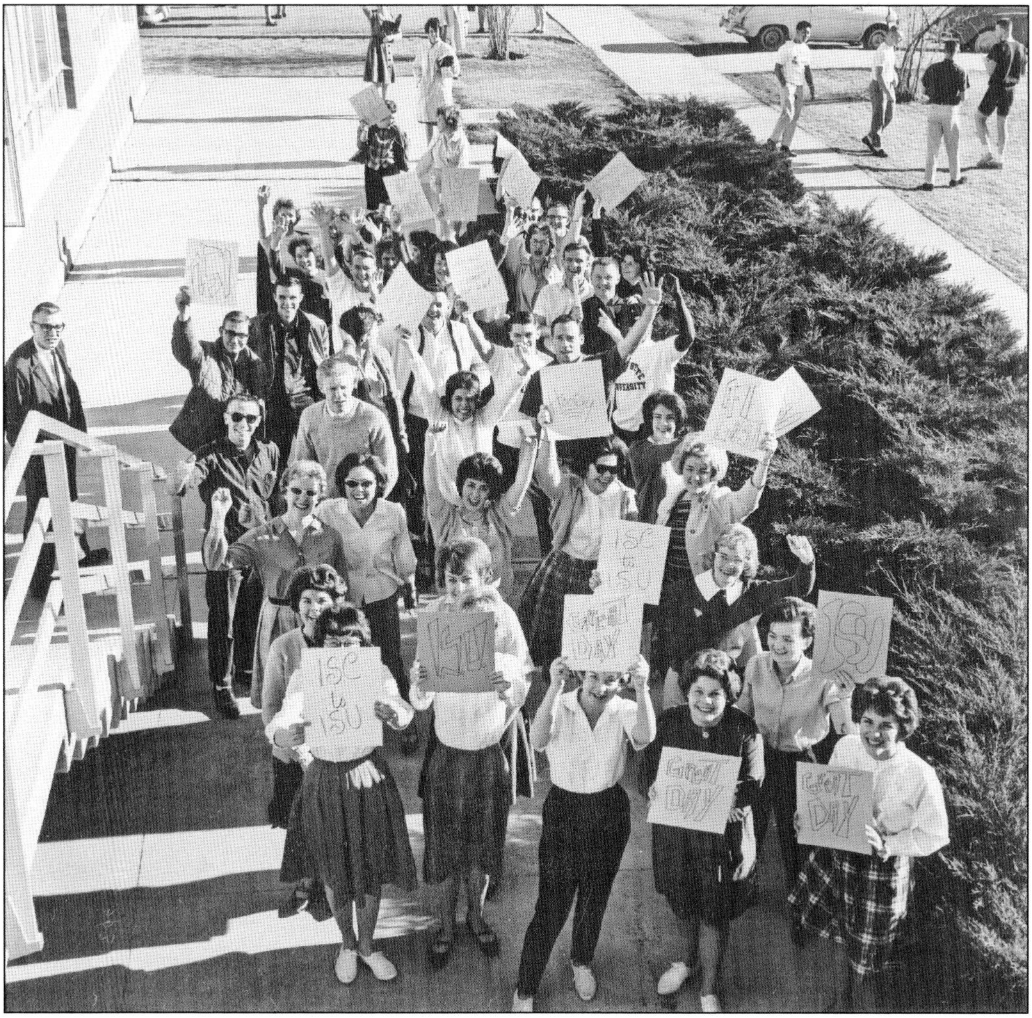

Throughout the 1950s, campus life at Idaho State College took on many dimensions. As programs flourished, the college's growth kept pace, and students advocated for university status in hopes of placing the college on a level playing field with the University of Idaho. The bill failed at the 1961 biennial session over concerns of "maturity." Student body president Jack Johnson wrote, "Honor, glory, tradition, and respect are not endowed by acts of legislatures . . . Idaho State University will not be born by the legislatures of our State. It is we who work, study, learn here now, and those who follow us who will give birth to Idaho State University." On July 1, 1963, the college was awarded full university status.

Two

ACADEMICS

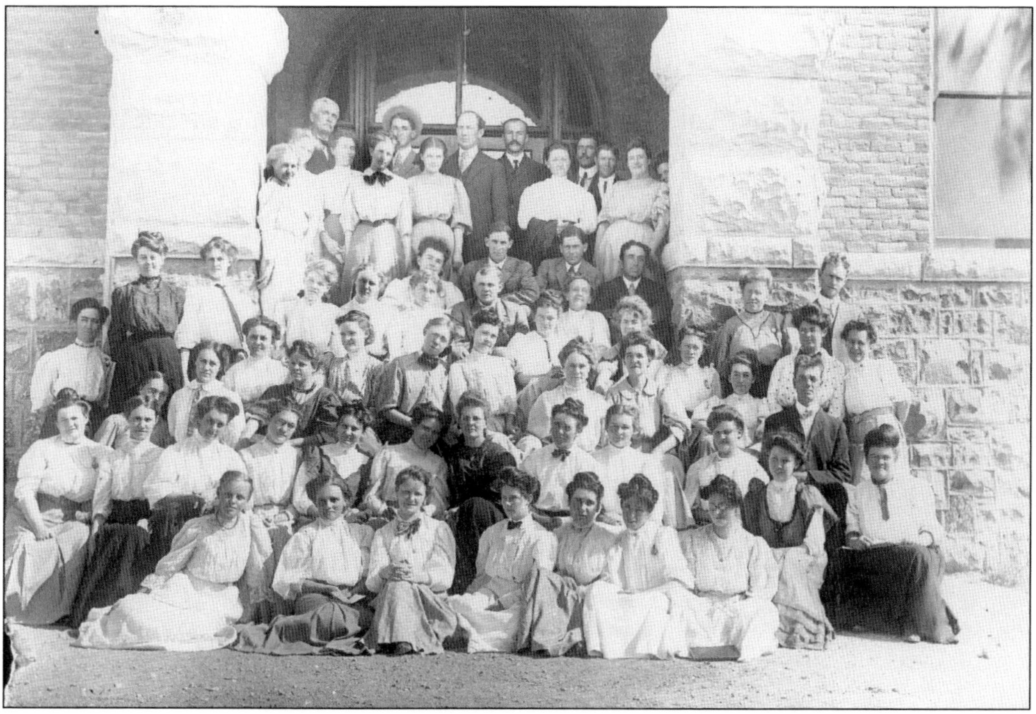

Established by Senate Bill No. 53 in 1901, the Academy of Idaho began offering limited coursework the following year in 1902. When this photograph of summer school students was taken in 1909, the Academy of Idaho offered college preparatory courses for local students lacking high school preparation, as well as technical programs in agriculture, mechanical arts, domestic economy, commerce, shorthand, and music. A few years prior in 1905, John W. Faris, the principal, began offering night courses and summer courses to better serve the so-called "special students" (now referred to as non-traditional students). This tradition of offering flexible course schedules in an effort to make education available to the community continues at ISU today, where the curriculum has expanded to include over 250 major programs.

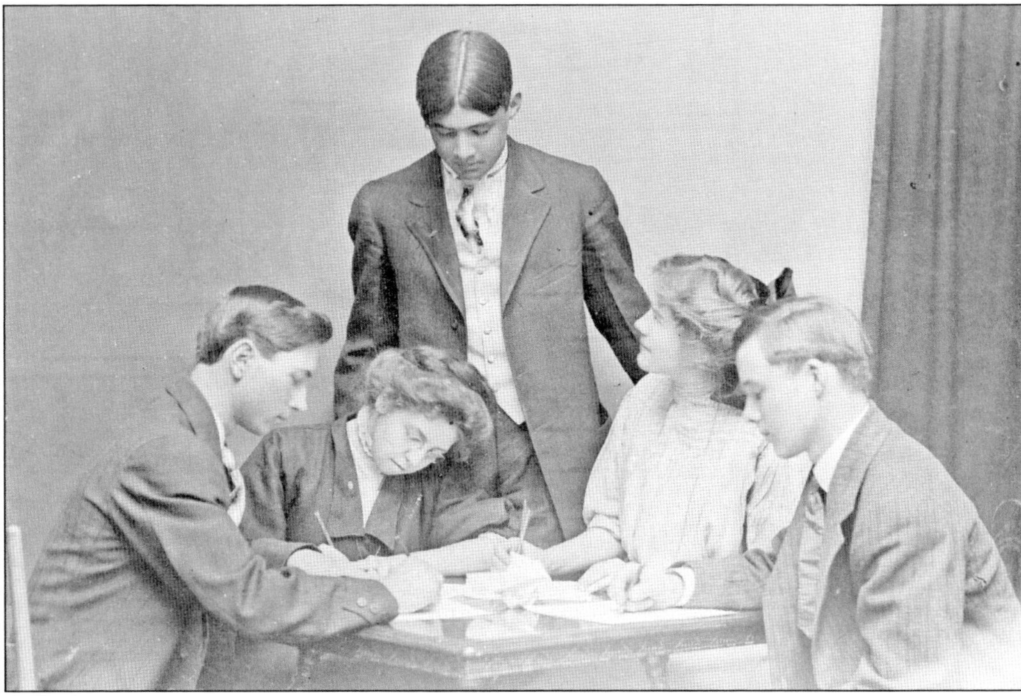

Students are pictured studying at the Academy of Idaho in its earliest days between 1902 and 1915. Pictured are Ray Bistline (standing), with Norma McMannas, Dell Sullivan, and two other students. Ray Bistline's father, John Bistline, was part owner of the extended Bistline family's Pocatello-based business Bistline Lumber. In the early 1910s, John was elected Pocatello's mayor on a platform of paving the city's sidewalks and modernizing its sewer and water systems. Ray graduated from the Academy of Idaho and went on to become a civil engineer.

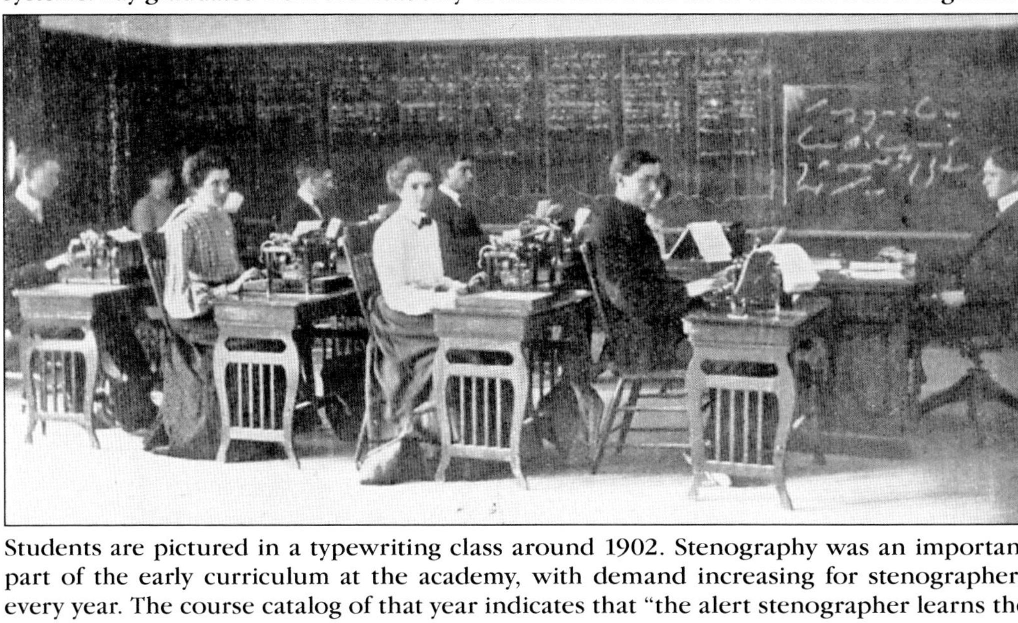

Students are pictured in a typewriting class around 1902. Stenography was an important part of the early curriculum at the academy, with demand increasing for stenographers every year. The course catalog of that year indicates that "the alert stenographer learns the secrets of his employer's success or failure from close observations made in the office" and that many business professionals "began their career as stenographers."

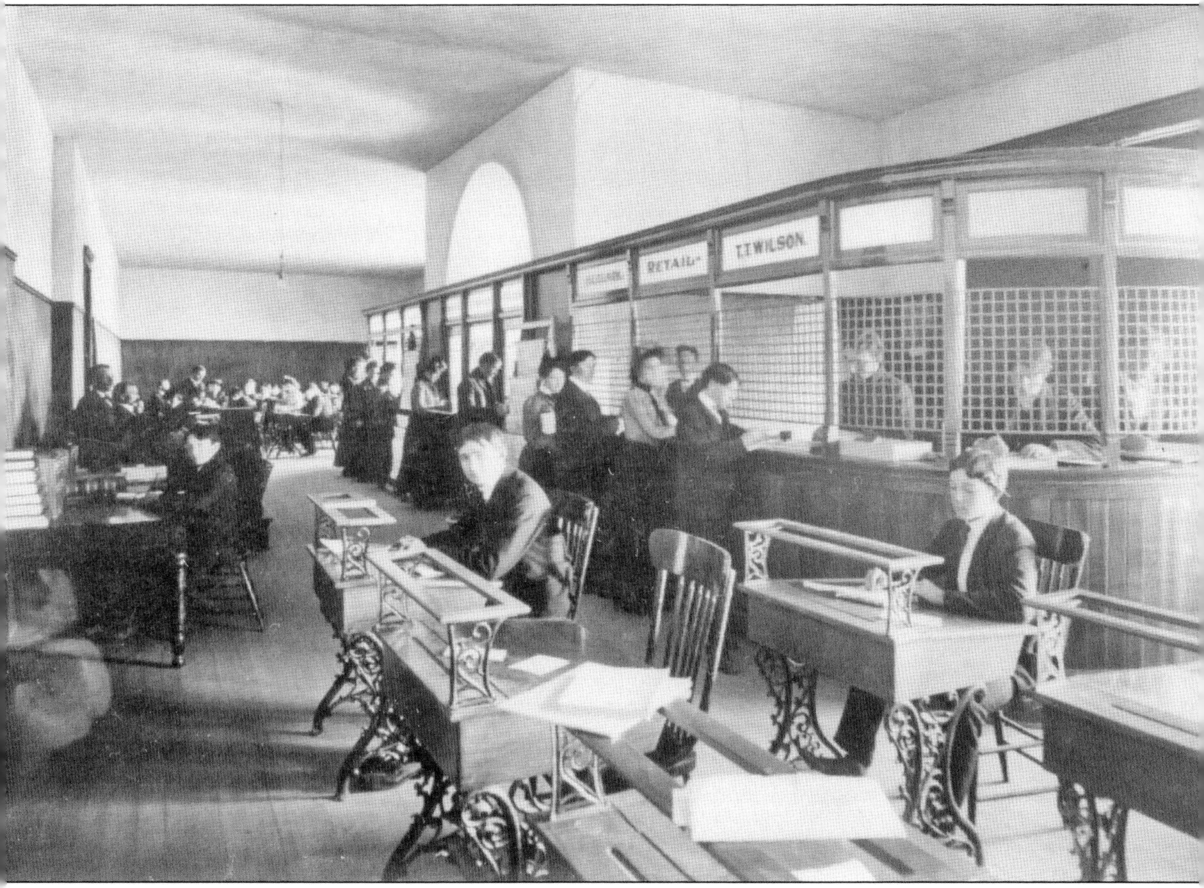

Included in the first course offerings of the Academy of Idaho were business and commerce courses, and soon after, a bookkeeping program joined the curriculum. This allowed local students to get some post-secondary business training. The 1902–1903 catalog discusses the commerce courses and the importance of business: "The aim is not merely to prepare young men and young women for clerkships or office positions. Every young person expects to conduct a business of his own or to practice a profession at some time, and without a business education he will be at a great disadvantage." The business programs have since evolved. After the institute was granted university status in 1963, the College of Business separated from Arts and Sciences and achieved its own separate accreditation in 1975, the first in the state, by the Association for the Advancement of Collegiate Schools of Business, which it maintains to the present day.

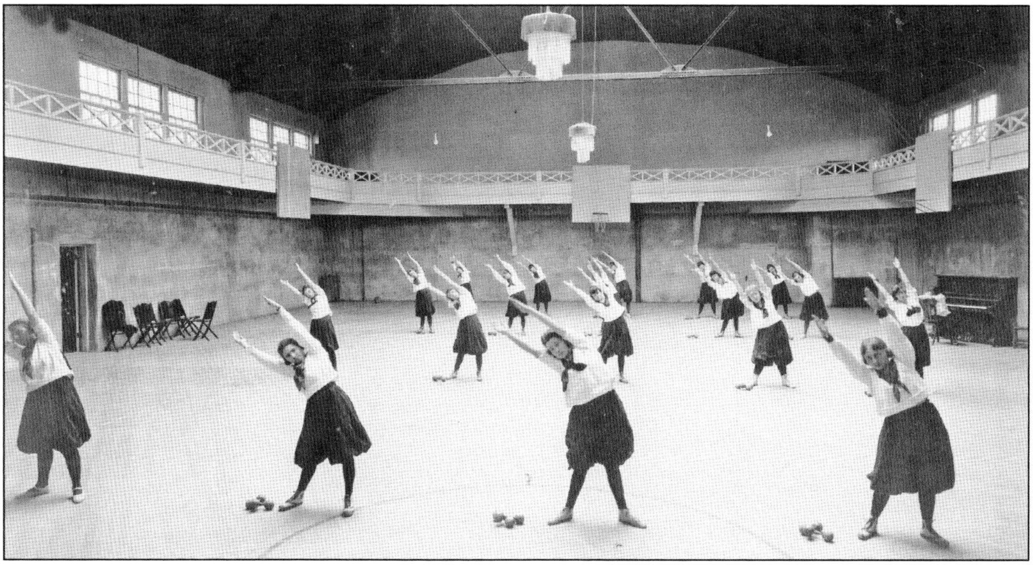

Students exercise during a women's physical education class at the Academy of Idaho sometime between 1902 and 1915. During this time, women were in the minority on college campuses across the United States, and many colleges did not allow women. In 1911, there were 295 students attending the Academy of Idaho, most of whom were men. But Idaho State University was ahead of its time in women's access to higher education. Both male and female students were able to attend the Academy of Idaho. In the 1902–1903 academic year, there were a total of 70 students, at least 27 of whom were female. In fact, the academy's first graduate was a woman, Helen K. Whittlesey Ferrer in 1904.

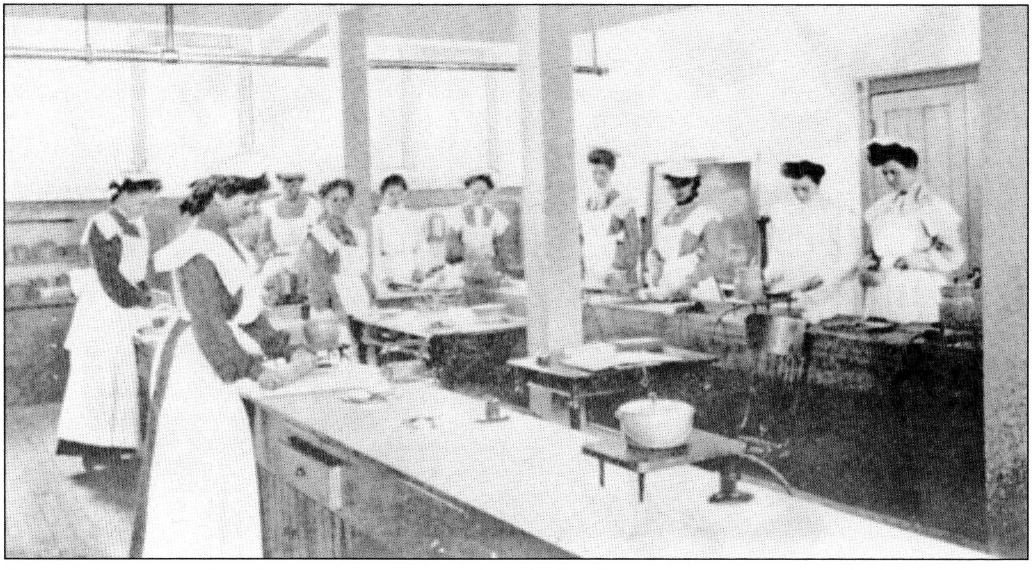

Domestic economics classes were a popular choice for women in the early 20th century. Here, students at the Academy of Idaho from around 1907–1908 gather to learn about cooking. The 1902–1903 course catalog describes the importance of the domestic economy program and that "upon it depend good citizenship, prosperity, happiness, and the future of the nation." Domestic economics courses do not exist in the same form today, but students can take a variety of related electives, including Dutch-oven cooking.

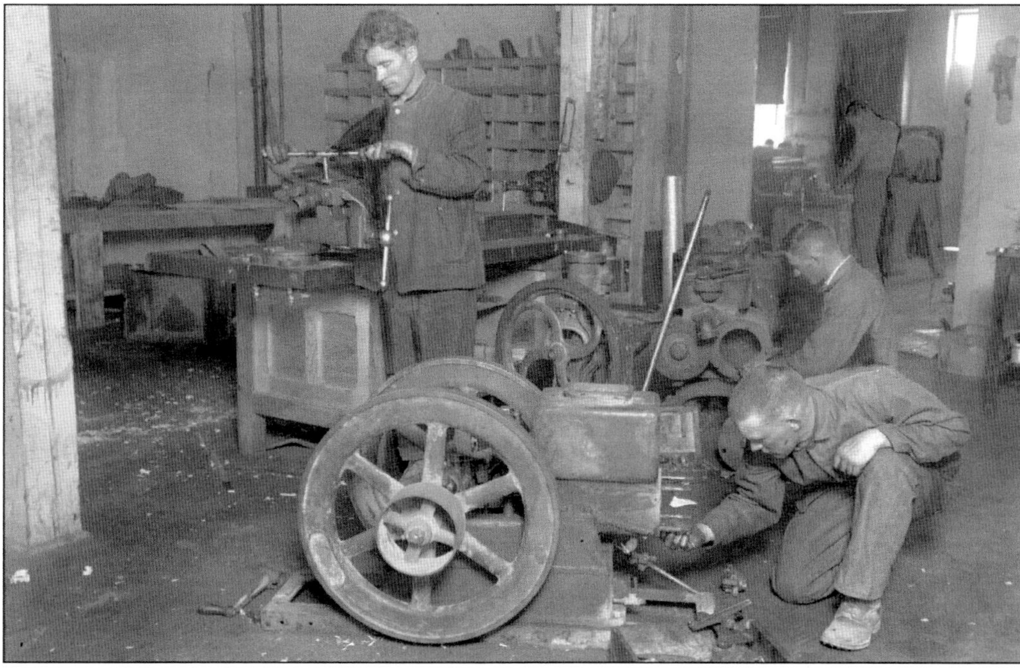

The military has a strong legacy at Idaho State University. In 1917, students voted unanimously in favor of requiring all male students to take ROTC courses, a requirement that continued until 1966. Pictured above are students in the first machine shop on campus around 1920, where many veterans returning from World War I learned automotive repair skills. In April of 1942, University of Idaho Southern Branch began taking part in the Navy's V-I program to help train aspiring naval officers. Over the next couple years, the V-5 and V-12 programs would be added. The photograph below, taken in 1953, shows students gathered at the gun plant in the naval apprentice school. A.L. Lillibridge was the instructor for this machinist trade theory course.

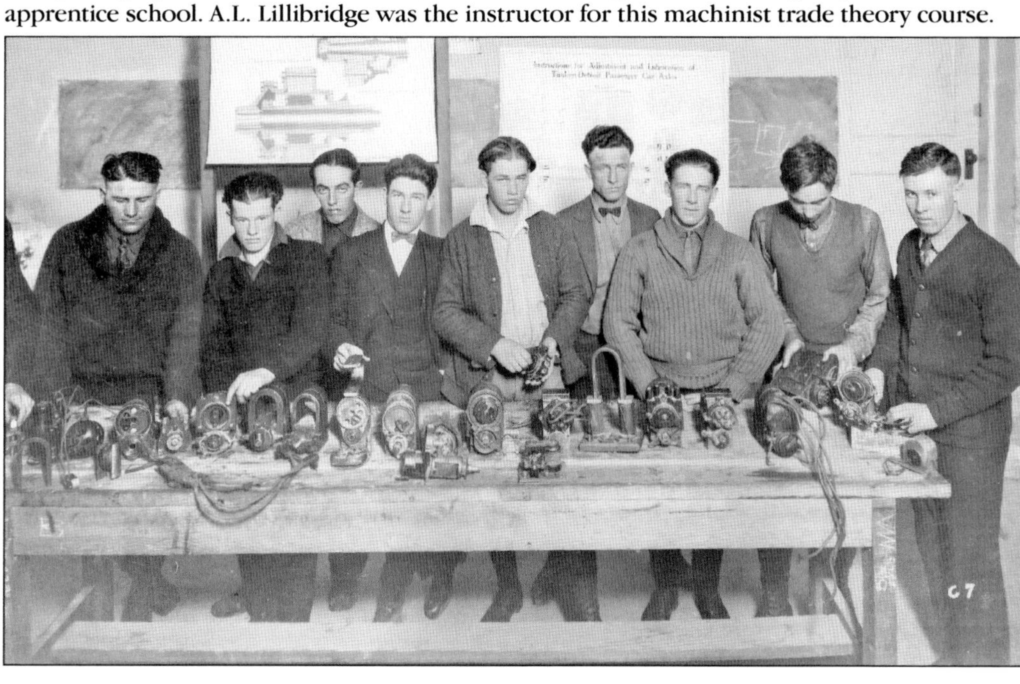

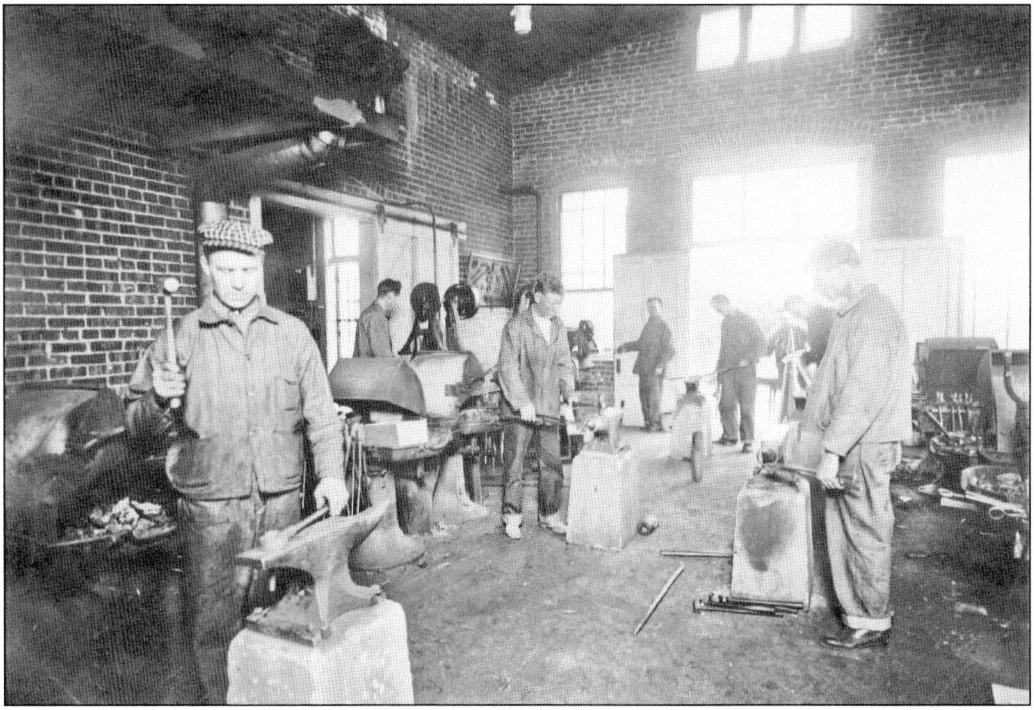

Idaho Technical Institute students gather in 1920 for training in forging. Those pictured are World War I veterans. After World War I, enrollment at the institute surged with returning veterans who were able to use government benefits to pursue education. This also led to another push for the institute to become a four-year school. By 1926, the "I" on Red Hill had been changed to a "4" to reflect the desire for four-year programs.

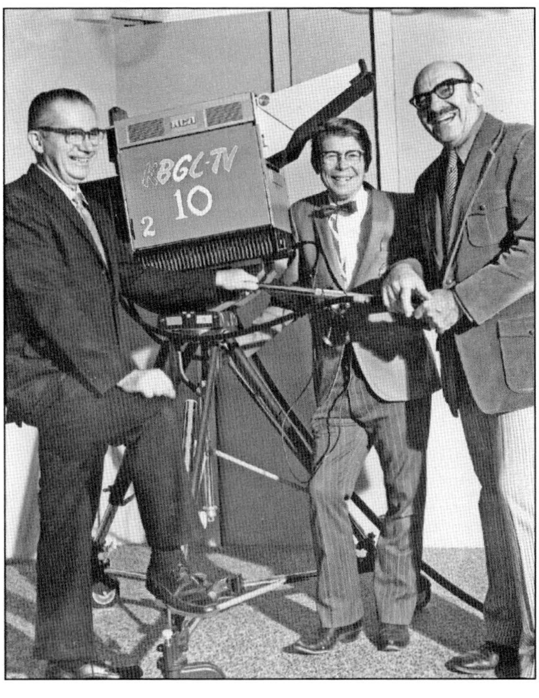

Idaho State University has often been at the forefront of new programs and new technologies. In the 1940s and 1950s, Bill Shiftlett, a television pioneer, helped establish a television filming program at the institution (a precursor to KISU TV). In 1950, C.E. "Chick" Bilyeu joined the faculty at ISU to teach classes in film production and speech communication. Together, Bilyeu and Shiftlett trained students to film and direct projects, and provided training in script writing and performance. From left to right are Bill Shiftlett, Herb Everitt, and Chick Bilyeu. (Courtesy of Diane Bilyeu.)

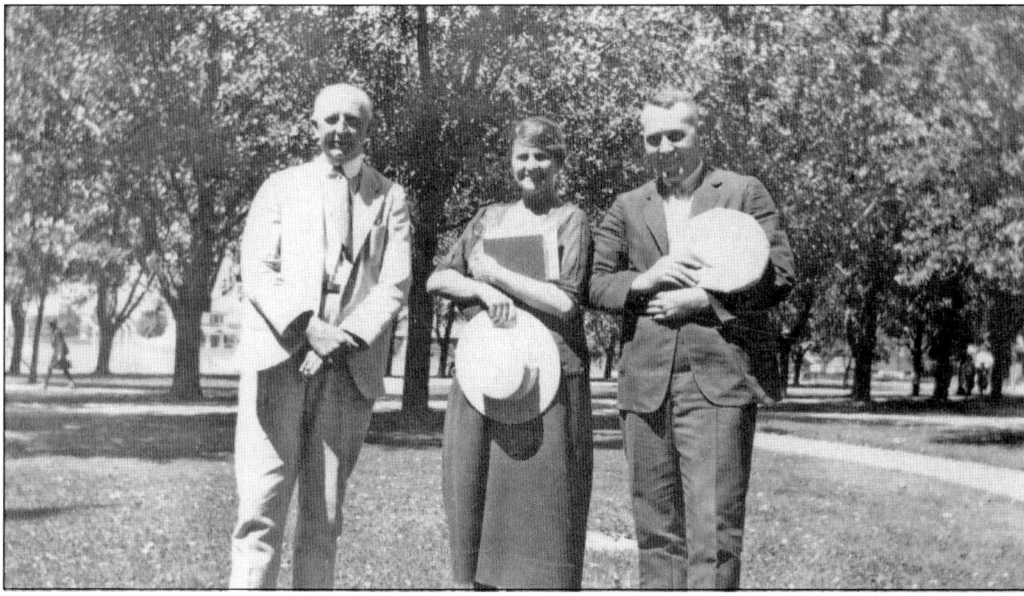

Faculty members were, and are to this day, an important part of the institution. The dedication of the faculty and staff helped propel and shape Idaho State University. Pictured above are three technology faculty members in 1921; from left to right are Professor Rutherford, Ms. Dayton, and Professor Atkinston. Pictured below are four faculty members on November 11, 1965, in a photograph taken by a Mrs. Gardner; from left to right are J.C. Gardner, music professor; C.R. Galloway, civil engineering professor; A.L. Lillibridge, technology and engineering professor; and Tom Dolmann, business management professor.

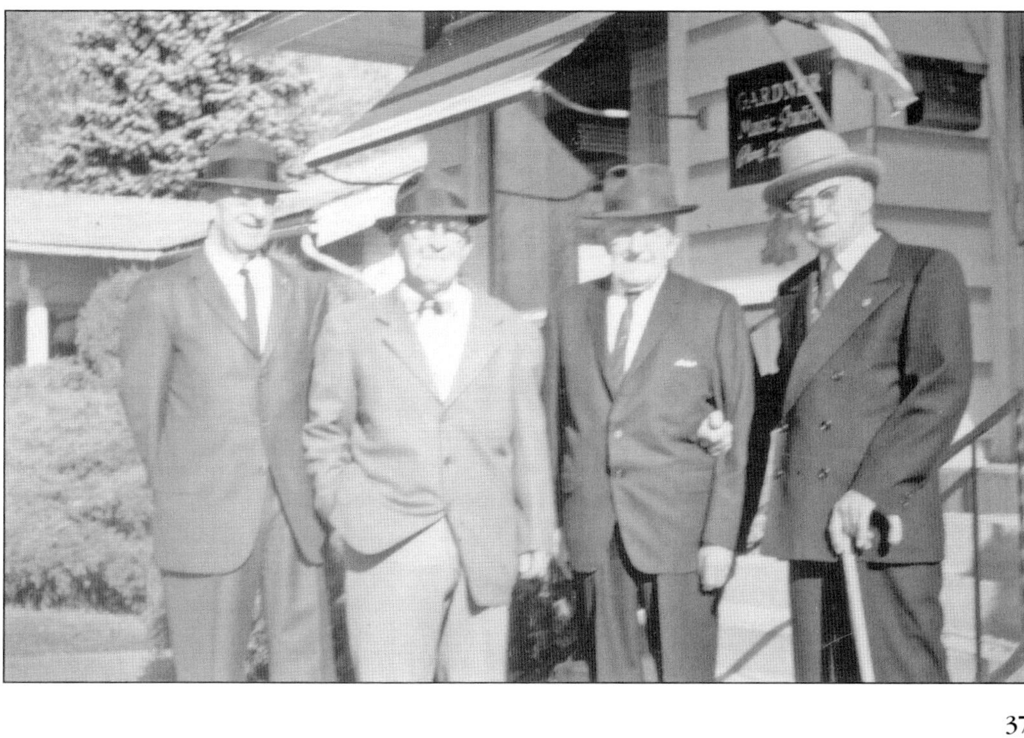

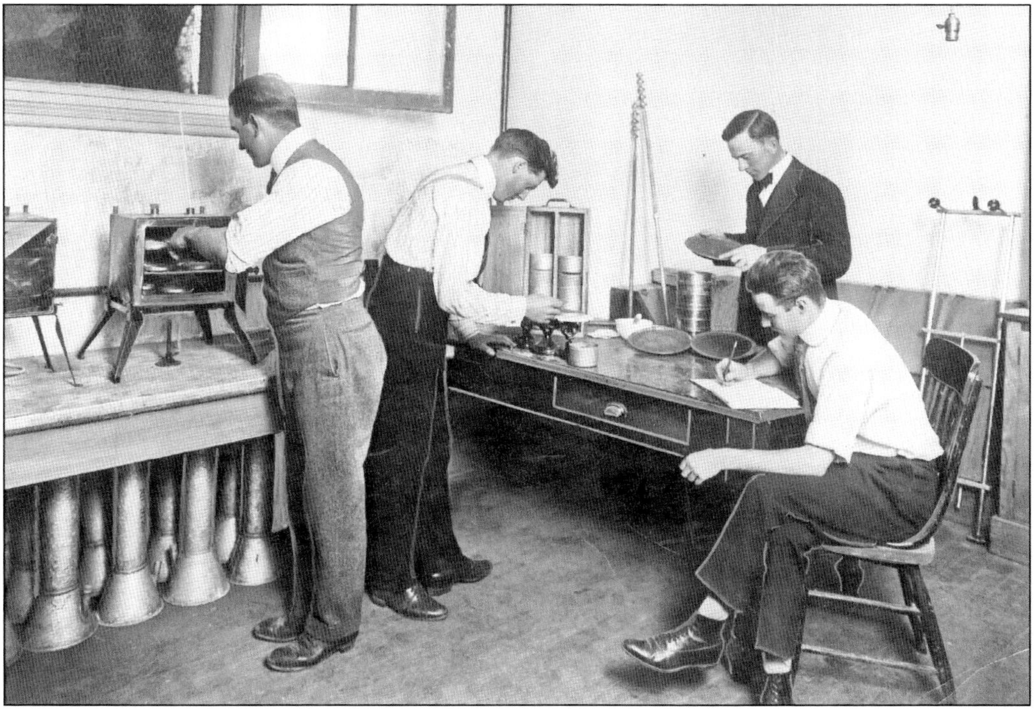

In this photograph, students engage in "a study of field perils" in the agronomy lab around 1923. Agronomy, the study of plants for their use in food, fuel, and other areas, was an important part of Idaho State University's early history. In 1909, Theodore F. Turner once again donated land to the academy, this time for a 160-acre farm. The so-called "Tech Farm" helped the Idaho Technical Institute create its Department of Agriculture. The agriculture department and its programs were disbanded when the Idaho State Board of Education decided that the state's land-grant institution, the University of Idaho, should be the only institution to offer agriculture courses.

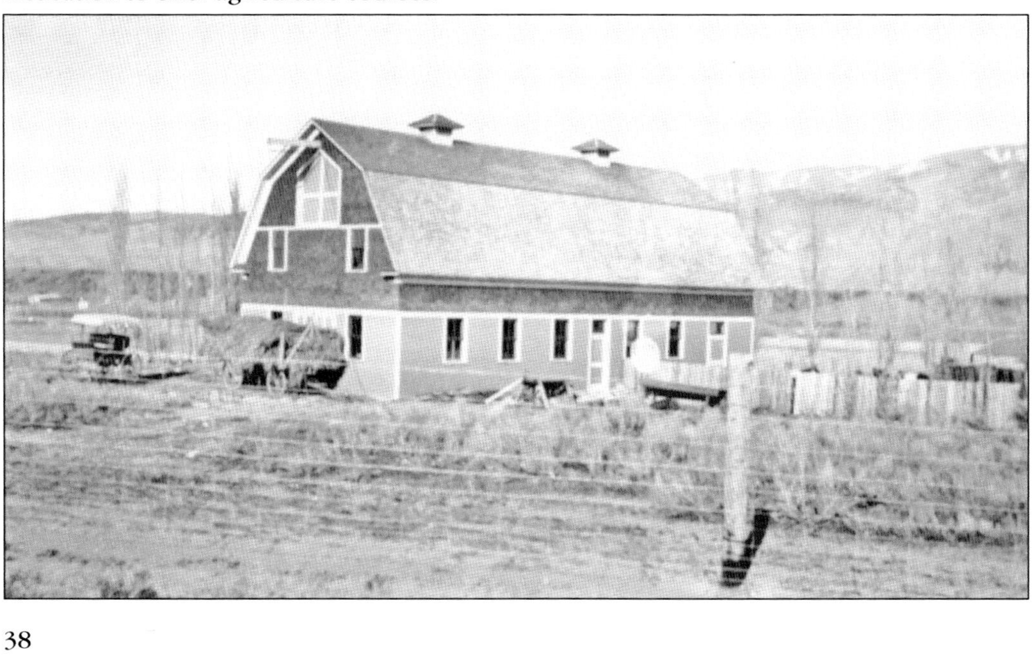

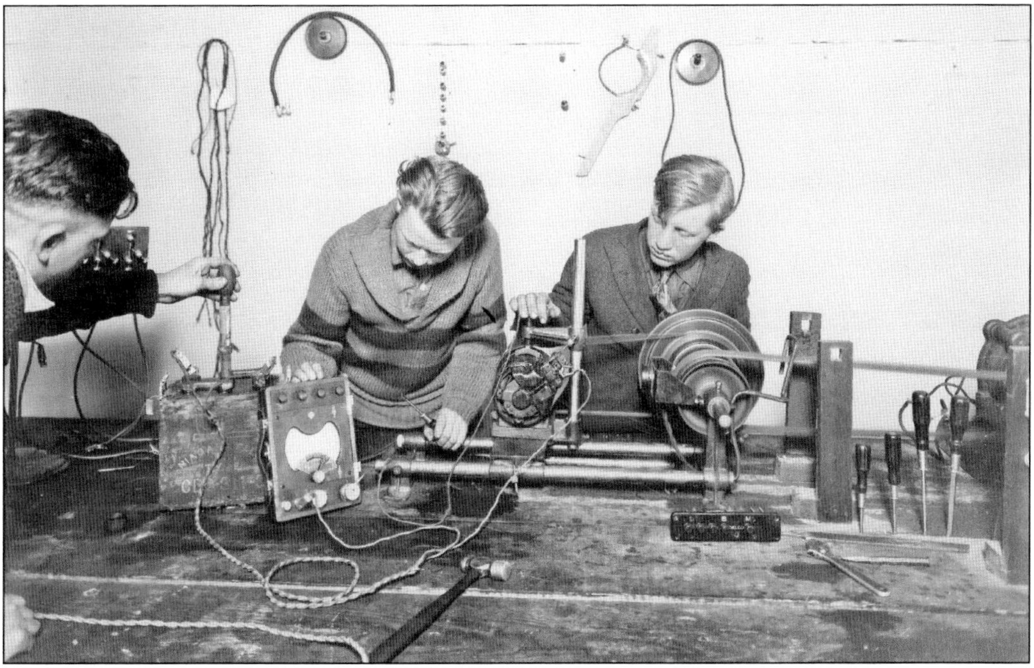

Several students work on a machine in the physics and electrical lab in 1923. Vocational programs have a long history at Idaho State University, starting in the Academy of Idaho's second year. By 1919, it was a formal department called the Division of Engineering and Trades, which was led by director A.C. Gough.

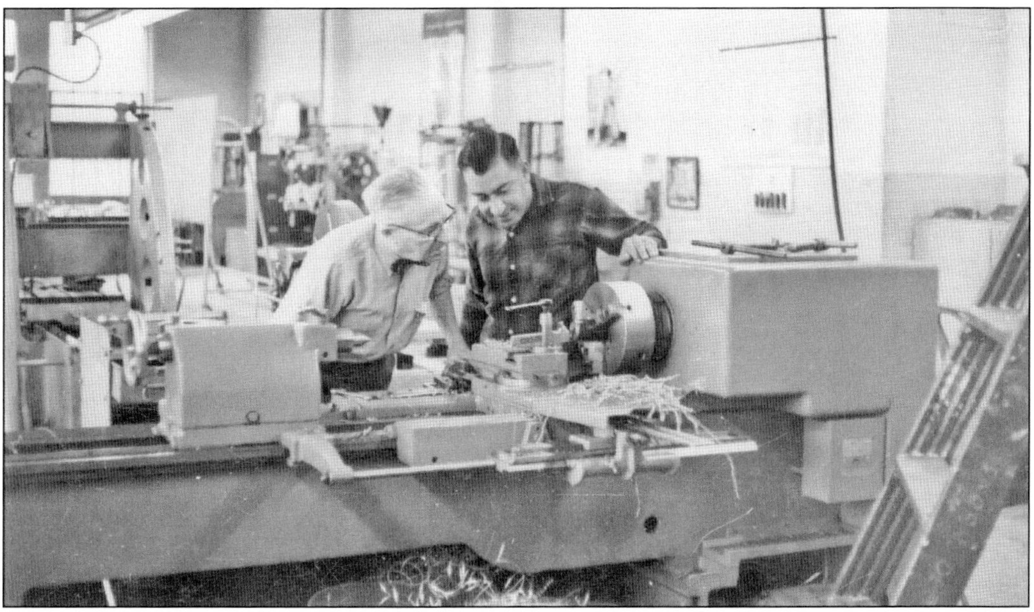

Technology and engineering instructor A.L. Lillibridge helps a student in the machinist shop. The naval V-12 program helped grow Idaho State University's programs and reputation with students from across the nation coming to attend the program. From 1943 to 1945, the institution would have been short on its operating budget by $50,000 without the V-12 program, which more than made up for that shortage.

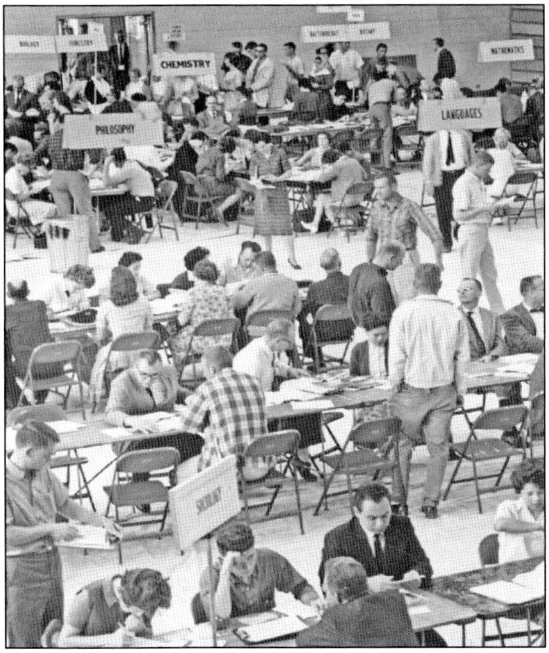

Prior to the advent of computers, registering for classes was not as easy as logging into BengalWeb and checking a box. Registration was accomplished by hand with punch cards. Students would gather in a large room, such as the gym or the student union ballroom, to grab a card for the course they wished to enroll in for the coming term.

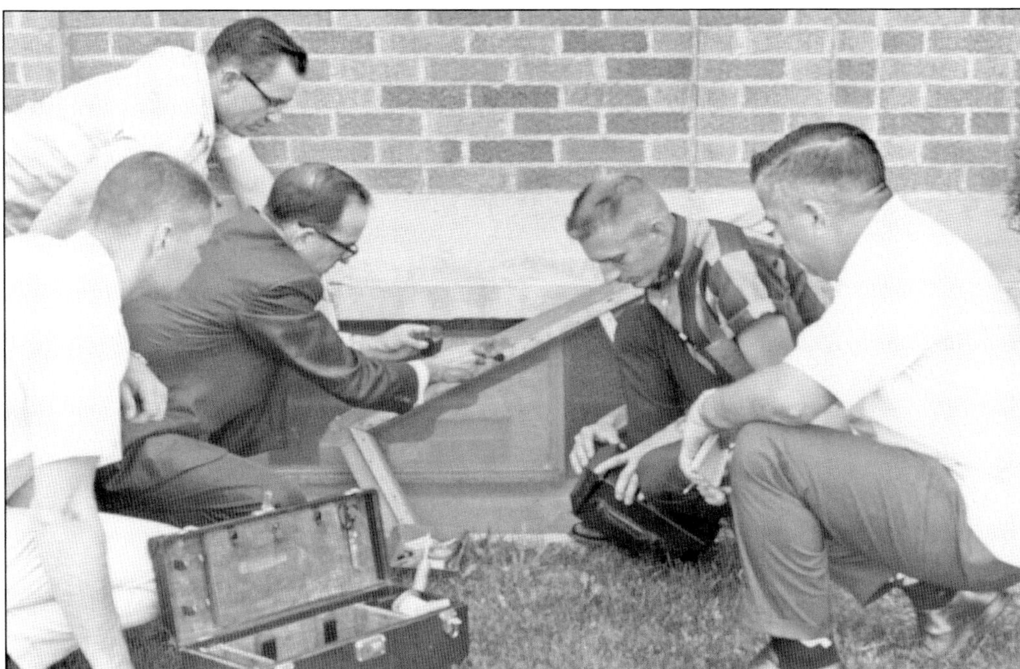

Students at the Idaho State College learn to check evidence at the window of a crime scene around 1950. Included in the photograph is Mountain Home deputy sheriff George Taylor and Walter Stohler of the Boise City Police Department. Law enforcement programs continue at Idaho State University today in the College of Technology, where students can earn a certificate or an associate of applied science in law enforcement, and in the College of Arts and Letters, where students can earn a bachelor of arts in sociology with a concentration in criminology.

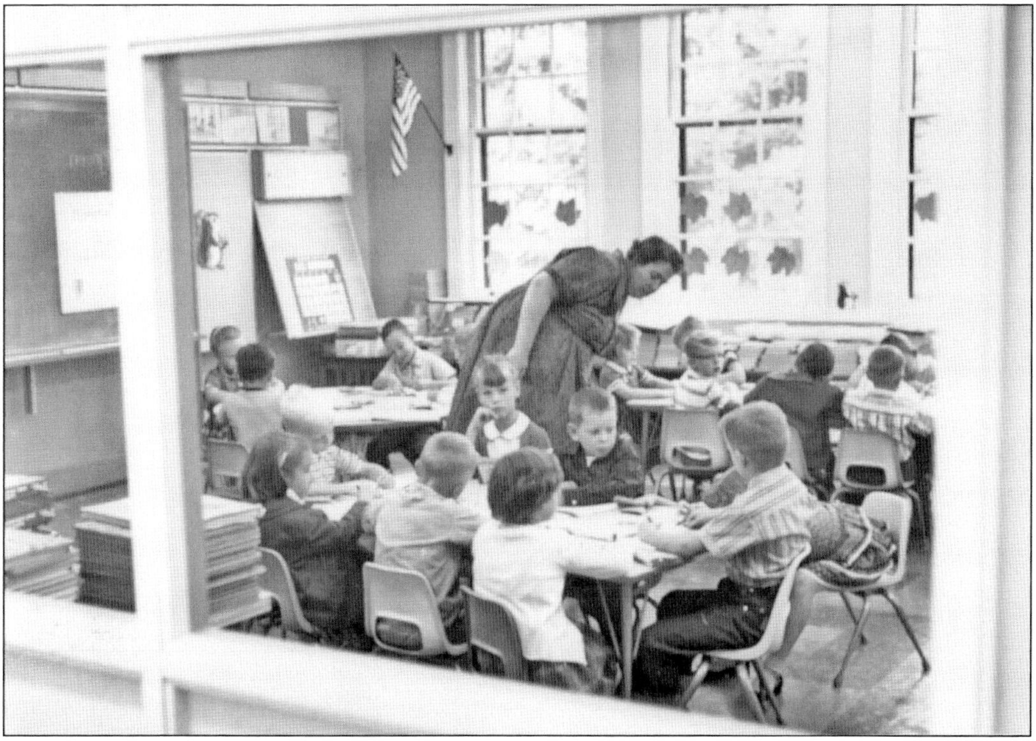

The Campus School, now called the Early Learning Center, was created as a primary school for young students where education students at Idaho State University could also do their training. This photograph, taken between 1947 and 1963, shows a teacher mentoring students at the school. Now, the school serves as a training school for the College of Technology's early childhood care and education program.

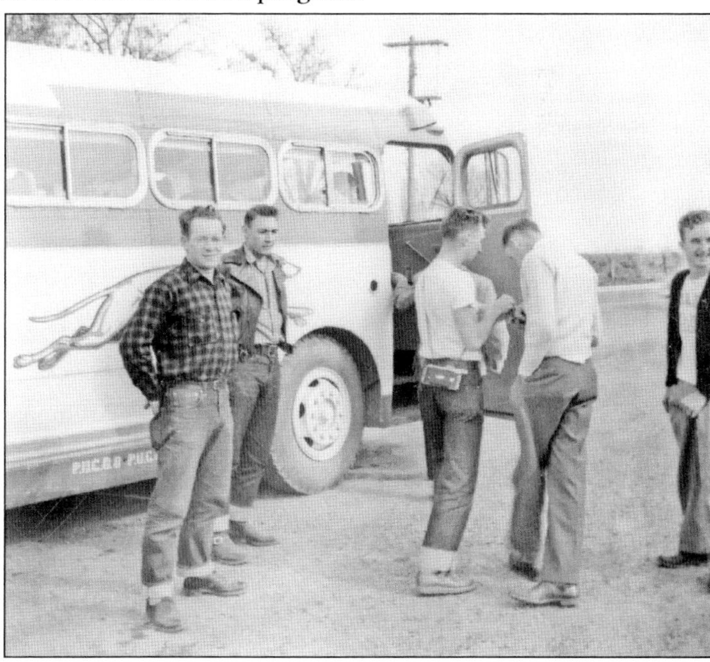

Idaho State College engineering students take a field trip to the Anderson Ranch Dam on May 7, 1950. Pictured from left to right are students Howard Brooks, Orville Drexler, Stanley De Stolinsky, Earl Capellen, and Wesley Kite. Engineering programs have expanded at Idaho State University and now include programs in civil, electrical, mechanical, and nuclear engineering.

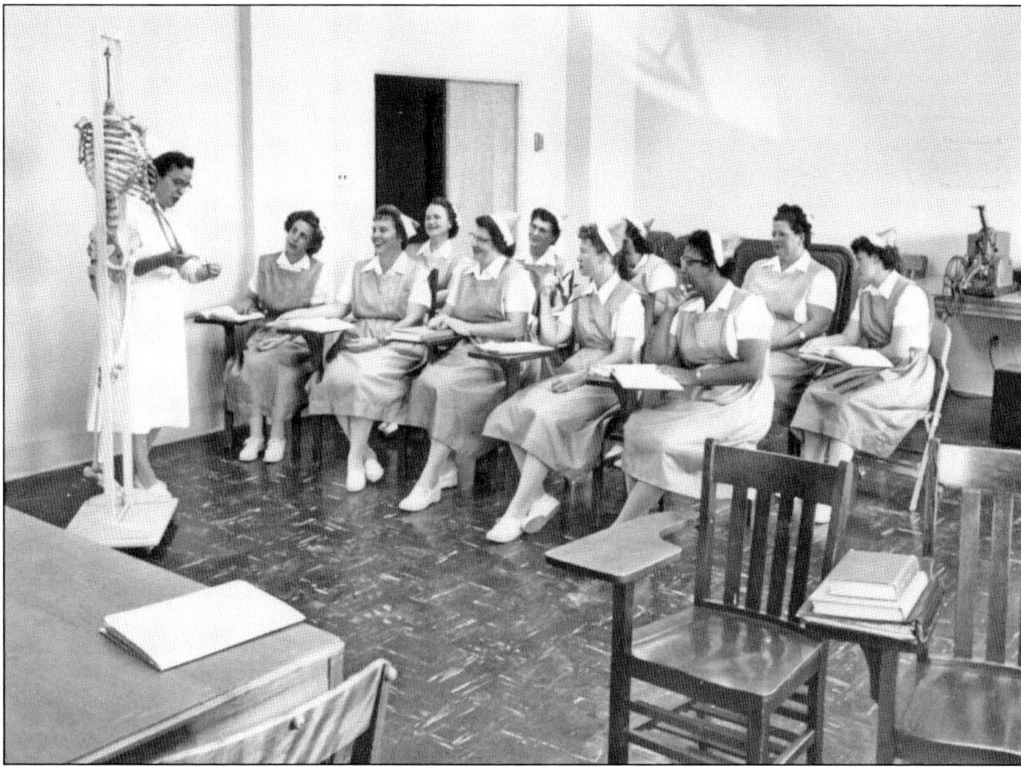

These students, pictured around 1956, receive instruction in human anatomy in the Idaho State College nursing program. A highly ranked program today in the Division of Health Sciences, the nursing department also offers the only PhD program in nursing in the state of Idaho. In 2016, the nursing program at Idaho State University celebrated its 60th year.

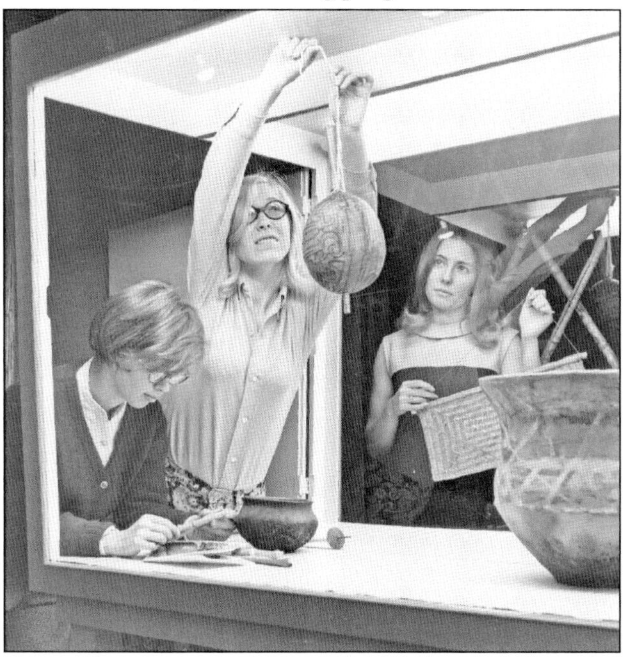

In the late 1960s, a group of students in a museum studies class, pictured here, created an exhibit with various South American objects at the Idaho Museum of Natural History (IMNH). The IMNH, established in 1934 on the ISU campus, has been a resource for students pursuing museum studies, anthropology, paleontology, life sciences, and earth sciences. It is also a popular destination for the public and school groups, with rotating exhibits that have even featured animatronic dinosaurs.

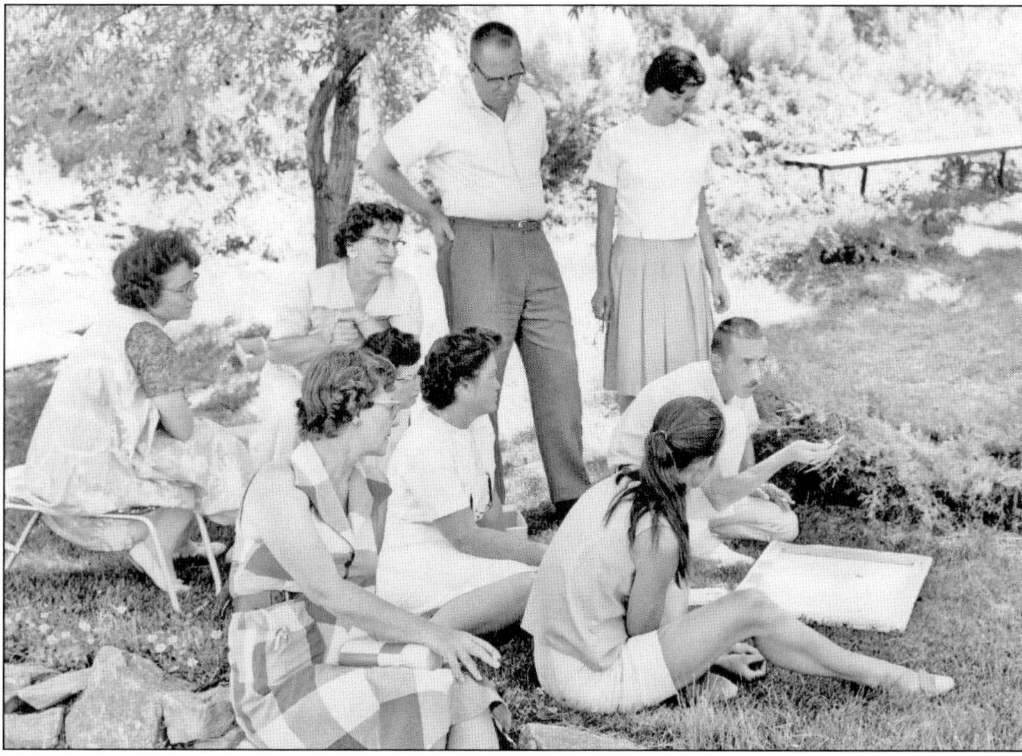

An art class heads outdoors in the early 1970s to learn more about outdoor artwork. The Idaho State University art department offers a bachelor of arts and a bachelor of fine arts with coursework in studio art, art history, ceramics, painting, drawing, and more.

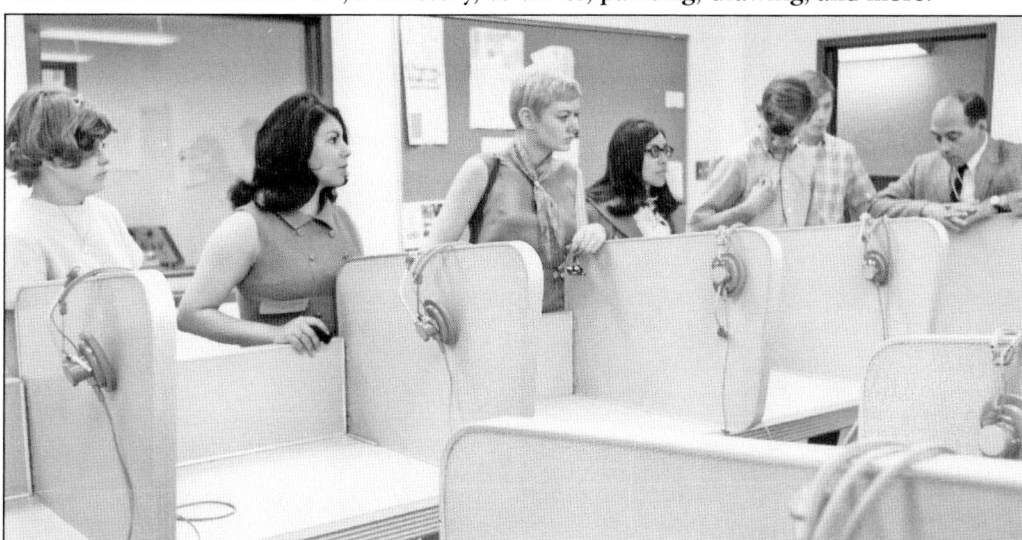

The Department of Global Studies and Languages at Idaho State University was created by joining the Department of Languages and Literature with the international studies program. Learning a foreign language opens the doors to study abroad through the university. In this 1970 photograph, students are eagerly learning how to use the equipment for their foreign language class.

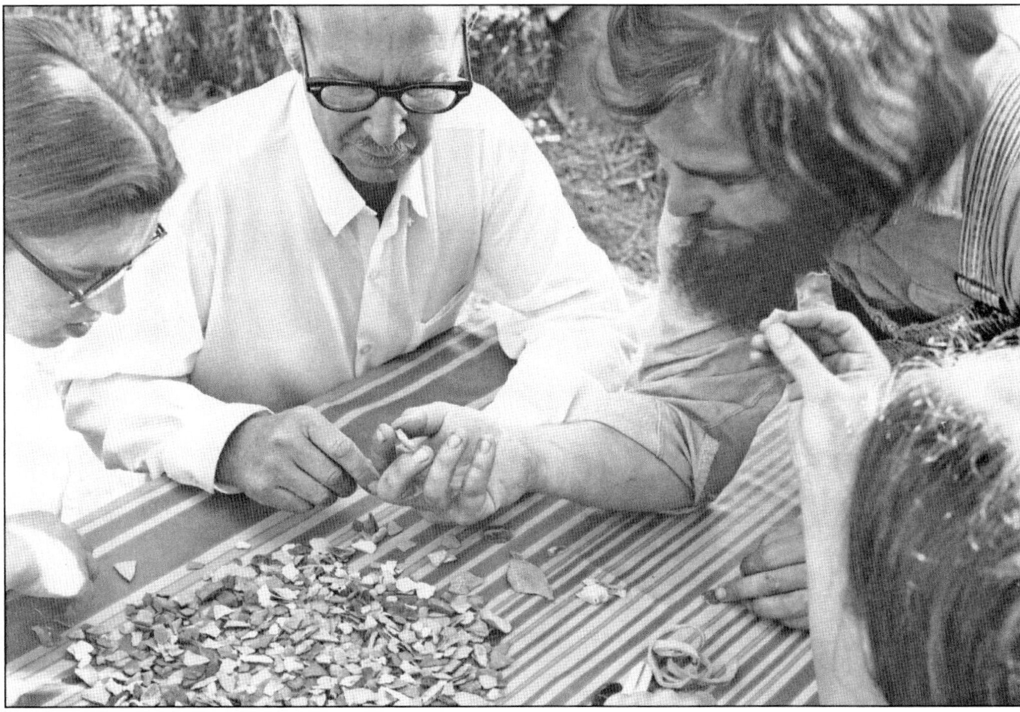

At Idaho State University, anthropology students have the opportunity to participate in fieldwork and gain hands-on experience. Students during the early 1970s are pictured here with Don Crabtree, widely known in the field as the "Dean of American Flint-Knappers," sifting for projectile points during a summer fieldwork project. Students were also able to learn from Crabtree how to craft a projectile point themselves. Below, students participate in a dig as part of a summer field school in the early 1970s.

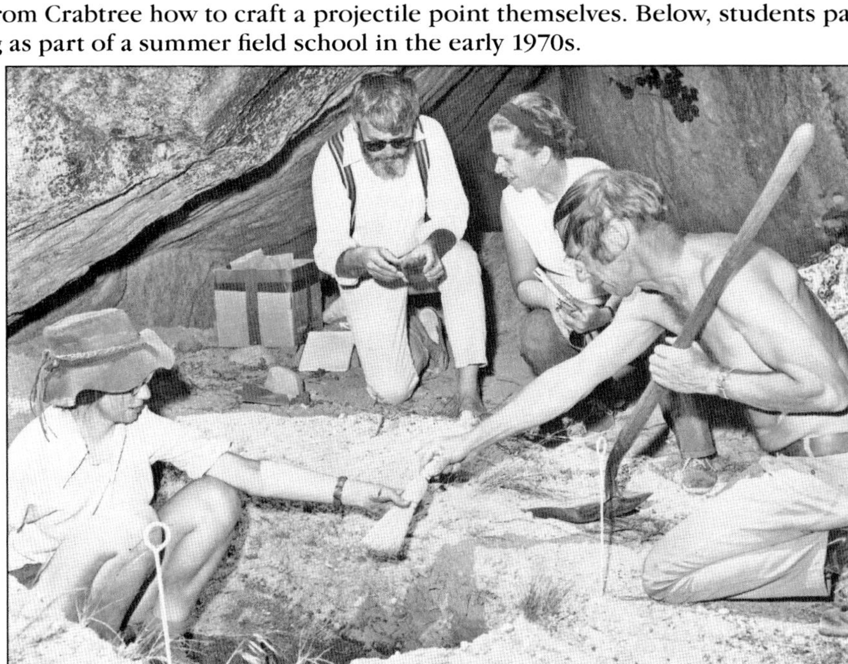

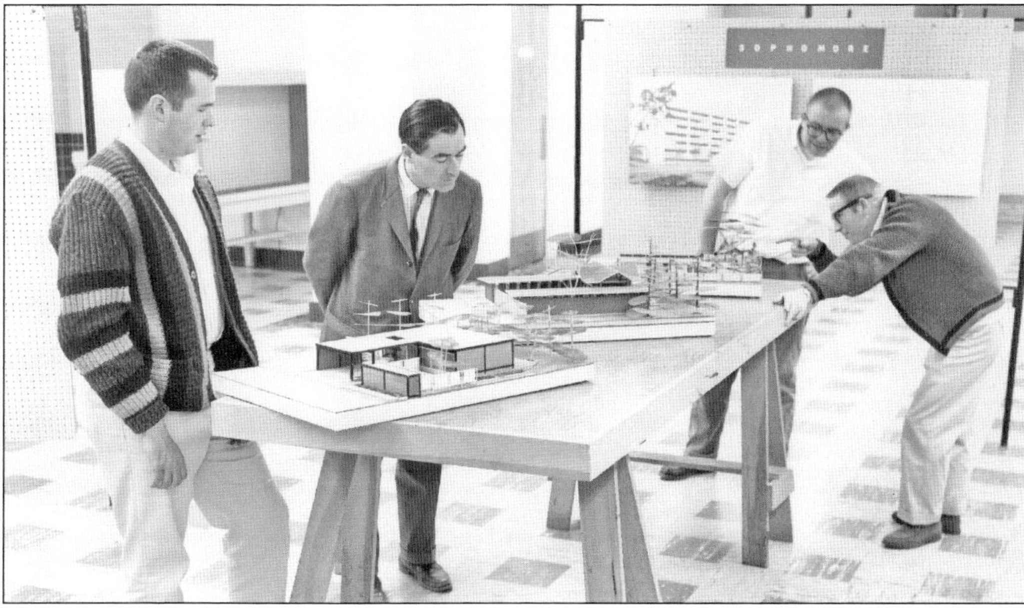

Architecture was formerly a very popular program at Idaho State University. Pictured here in 1971 are the final class projects of some of the architecture students, showcasing their building models while a professor reviews their progress. Below, students work at their drafting tables to bring their ideas to life. The four-year program in architecture was eventually eliminated from ISU after much contention at the state level.

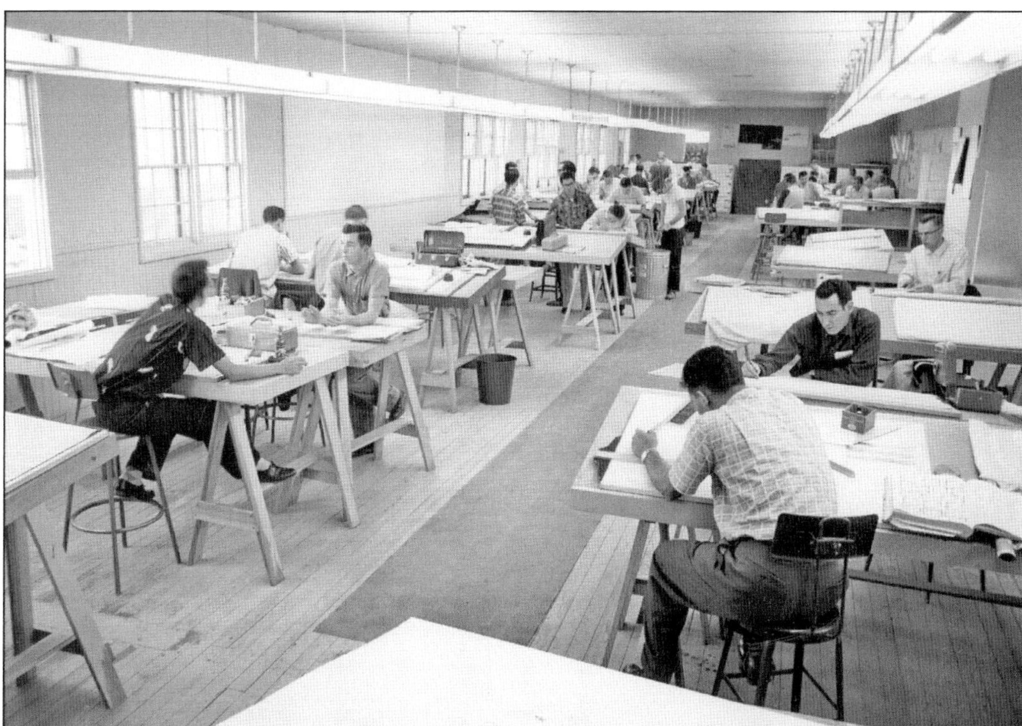

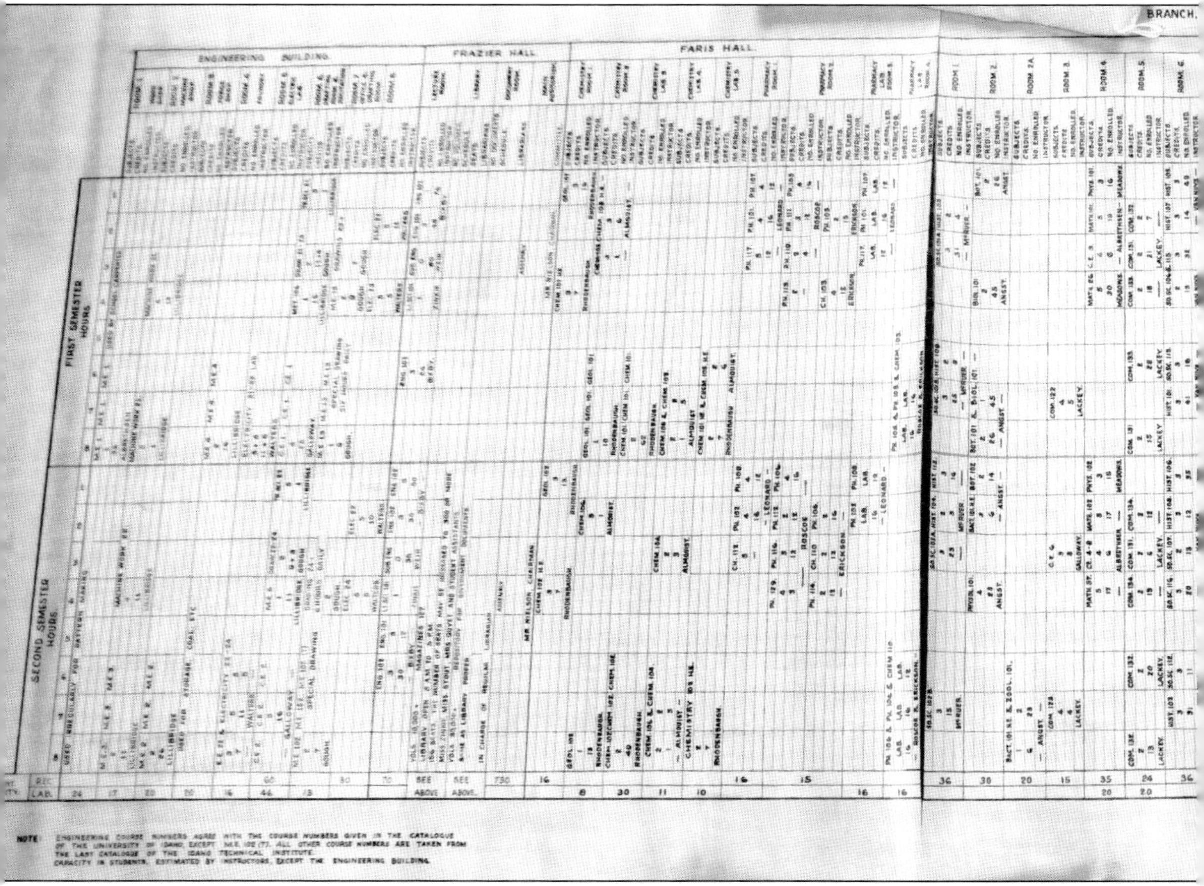

Creating the course schedule has always been quite the feat for Idaho State University. Juggling class times, meeting rooms, and professor schedules with the needs of students has always been important. This image shows a course-planning document from the University of Idaho Southern Branch, complete with faculty names, classrooms, and time slots. Today, these schedules are created by departments with a computer spreadsheet and

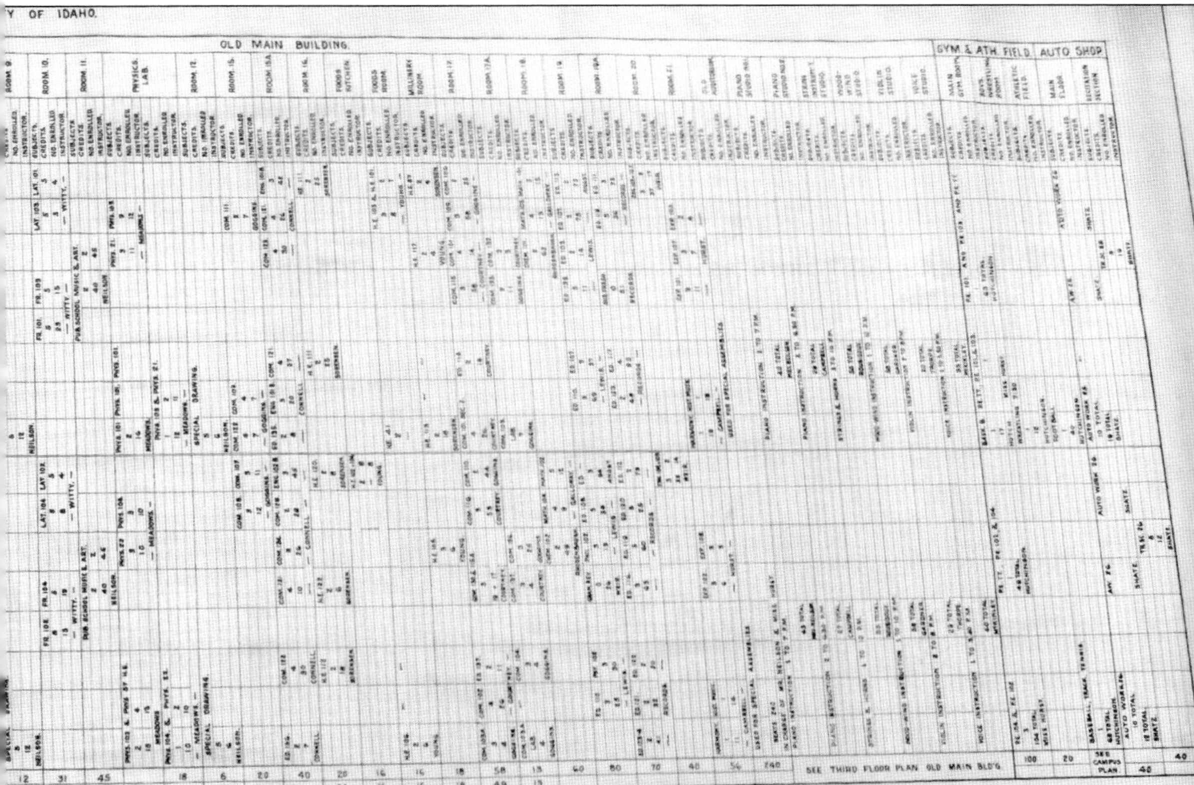

then compiled together by the registrar's office. It is still a challenge today, but creating them electronically is certainly much more efficient. Crafting a schedule that meets student needs with a variety of course times, online classes, and evening classes is still essential to the university—both for the main campus and the ISU outreach campuses in Idaho Falls, Twin Falls, and Meridian. (Courtesy of Kelsey West.)

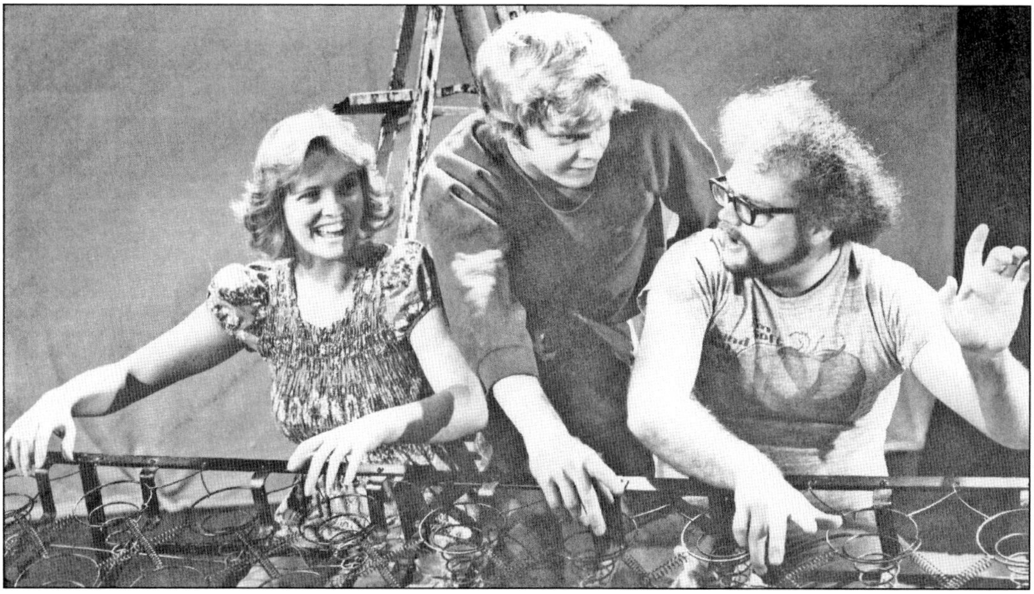

Three theater students work together to prepare for a play during their theater class in 1976. The theater department has a long history at Idaho State University, with performances early on at the Academy of Idaho. The department was located in Frazier Hall upon its completion in 1924. Since then, the program has moved to the new Stephens Performing Arts Center and offers a bachelor of arts, bachelor of fine arts, bachelor of science, and master of arts degrees in theater with a variety of emphasis areas. Just two years after this photograph was taken, the ISU student dance company Danson formed under the Associated Students of Idaho State University (ASISU).

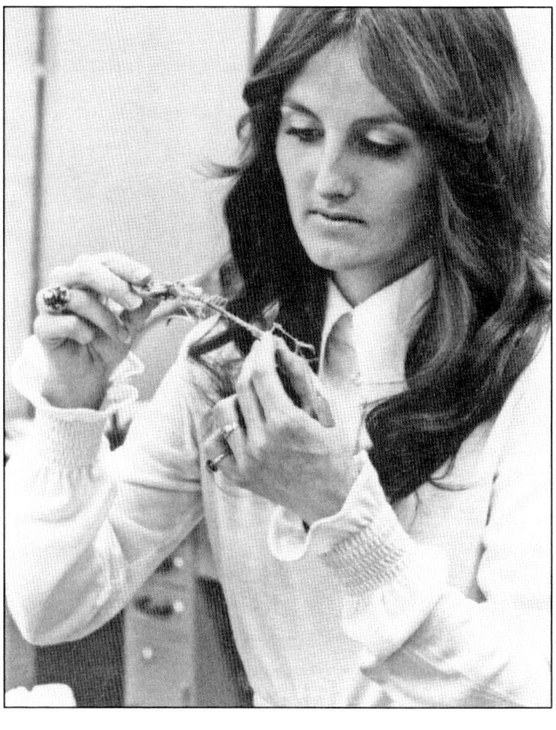

A student in the early 1970s works on a biology research project for which she was granted funding. Research has a long history at Idaho State University. Both undergraduate and graduate students have the opportunity to conduct their own research and work with faculty on their projects. ISU is classified as a Doctoral Research University by the Carnegie Foundation.

Three

Student Life

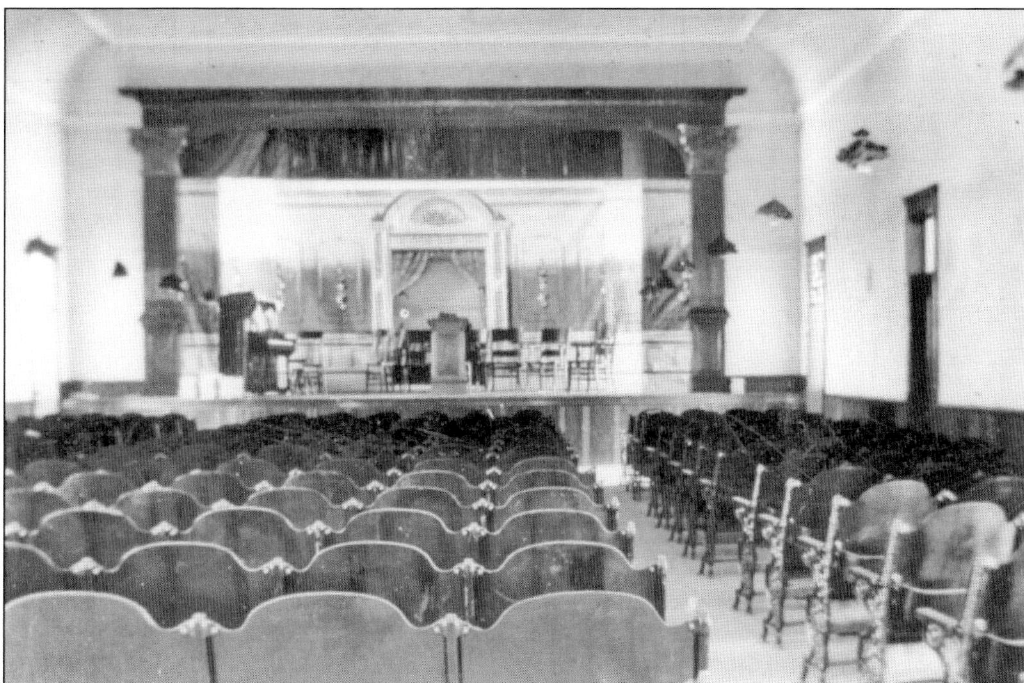

Since the very beginnings of the Academy of Idaho, students not only achieved an education, but they also pursued social growth through student involvement on campus. Some of the earliest student events happened on the very stage pictured here, centered in Swanson's assembly hall. From student body assemblies to orchestra performances to a student production of *Ivanhoe*, this stage served as a center of student life.

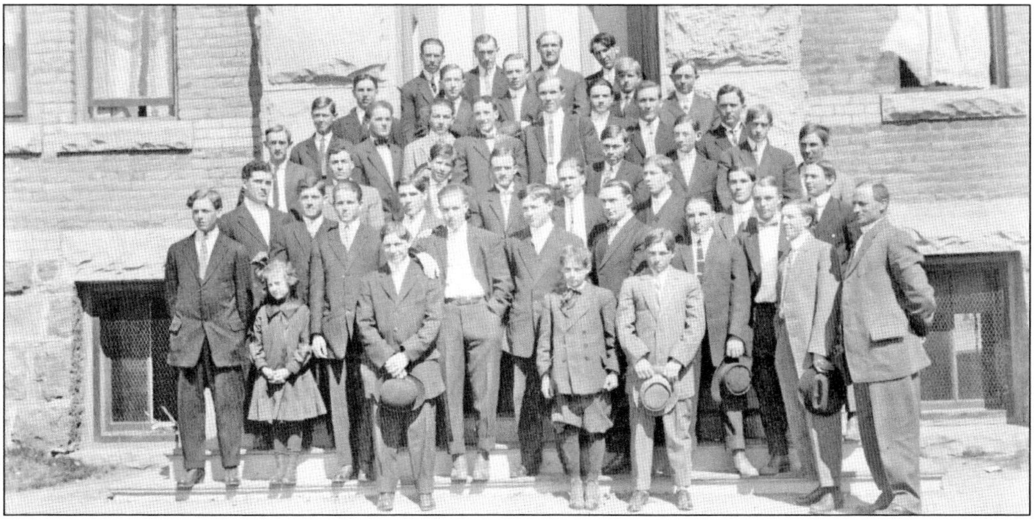

Pictured here is one of the earliest groups of students living on campus. These men lived in Faris Hall, the first men's dorm on campus. After the first year of classes, during which students boarded with local families, at a cost of $3 to $5 per week, Faris Hall was opened and housed 50 men. Shortly after, the Girl's Dormitory (later renamed Turner Hall) was completed to house women, and from that point on, all students have been able to live and learn on campus.

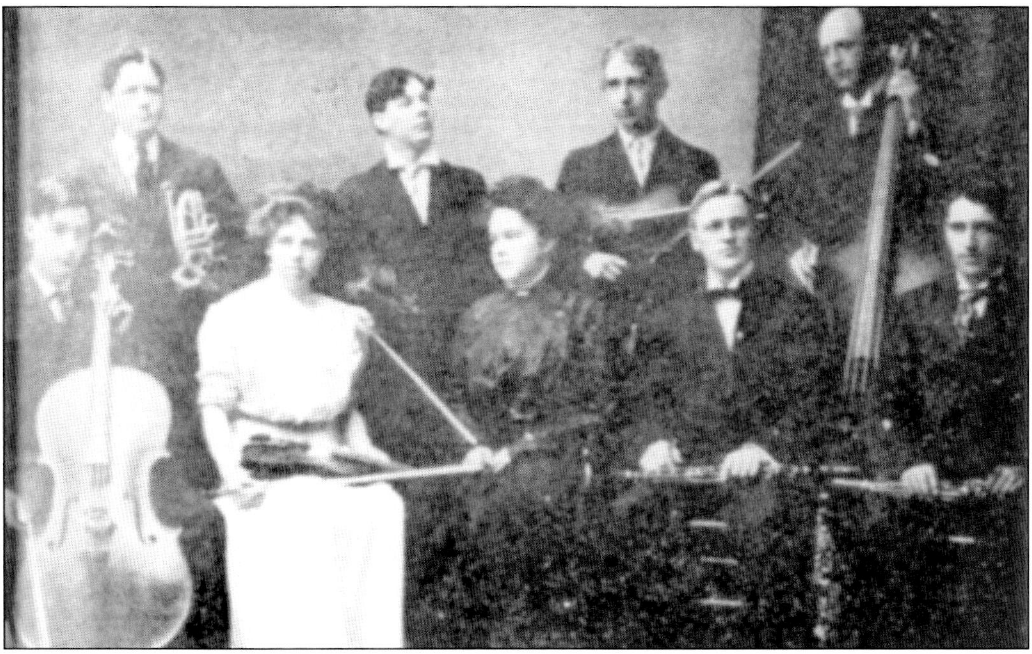

Student involvement really began to thrive in 1907. New organizations were started including Mu Theta, debate club, and the first orchestra. Students were especially interested in the arts and could often be found in the Auditorium Theatre on the weekends where they enjoyed plays and musical performances like the one pictured here. Students also printed the first student annual: the *Wickiup*. The *Wickiup* would be published almost every year until 1981, when a final subscription copy was sold without breaking even. The *Wickiup* served as a way for students to express sentiments and memories for almost 70 years.

One of the earliest fraternities was started on campus in 1909. The "Bachelors' Club" originated in the men's dormitories and was focused on "promoting a general good feeling among those boys who were afraid of the gentler sex." The club's one and only rule was that each member, over the course of the school year, should escort a girl to two functions only. Anyone disobeying the rule would be unfit to associate.

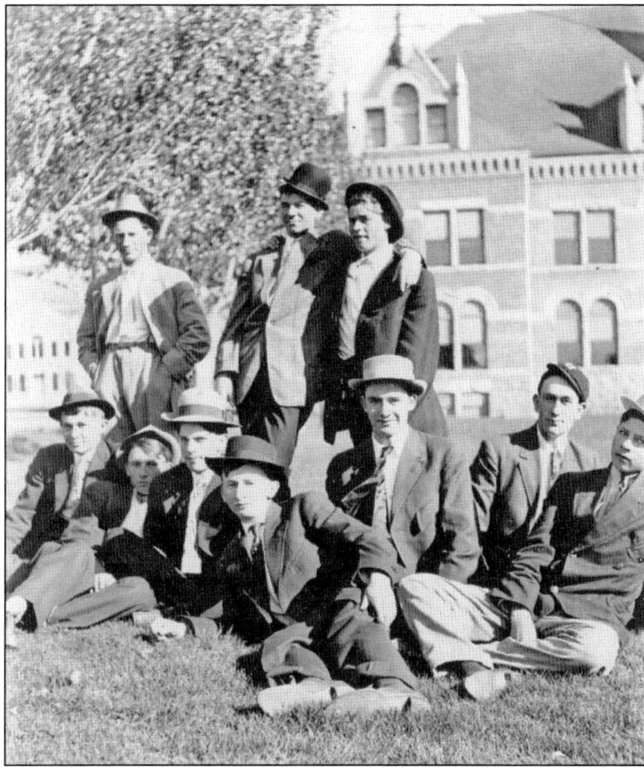

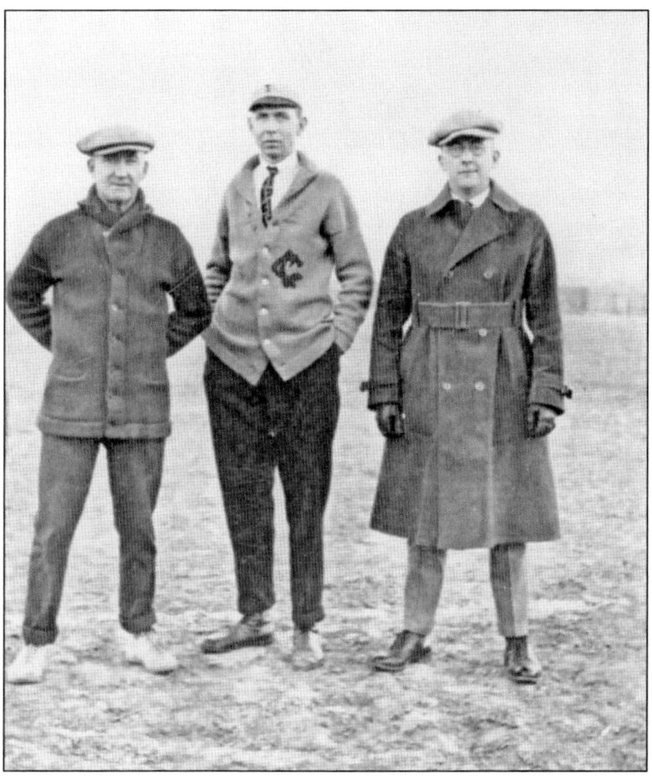

The first student newspaper, the *Techniad*, was published on November 24, 1910. Although it has been through several name changes since, it has been the main source of information about student life and opinion for more than a century. The following year, the first student government, the Associated Students of the Academy, was also formed. Enrollment was increasing, and students' voices were growing. Pictured here are three academy students, including Fred Turner (center), the son of Theodore Turner.

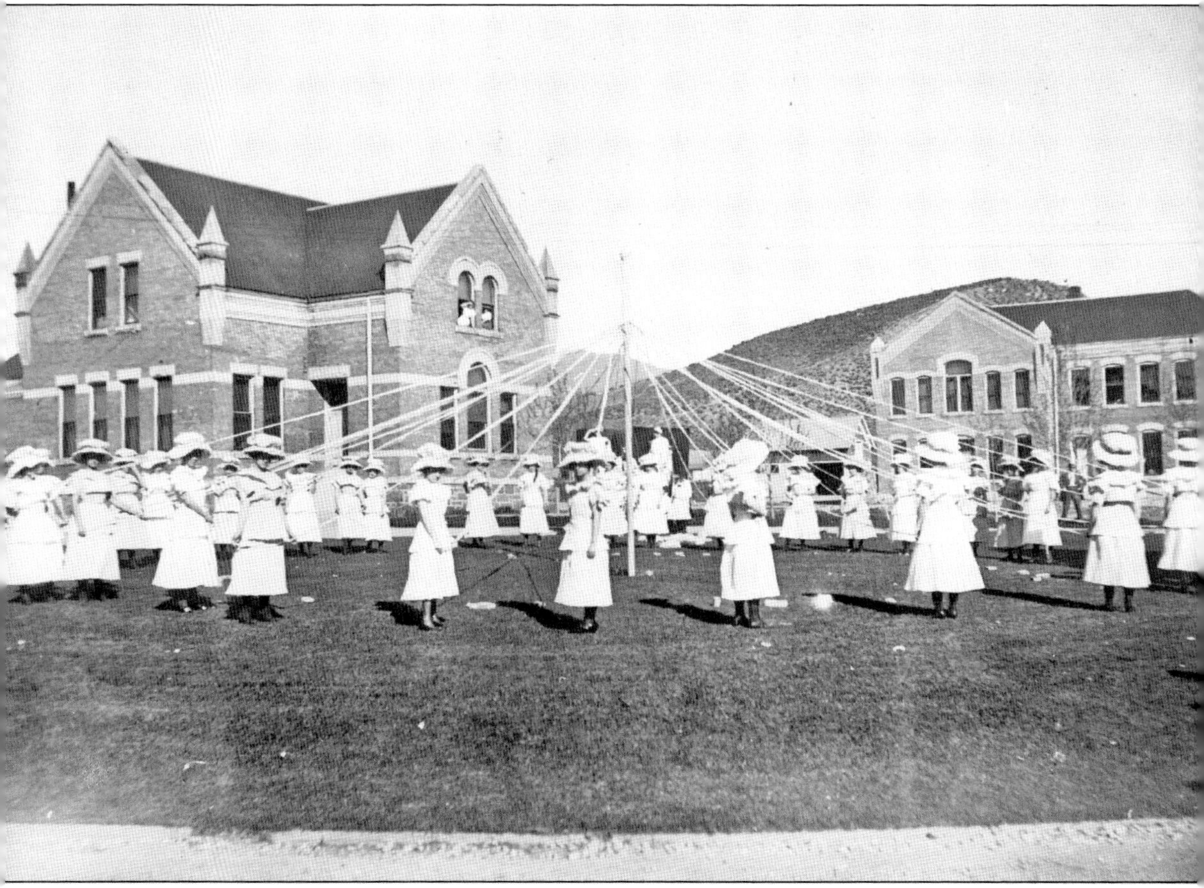

One of the most elaborate student life events was the annual May Day celebration. Started in 1912, the academy's Young Women's Christian Association fundraiser was a celebration that included a choreographed May Pole dance and May queen crowning. Pictured is the inaugural event where Emily Whittlesey was crowned as the first "Queen of May." Hundreds of townspeople would come to campus to join in the festivities, making this one of the earliest and largest examples of Pocatello community members and Academy of Idaho students coming together on campus.

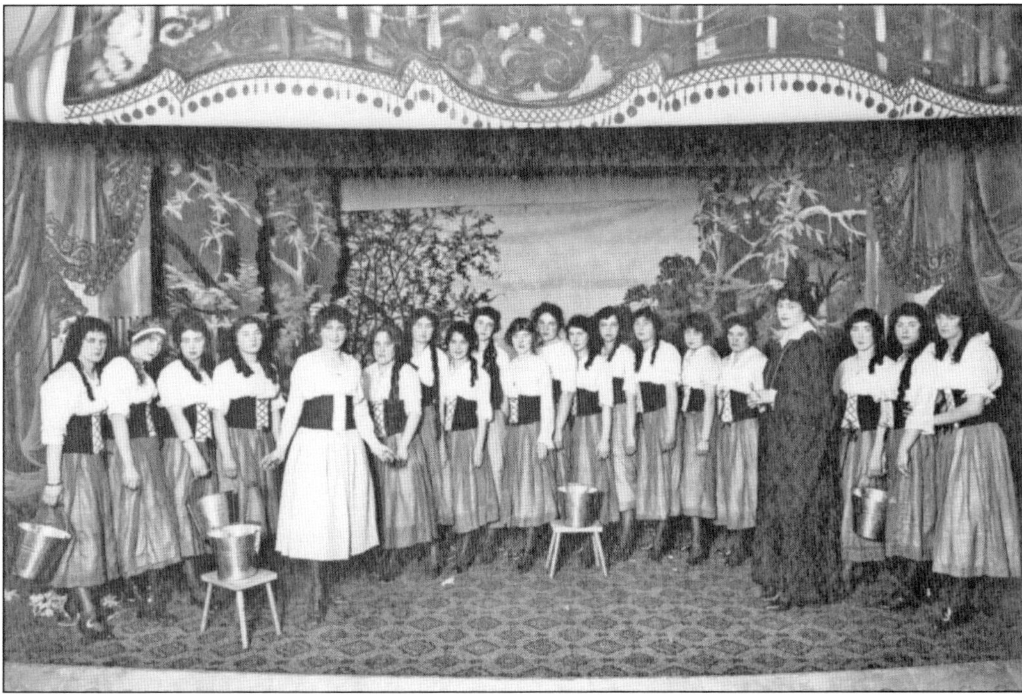

Throughout the years of the Academy of Idaho, student involvement in campus activities was a guarantee. Plays, like the one pictured here, as well as picnics, athletic games, dances, and band performances were all fully attended by both students and faculty. A strong sense of community and camaraderie was always present at the academy.

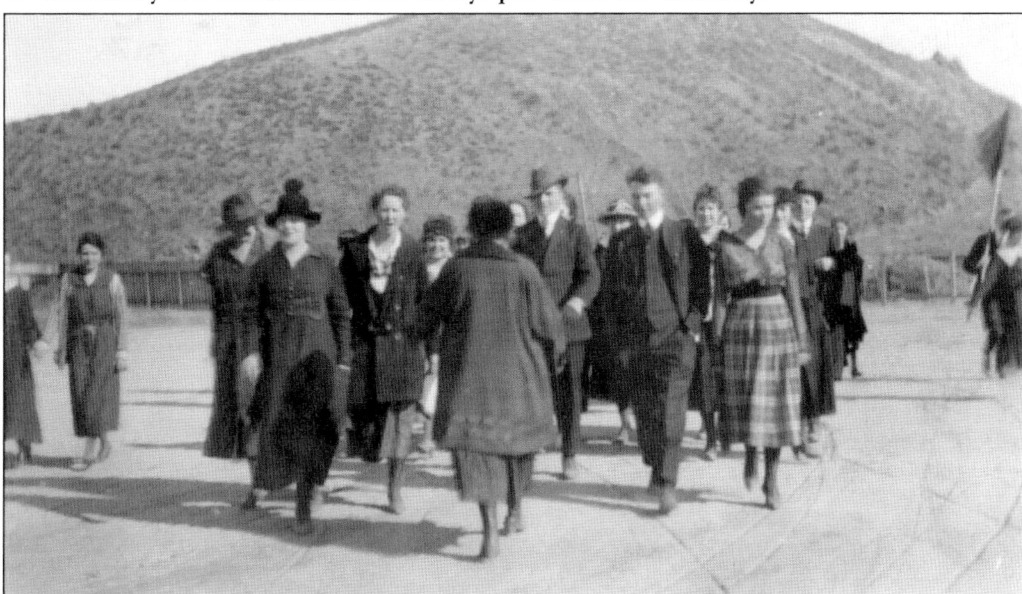

Excitement and involvement skyrocketed in 1915 when the school was renamed the Idaho Technical Institute. This landmark change was commemorated with a "Tally-Ho" parade, helping the exhilaration spread through the entire town. The celebration ended with students marching up Red Hill to whitewash a "T" on the rocks.

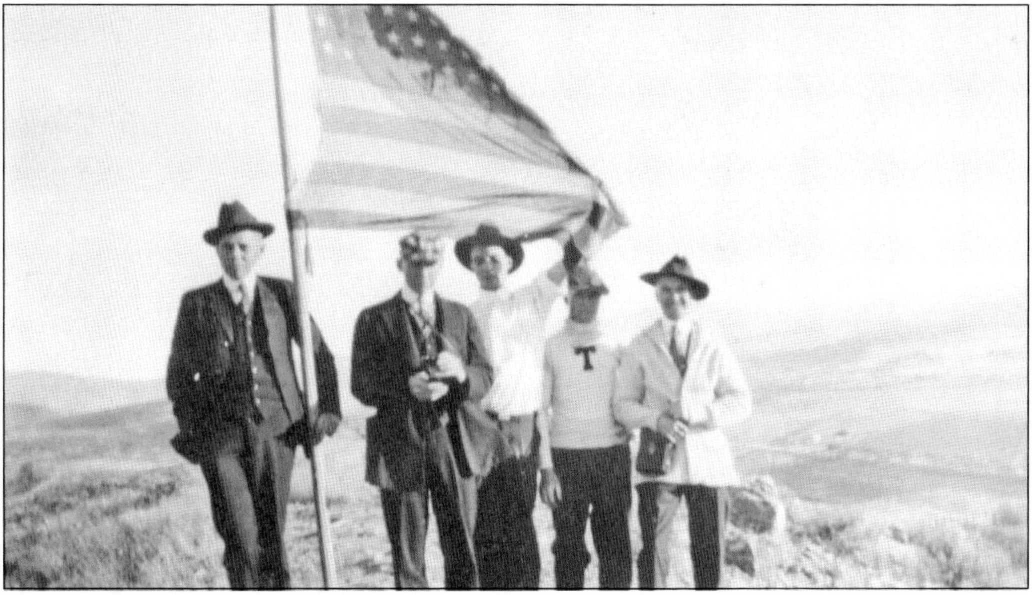

The increase in involvement was short lived, however, because student life took a short decline as the United States entered World War I. Spring break and commencement were cancelled, and students took examinations early so they could leave to attend to wartime demands. Though student life had diminished, the annual "T" party began as a new tradition for students to celebrate the anniversary of the Tech Bill. Students would hold a pep rally, bonfire, and dance after cleaning the campus and climbing to the top of Red Hill to whitewash the "T."

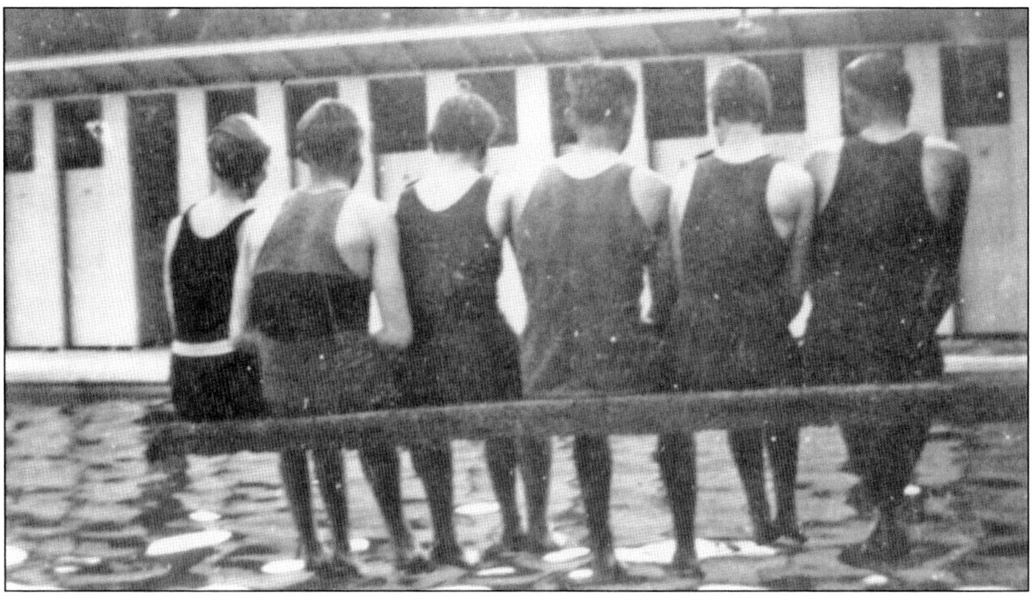

After the war came to a close and enrollment went back up, the 1920s brought more excitement to campus. New clubs were formed, including the "I" Club, pictured at a retreat to Lava Hot Springs, which is still a popular hangout today. The "I" club was made up of lettered athletes who promoted athletics, school spirit, tradition, and sportsmanship. It remained one of the longest-standing clubs on campus.

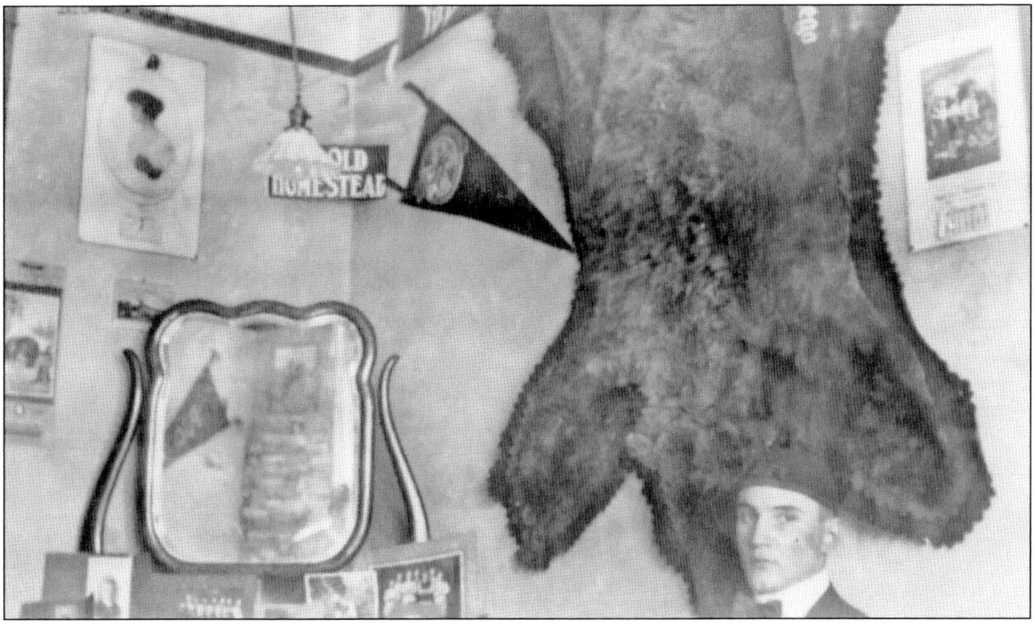

Life continued to thrive within the dormitories. The excitement of moving away from home and taking a step toward independence was immortalized in how students chose to represent themselves in their dorm rooms. Pictured is one young man's dorm room from March 31, 1918. While students may not display bear pelts in their dorms anymore, little else has changed. Family photographs, mirrors, and sports paraphernalia still adorn dorm room walls.

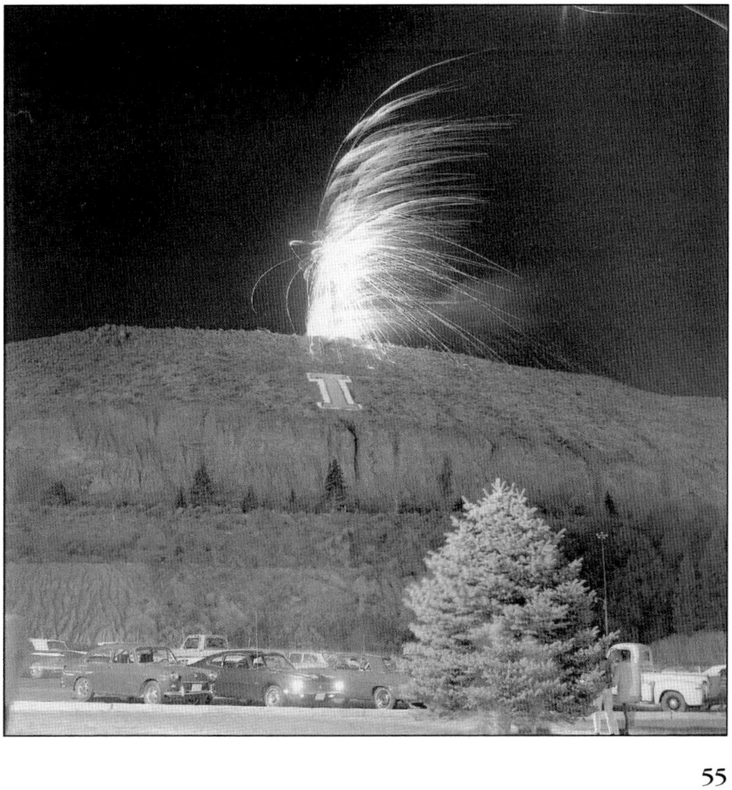

During the 1920s, students felt frustrated about not being afforded the status of a four-year institution, so they trekked up Red Hill to change the existing "T" to a "4." After lengthy protests, the decision was made to incorporate the school with the University of Idaho, and the Southern Branch was born. Students marched up Red Hill once more to change the "4" to the longstanding "I."

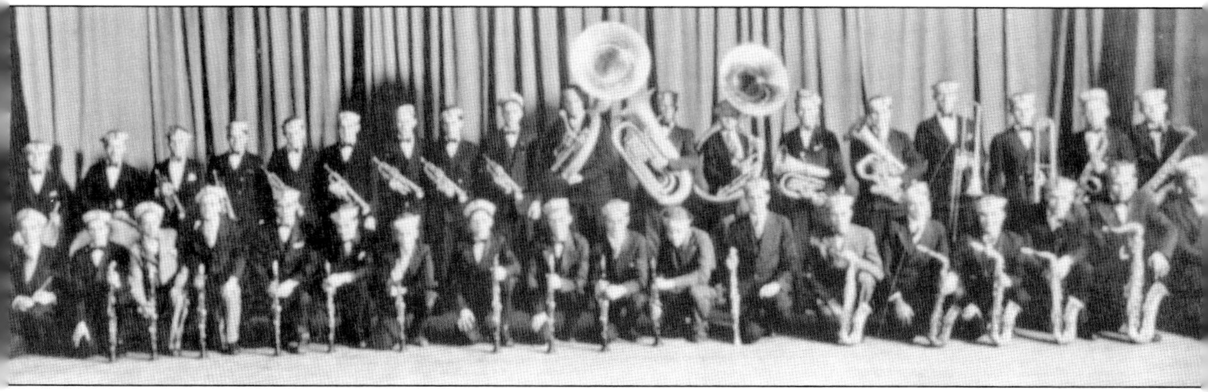

As the school transitioned into its association with the University of Idaho, campus life flourished. Student clubs grew to include an agriculture club, Sigma Sigma Beta, Sigma Alpha Psi, orchestra (pictured here), and the first pep band. The orchestra soon became the Pocatello Symphony Orchestra in the 1930s, and talented musicians from the community were invited to join the students. During this time, the relationship between students and the community grew, and campus events were enjoyed by all of Pocatello, as long as participants were not caught violating the laws of Prohibition.

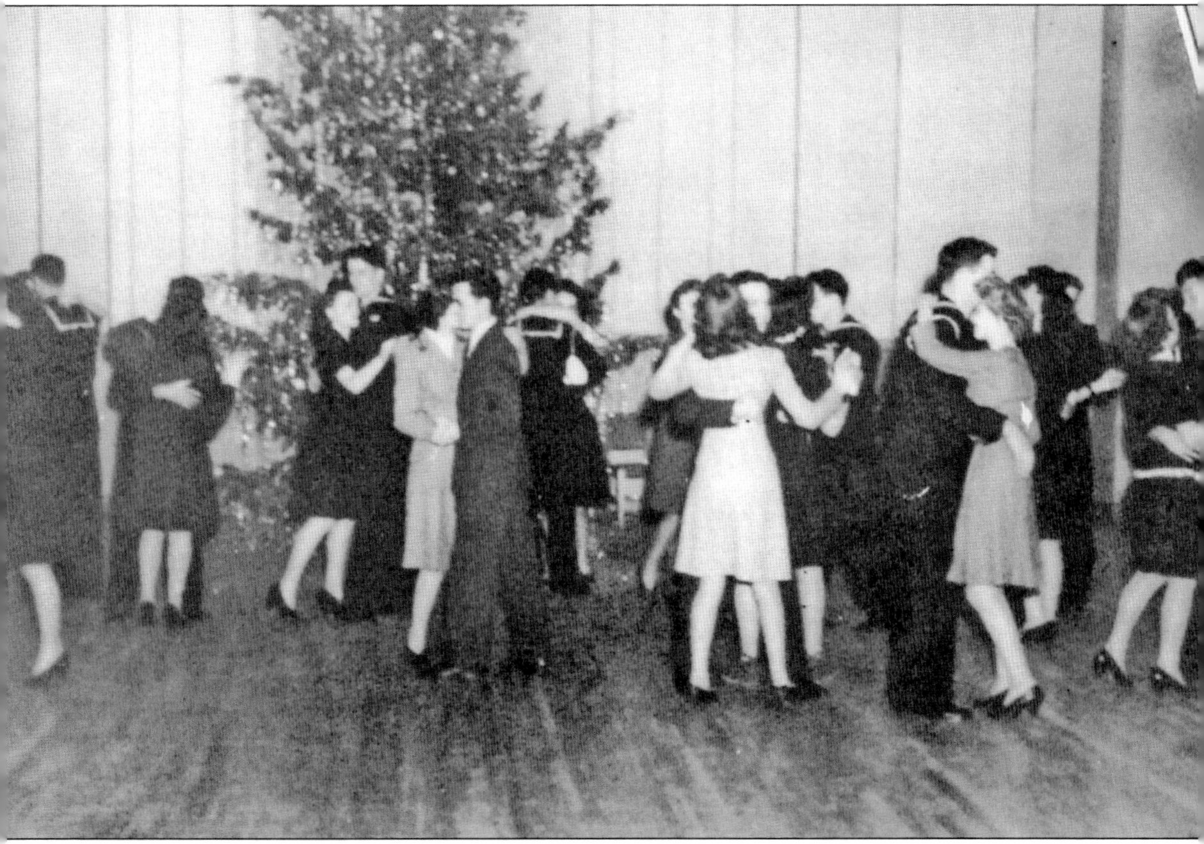

In the 1930s, the student population became more nontraditional, including at least eight married students, a 15-year-old student, and its first blind student. The student population also included many more working students as they tried to work off the burdens of the Depression. Although the Depression brought hard times for the students living in Hooverville, student life continued to grow and thrive. Pictured here, students continued to throw annual dances and events, including the Christmas formal. A student "mini-government" was formed, and although money was tight, they established a bookstore, donated funds to the Community Concert Association, sponsored recruitment trips, and continued to finance the four-year movement. They even approved a salary for the president of the associated student body.

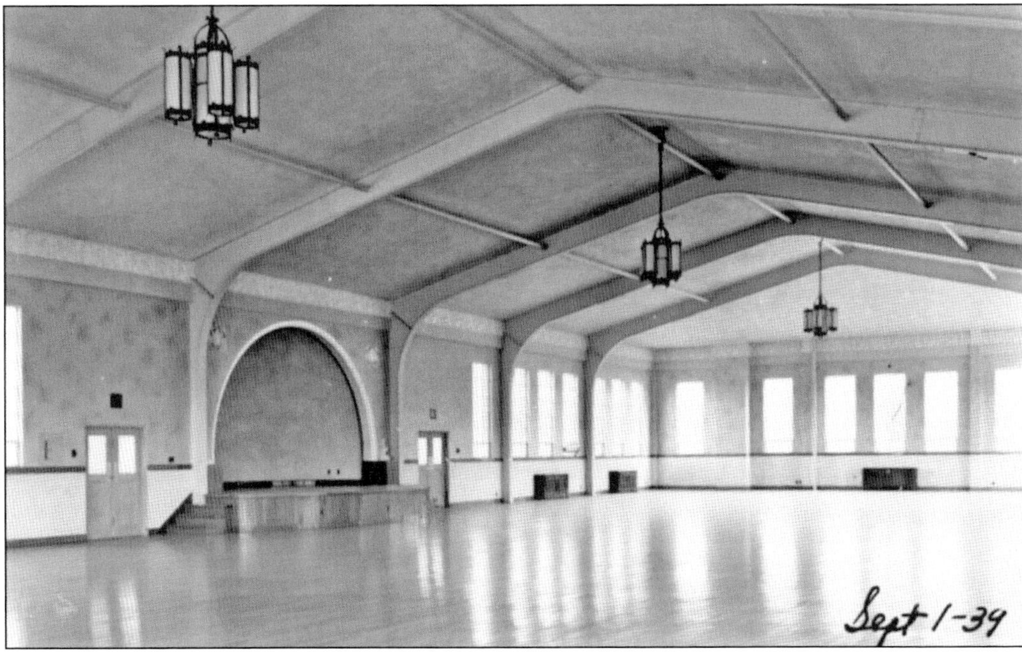

Toward the end of the Depression, the student council assumed much more responsibility, including the financial burden of a new student union building. Since most functions were being held in the dilapidated gymnasium—or on special occasions, the Bannock Hotel—this marked an exciting time to be a student with increasing student activities and the bringing of a center of student activity to campus. Pictured here is the finished interior of the student union, a home for dances like the annual Sweetheart formal, pageants for homecoming queen, and even contests for the famed "Ugly Man."

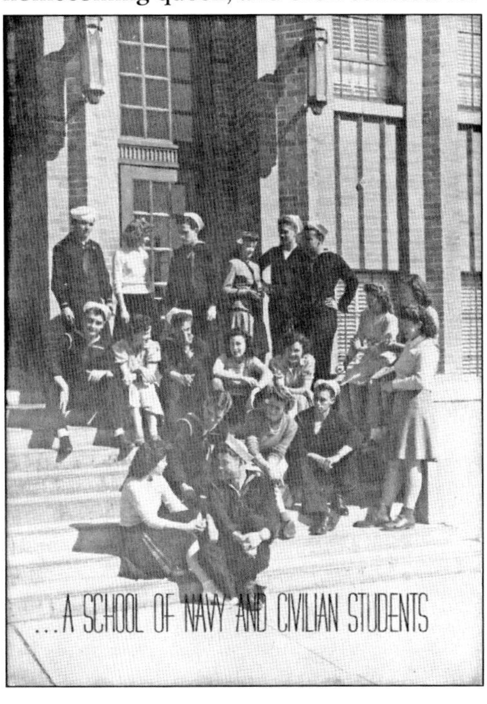

The beginning of the 1940s plunged the campus into wartime once again, but the installment of naval training programs helped grow enrollment and involvement. Military students were sent to campus and acting dean Ernest J. Baldwin reported that the cadets had "entered wholeheartedly into our student activities." Although the *Wickiup* yearbook was suspended during the war, a magazine called the *Dittybag* was published and recounts many stories of military and civilian students joining together in student plays, choral groups, dances, and many other activities.

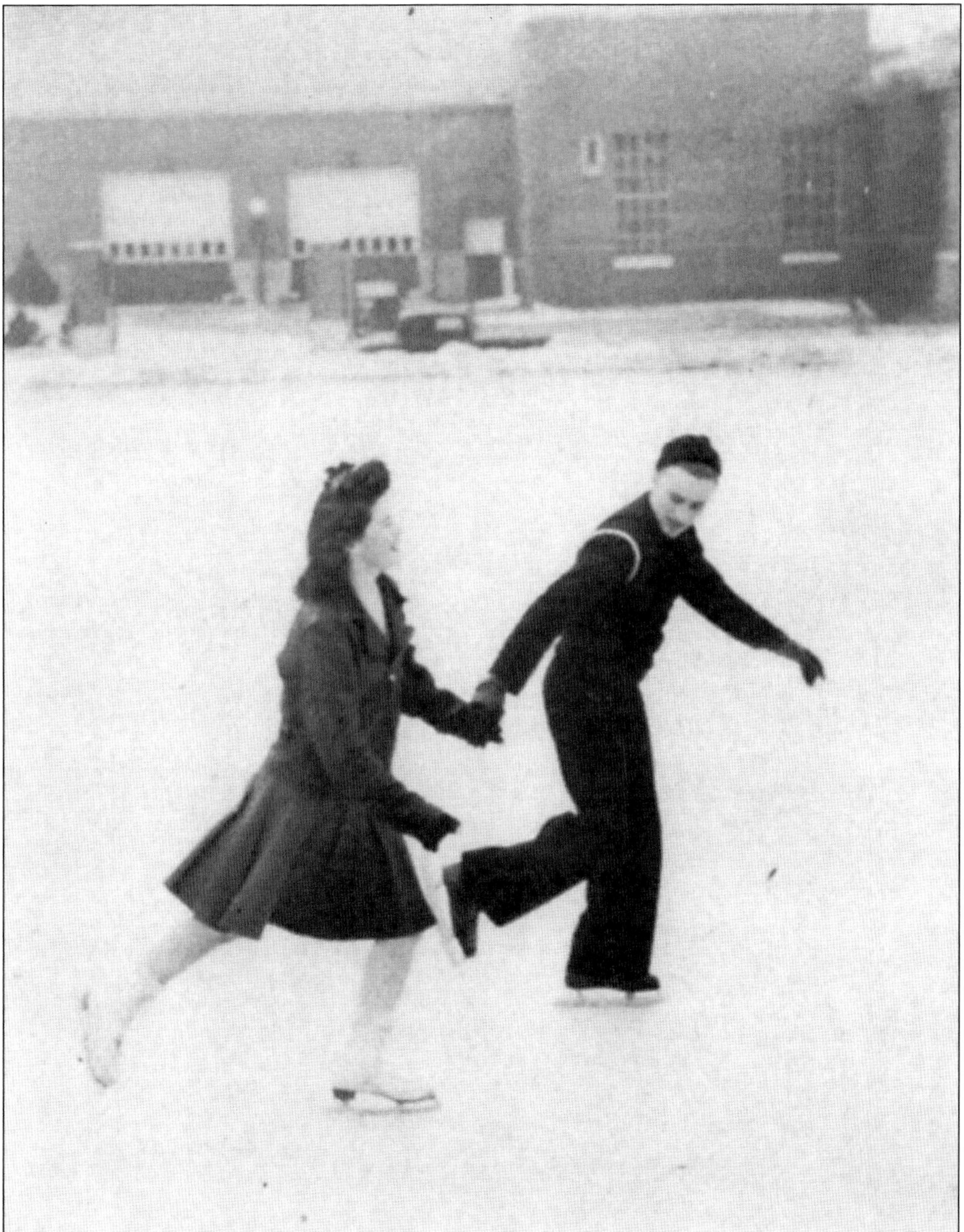

Despite limited funds during wartime, student activities remained constant and plentiful. Students gathered together for "send-off" dances for departing cadets, celebrated Sadie Hawkins Day, and continued many annual traditions like the All-College Ball and the freshman "green beanie" ritual. There was a regularly scheduled Navy Happy Hour, which featured boxing and music. The infamous Blue Room opened in 1944 and became an instant favorite hangout for all students on campus. Another popular activity for students was skating on the on-campus ice rink (located near the present-day Fine Arts Building).

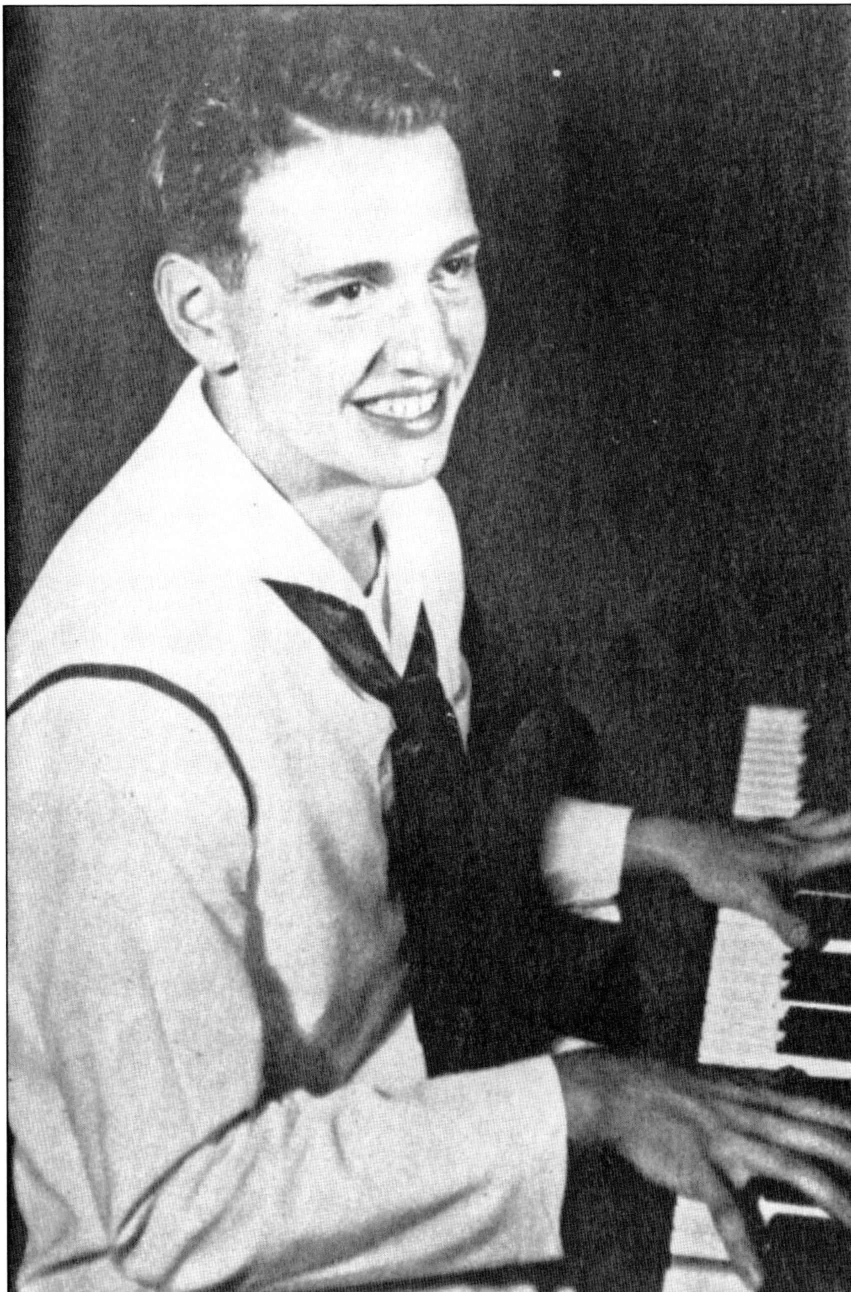

In 1944, the V-12 program brought a very special student to campus. Pictured here is Louis Weertz, who would later be known as the famous pianist Roger Williams. Though his schedule was filled with vigorous workouts, including a regularly scheduled obstacle course up Red Hill, he spent long nights and weekends in front of the piano while fellow students enjoyed social activities. His hard work and dedication paid off, and he made a lasting impression on the Southern Branch and Pocatello. Many alumni still recall seeing him perform at the Bannock Hotel and in the student union ballroom, where more than one student proposed to their sweetheart during his captivating performances.

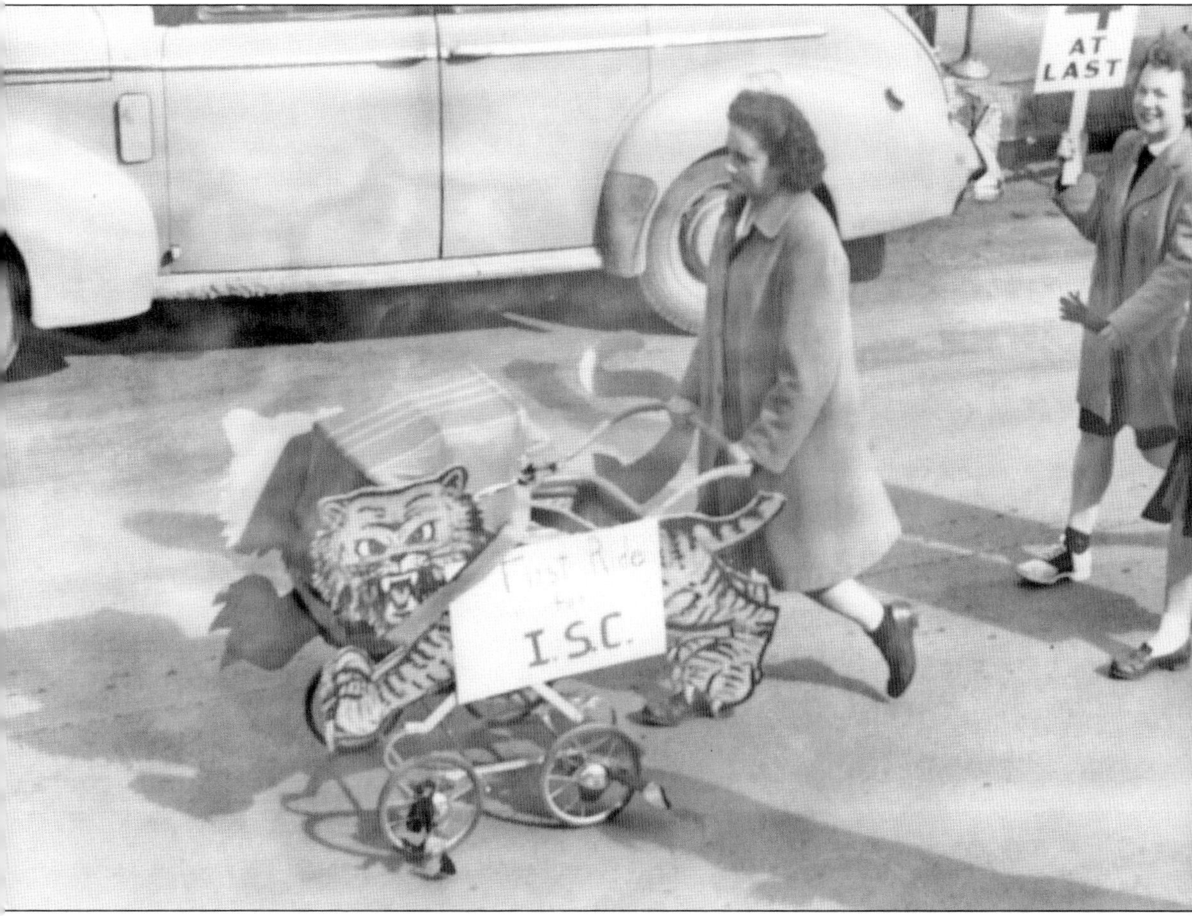

Student pride completely exploded in 1947 when four-year status was granted at last. Pictured here is student Melba Mack in a parade celebrating the bill passing. Just before the bill passed, students John Foreman and Jay and Del Slaughter organized a musical variety show to increase public interest in the four-year cause. This morning assembly included an orchestra and several actors who performed a musical extravaganza. Two months later, Idaho State College became a reality. This event, which was called the "Great Day," ended in 1950, but it provided students with an institutional celebration to show off their new school pride. The last Great Day also blessed Idaho State College with one of its more enduring traditions: the fight song.

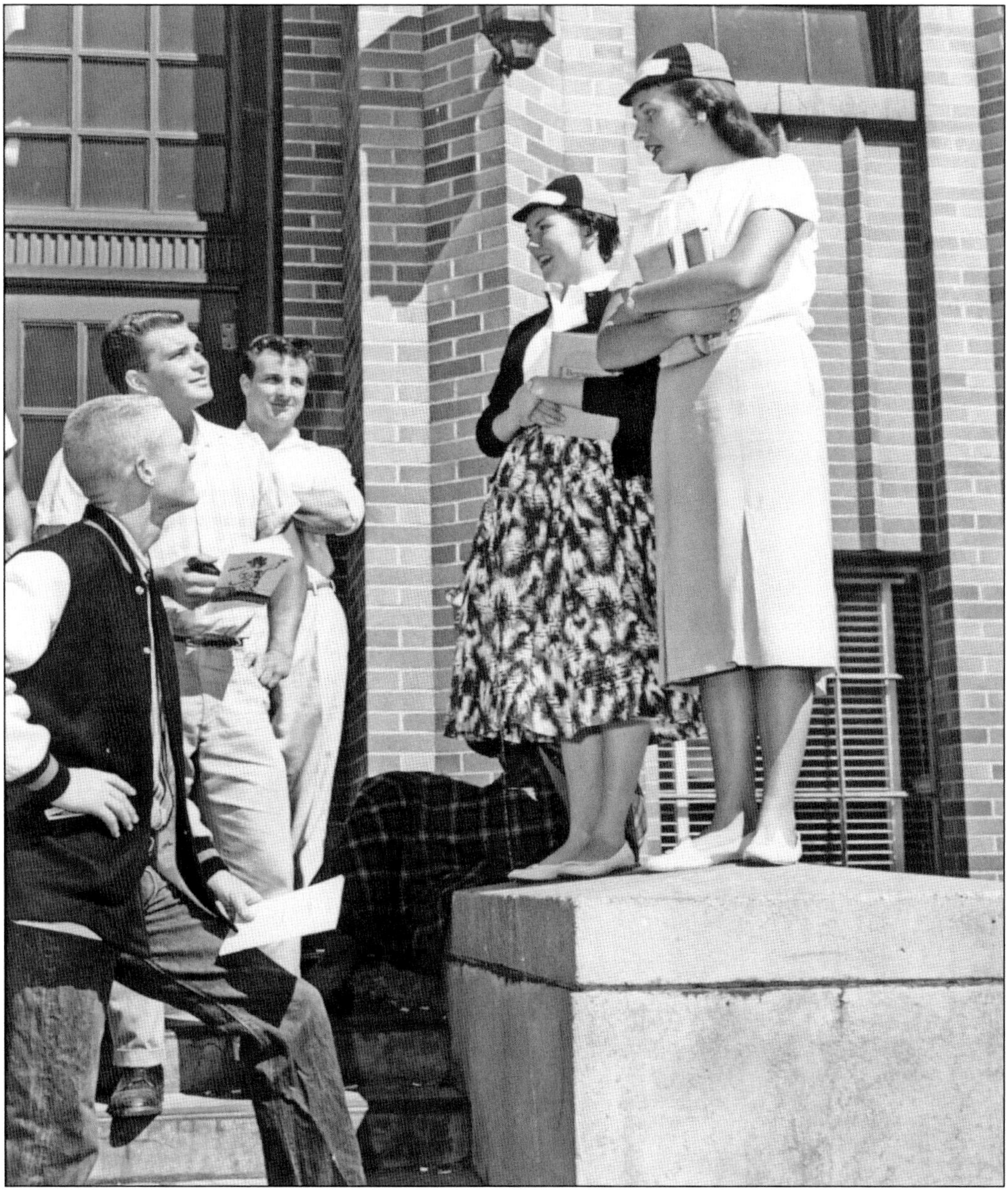

With newly expanded school pride, traditions like homecoming took on an even greater significance. The freshmen initiation process returned, and initiation rituals were outlined. Freshmen beanies, which were now black and orange, were required at all times, and a giant freshman beanie was to be constructed by homecoming time when it would be burned at the game. During initiation week, freshmen were not allowed to be seen within the vicinity of Graveley Hall or in the company of women, and they were not to sit in the Blue Room unless it was on the floor. Initiation ended with freshmen sitting in a segregated section at the homecoming game and finally removing their beanies.

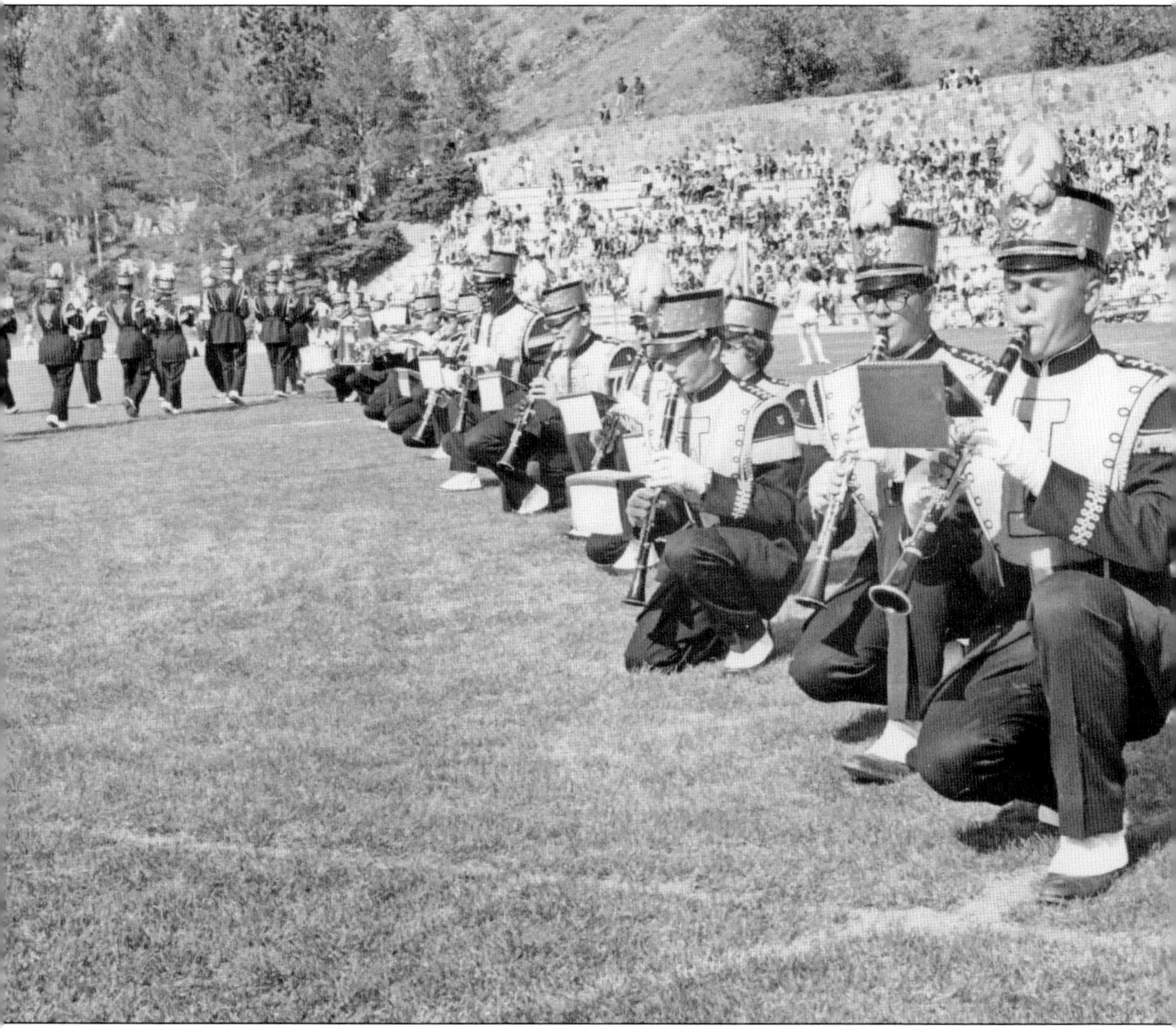

Although the original marching band was organized in 1923, wartime had caused its demise. Thankfully, in 1948, Idaho State College appointed Wesley Harris as band director, and the marching band reappeared. They enhanced school pride with their performances at games and events. Harris worked hard to get donations, and a booster, Danny Pullos, sponsored the band's first trip. From that first journey, the Alma Mater Hymn was born. The band continued to flourish and even performed on Idaho Day at the 1962 World's Fair in Seattle. Pictured here is a later photograph of the Idaho State College marching band performing in the Spud Bowl. Though the program was once again eliminated in the 1980s, it was reborn in 1998, exactly 50 years after its first revitalization.

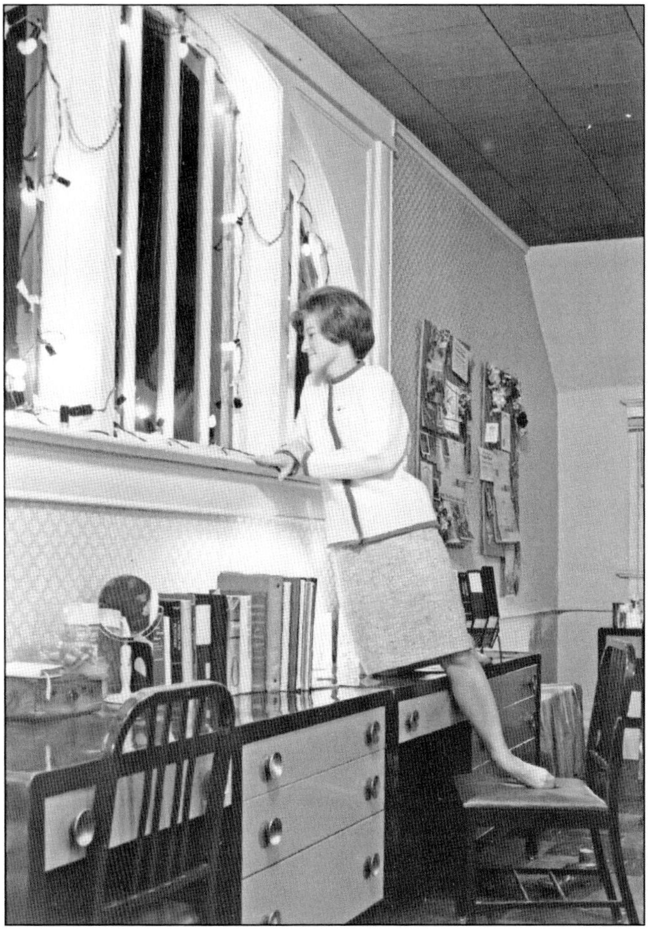

Student housing at Idaho State College (ISC) was as popular as ever. Rules were strict for coed housing, and Graveley Hall residents had a manual that outlined quiet hours, telephone calls, dress code, and appropriate behaviors when being "serenaded" by male students. Despite regulations, Graveley Hall remained a center of life and excitement for ISC women, and many students found great fun in sunbathing on the roof or sneaking last-minute goodnight kisses before getting caught by their housemothers. By 1951, the women had gained more freedom, and they asked that they be allowed to vote on their own house rules. That same year, the ISC student body elected their first-ever female president, Dorothy Wagoner.

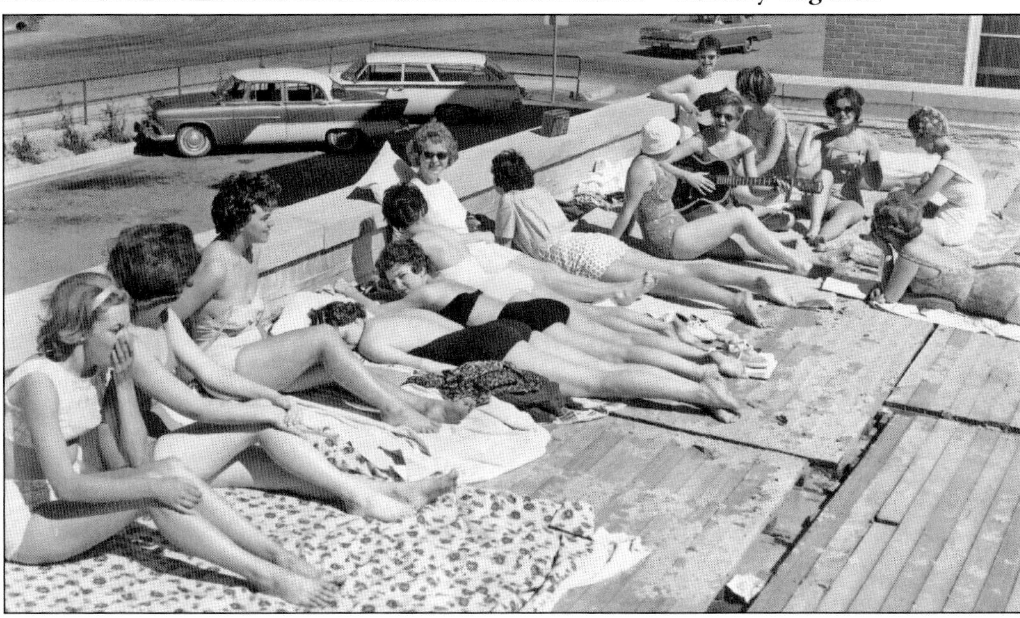

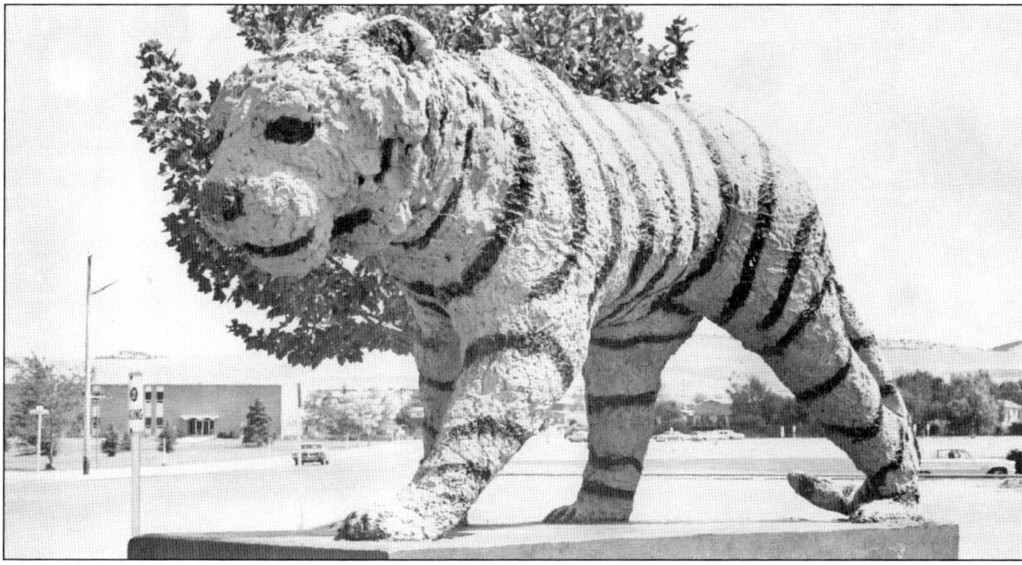

Homecoming on campus has been a longtime pillar of spirit and celebration. Homecoming parades have historically featured elaborate floats made of papier-mâché. Although many of these floats were a bit flimsy and did not hold up well in wind and cold precipitation, some were surprisingly durable. This Bengal tiger was part of the award-winning float constructed by Phi Sigma Kappa for the 1953 homecoming parade. Made of papier-mâché on a wire frame, the Bengal was preserved and mounted in front of Reed Gym for decades.

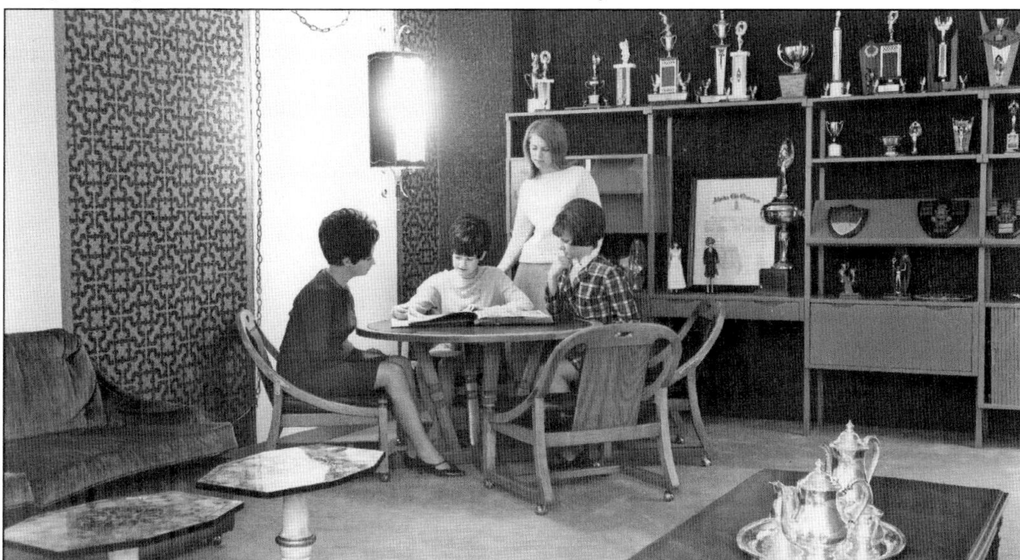

During the time of Idaho State College, the number of student clubs and organizations continued to grow. With more than 30 clubs offered by 1955, there was certainly no shortage of options for students to get involved. Clubs like Intercollegiate Knights, cadets, and the "I" club remained popular, while the number of sororities and fraternities grew. Pictured here are student members of Alpha Chi Omega meeting in their chapter room. Through their expansion in the 1950s, the fraternities and sororities had developed their annual Greek Weekend into the seven-day Greek Week celebration of today.

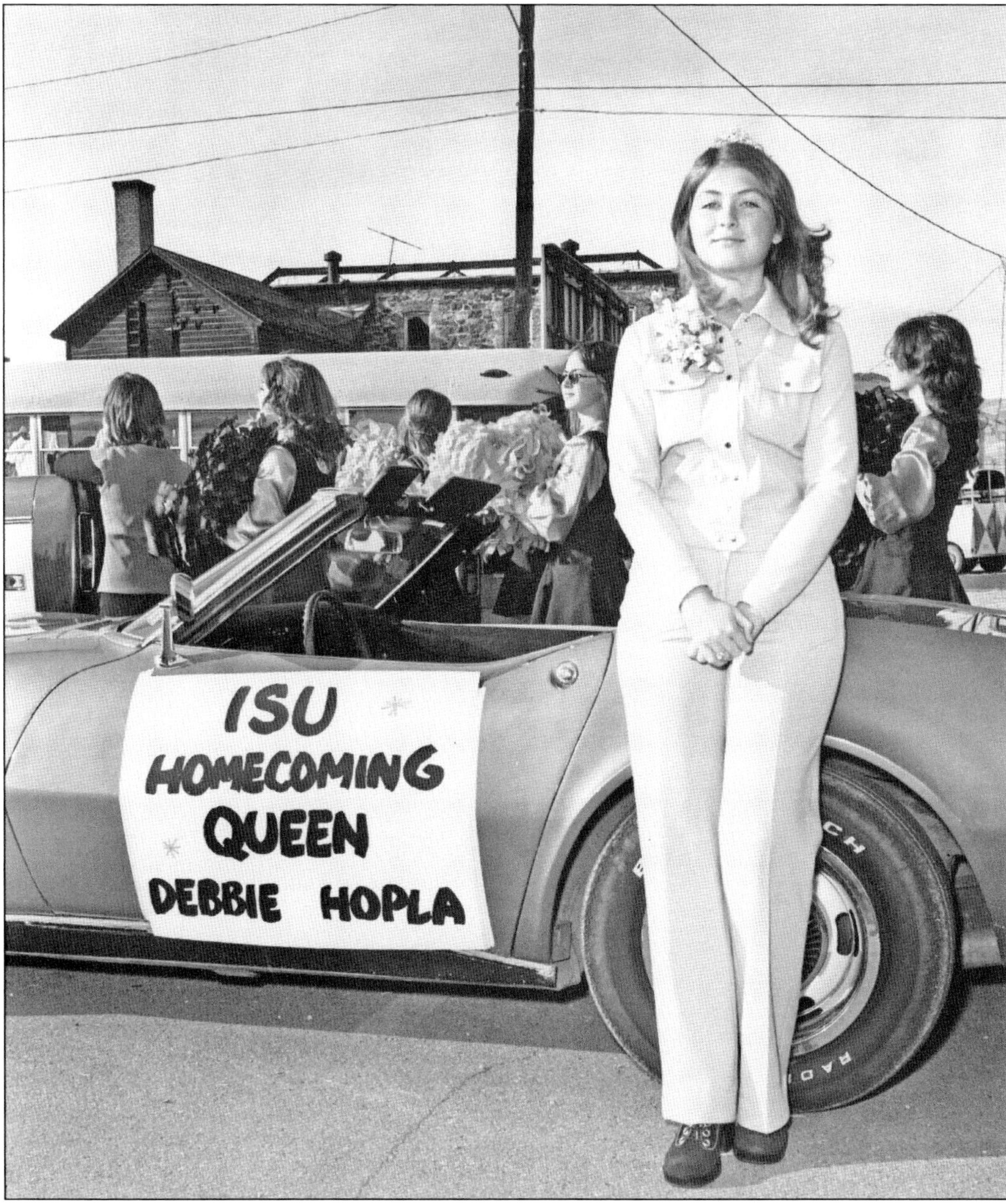

In 1963, the students rejoiced once again when they finally earned the beloved name of Idaho State University. Along with this change of name came a new and more vocal student body. With the impending Vietnam War, many students began questioning authority and desiring control of their own destiny. There were many peace rallies across campus, marches through Pocatello, and the *Bengal* newspaper, formerly known as the *Techniad*, began publishing its first political cartoons. The student government reformed from a student council to a student senate with representation based on enrollment. This similar structure that is known today was established in the 1960s, and the students have since had a much louder voice across campus. When the senate was established, one of its first acts abolished the women's dress code. Pictured here is Debbie Hopla, reigning as an ISU homecoming queen, in a fashionable pair of pants.

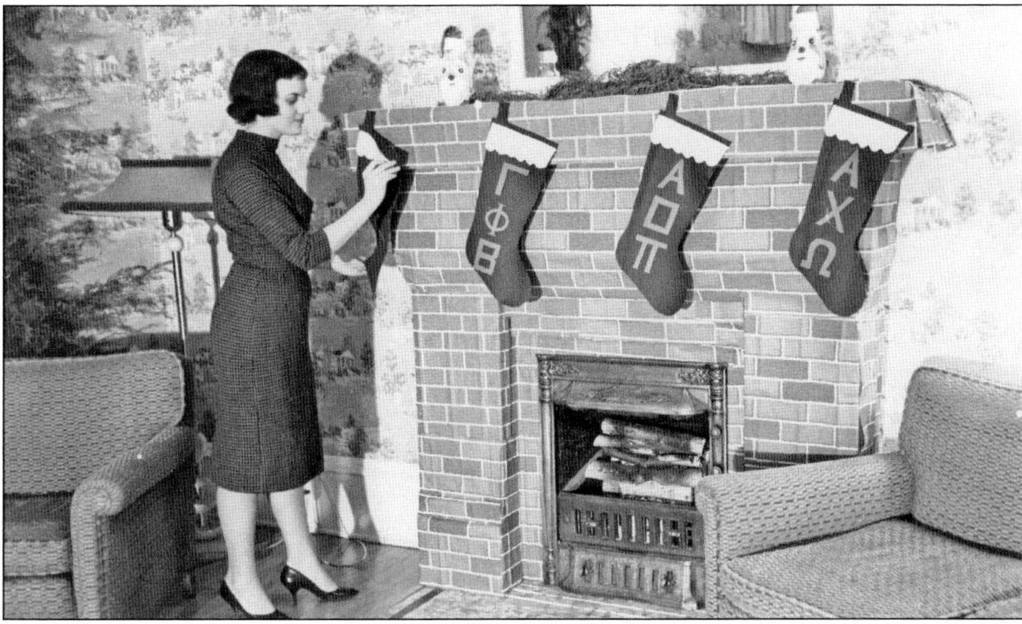

Christmas brought out large amounts of student involvement across campus. Pictured here are sorority girls showcasing their holiday spirit by decorating their chapter rooms and residence hall rooms. It was always popular to decorate the residence halls and celebrate for weeks leading up to the Christmas break. The students would open up their halls to the community for their annual open house, where everyone across campus could enjoy the decor and refreshments. The annual Christmas ball was also a popular formal that gave students a chance to dress up and dance the night way.

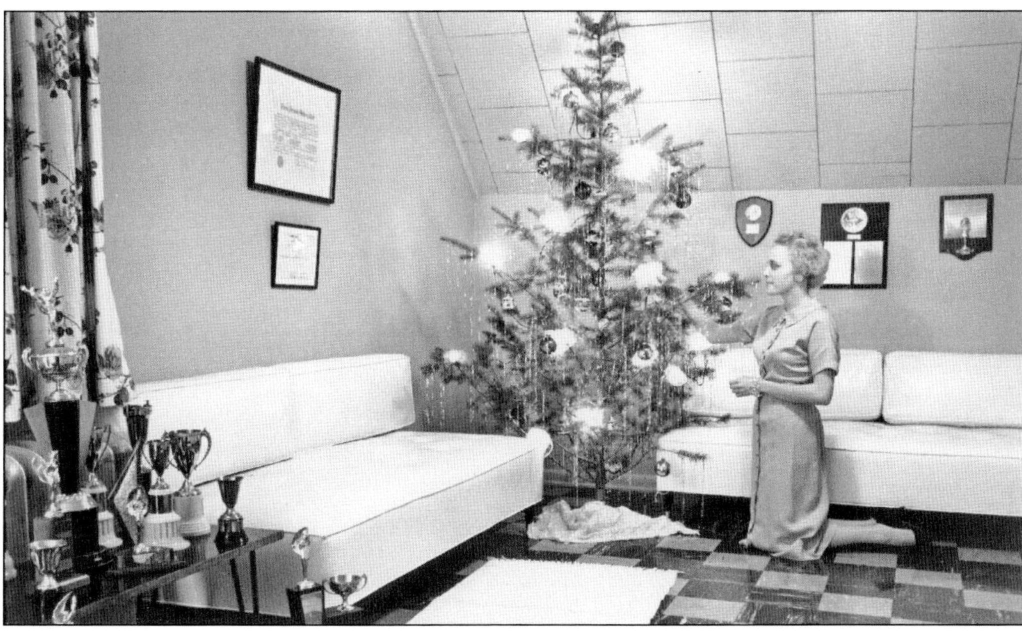

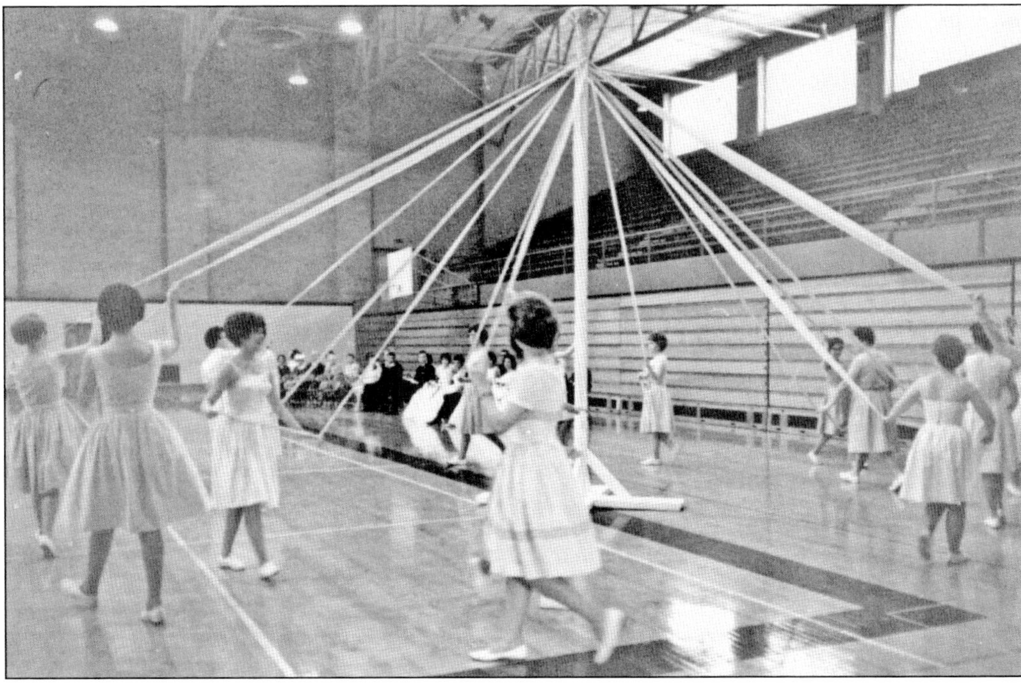

May Day remained a longstanding tradition and popular event celebrated during parents' weekend on campus. Here, students participate in a May Pole dance in Reed Gym. Other popular and traditional events included the Kickapoo Gardens Dance sponsored by the Intercollegiate Knights, the annual barn dance, the Christmas formal, military ball, Sweetheart formal, and, of course, homecoming.

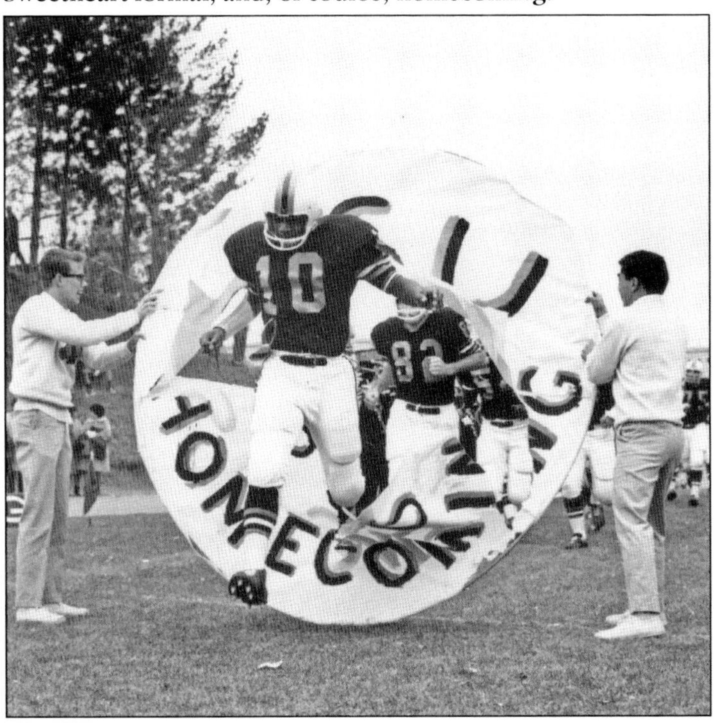

Idaho State University Homecoming Saturdays today look a bit different from Homecoming Saturdays of the early 1960s. In this photograph, the ISU football team breaks through a sign as they charge onto the field at the start of the homecoming game. Whereas homecoming used to be played in mid- to late October outdoors on the grass at the Spud Bowl (now Davis Field), often in inclement weather, today's homecoming game takes place indoors at Holt Arena on a state-of-the-art SporTurf field.

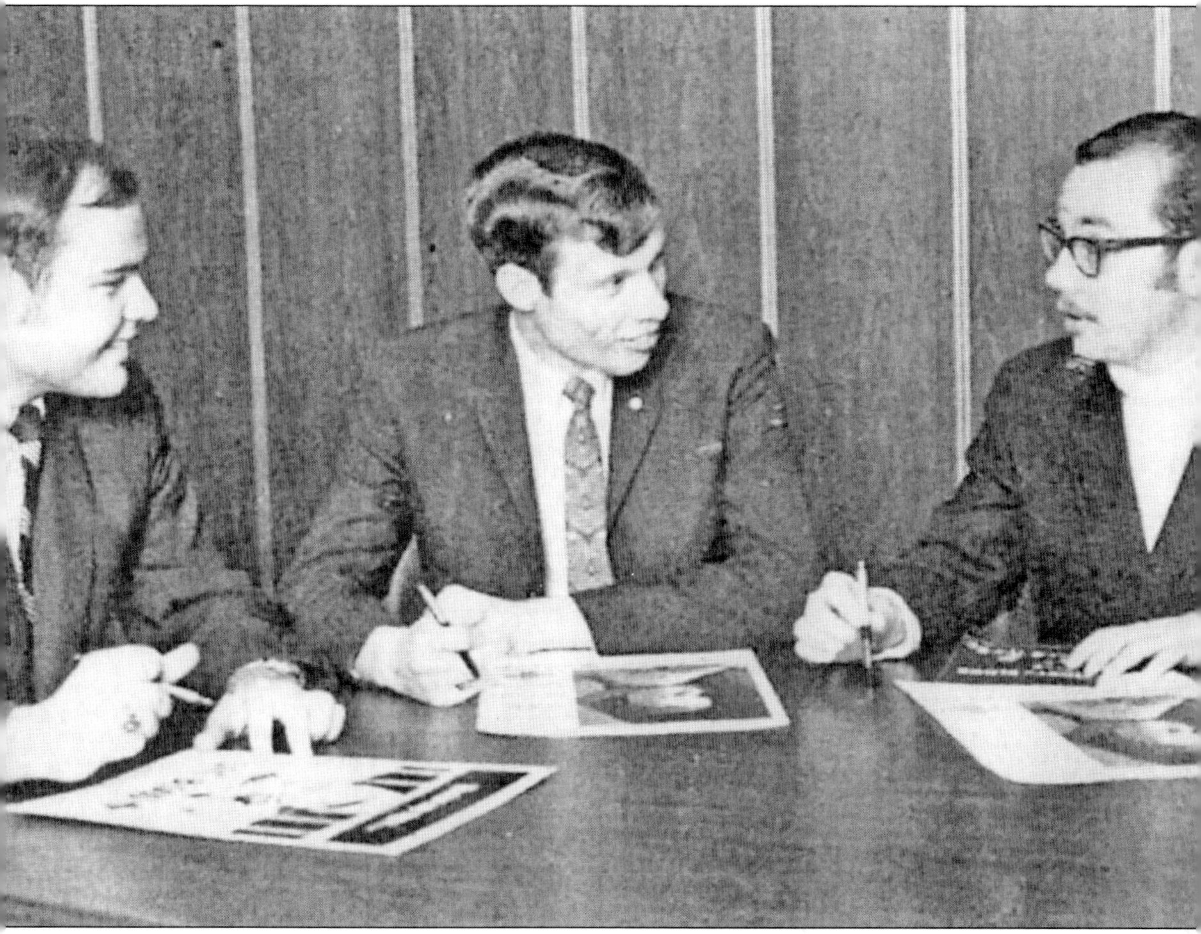

Members of the Idaho State University Circle K Club, a university equivalent of the Kiwanis service club, plan for the annual Red Cross campus blood drive in December 1968. ISU's club proposed a friendly competition with the Circle K clubs at the University of Idaho and Boise State College, as well as among social and service clubs on ISU's campus, to increase blood donations during the Vietnam War. Service organizations thrived on university campuses in the 1960s, and ISU was no exception. Pictured in this photograph from left to right are Ron Bolinger, John Kash, and David Hegsted.

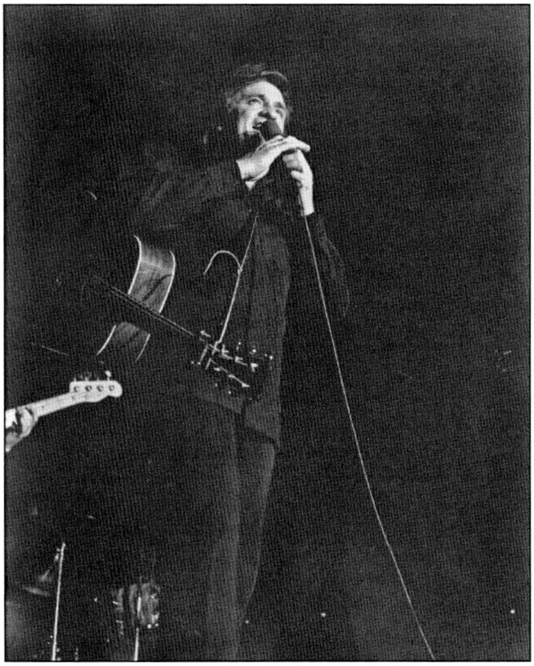

Transitioning into the 1970s, the student population was becoming older, with more students holding full-time jobs and raising families. Student life slowed down because of this strong influx of a more nontraditional student population, but many students were still involved in Greek life, student clubs, and organizations, and they still loved attending events and dances on campus. Some of the most popular events in the 1970s were the concerts in Holt Arena. Performers included Neil Diamond, Johnny Cash, and Chicago. In this photograph, Johnny Cash performs during the 1973 ISU Homecoming Week.

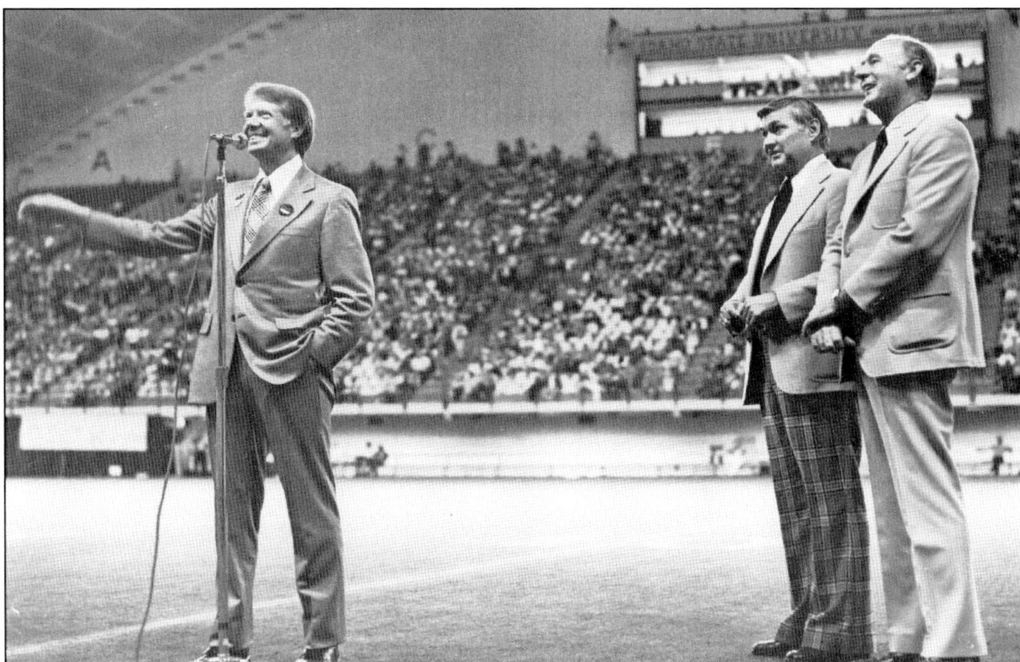

Because of its strategic location at the junction of multiple railroads, Idaho State University's home city of Pocatello has hosted a number of presidential candidates, including William Howard Taft, Harry Truman, John F. Kennedy, and Jimmy Carter. A year after his 1976 election, Carter returned to Idaho with his new secretary of the interior, former (and future) Idaho governor Cecil Andrus. Carter spoke to a crowd gathered at ISU's Minidome (now Holt Arena) and also rafted the Middle Fork of the Salmon River during his visit.

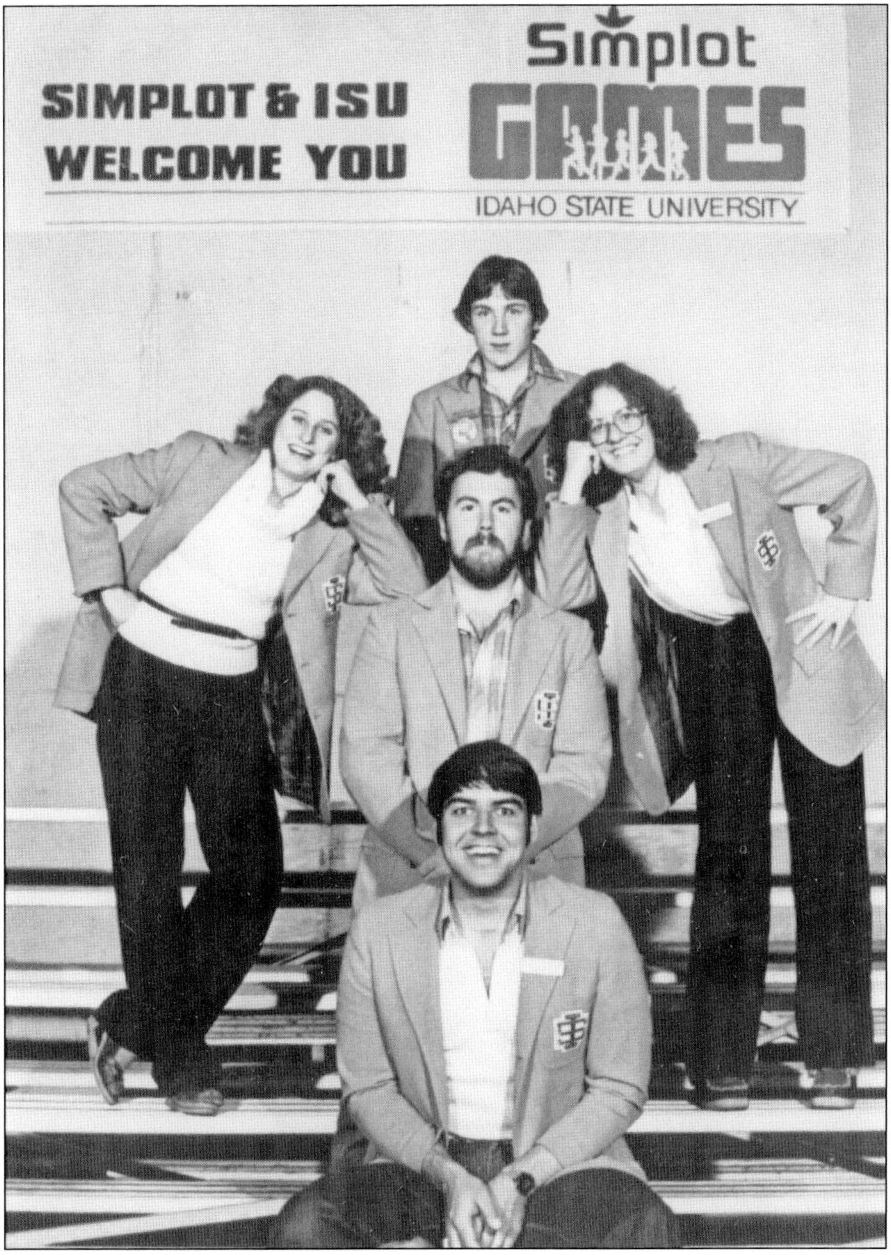

In the 1980s, the student population grew even more nontraditional and student life became less lively. Though there were still annual homecoming celebrations, dances, and many student organizations, the Greek life on campus started to collapse with fewer and fewer students choosing to rush. To help replace the spirit and student involvement on campus, the Idaho State University Ambassadors organization was born. The ISU Ambassadors were founded by Charlie Clark in March 1980 to promote ISU on campus through giving tours to prospective students and their families, ushering at concerts and performances, and providing other services to the university and the Pocatello community. Pictured in this photograph are, from left to right, (first row) Clyde Brinegar; (second row) Tammy Hartman, Jim Goes, and Anne Harding; (third row) Mark Evans.

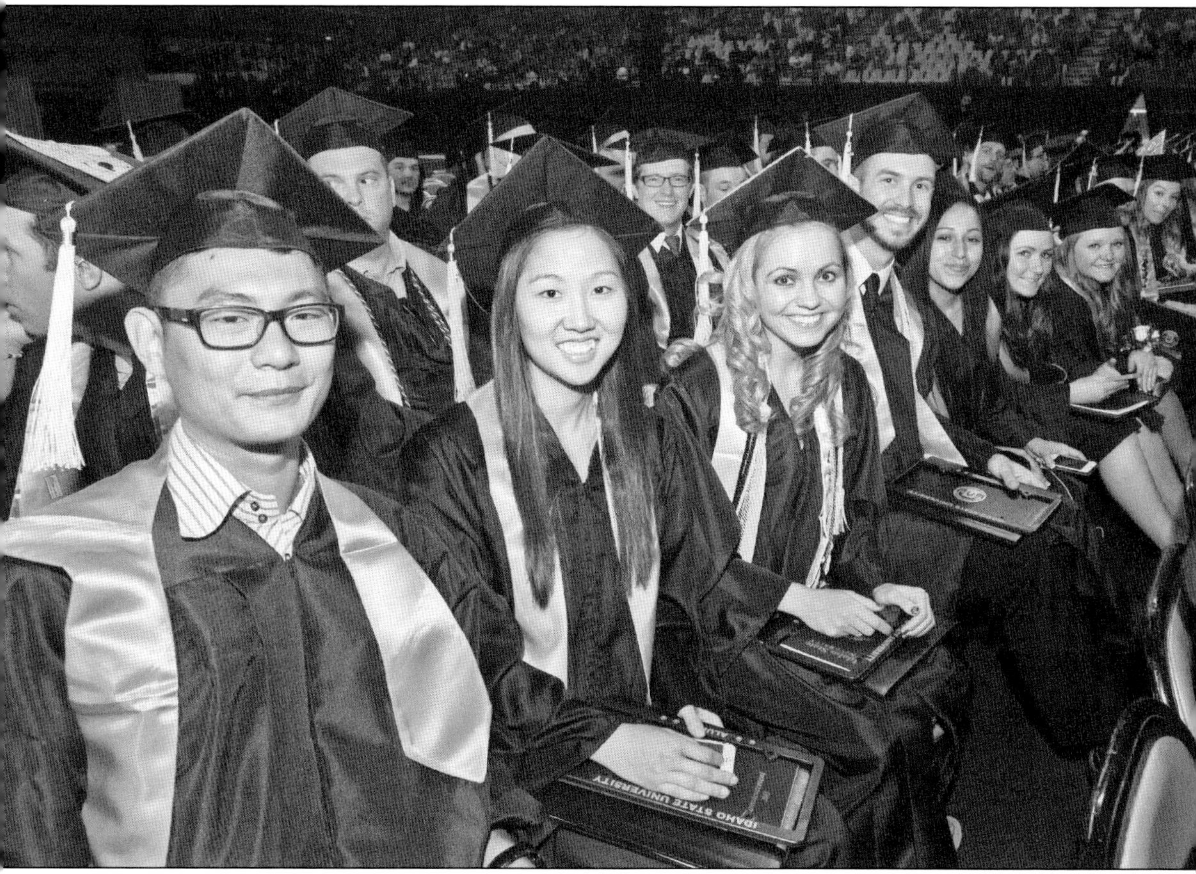

Since the 1980s, student life has continued to change and adapt to fit the demands of the student body. The school still has many clubs and organizations, hundreds of campus events, the annual homecoming celebration, and many other things for students to get involved with. Being involved on campus and participating in traditions helps to tie students to the university, and many students, while they may be unable to recall all of their classes and tests, will always remember the school spirit and good times they found here.

Four

Athletics

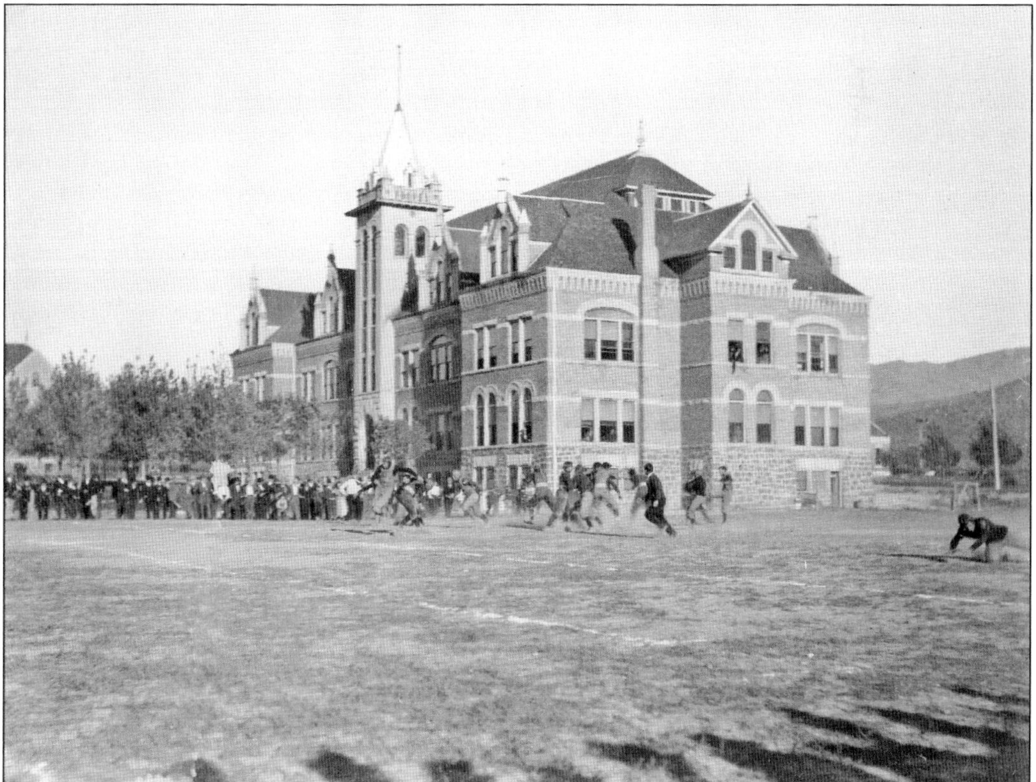

Since its inception, sports have played a vital role in the history of Idaho State University. During the opening school year at the then Academy of Idaho in 1902, the school fielded its first football team. Originally, the team was small, with many athletes also playing in other sports; there were no scholarships, and the coaches were volunteer faculty members. Travel was inconvenient and expensive, and in the beginning, the school mostly played surrounding area high schools. Pictured is one of the early football games played on what is now the campus quadrangle against Boise High.

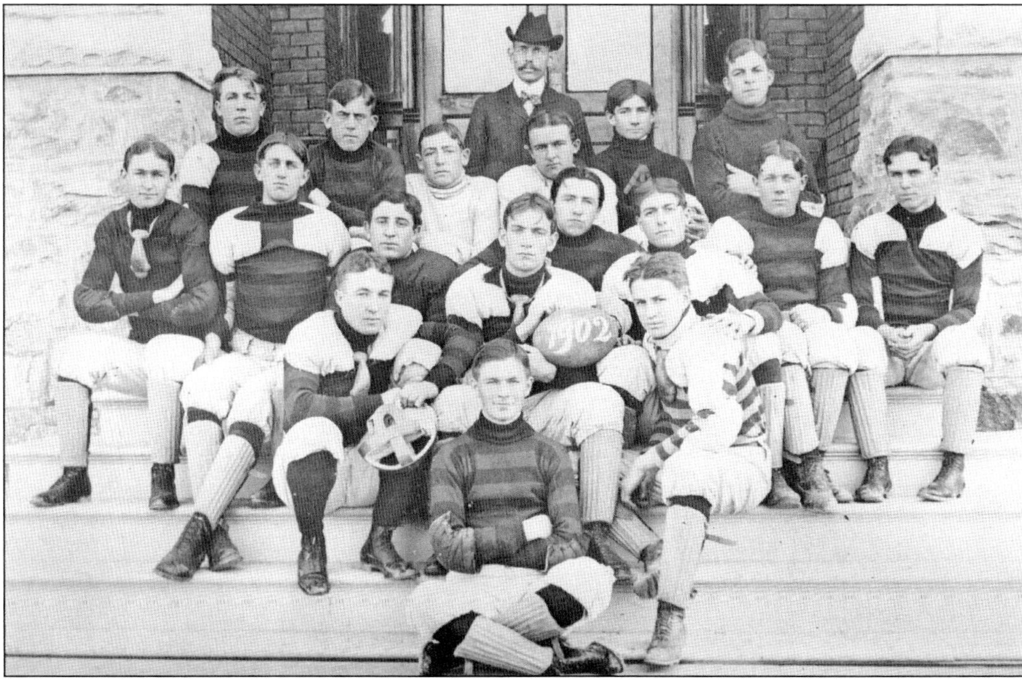

Pictured above is the first men's football team from 1902, while below is one of the first women's basketball teams. Women's basketball was very popular from the earliest years of the Academy of Idaho. The success of the women's teams at the dawn of the 1900s foreshadowed Idaho State University's success in women's basketball in the Big Sky Conference a century later.

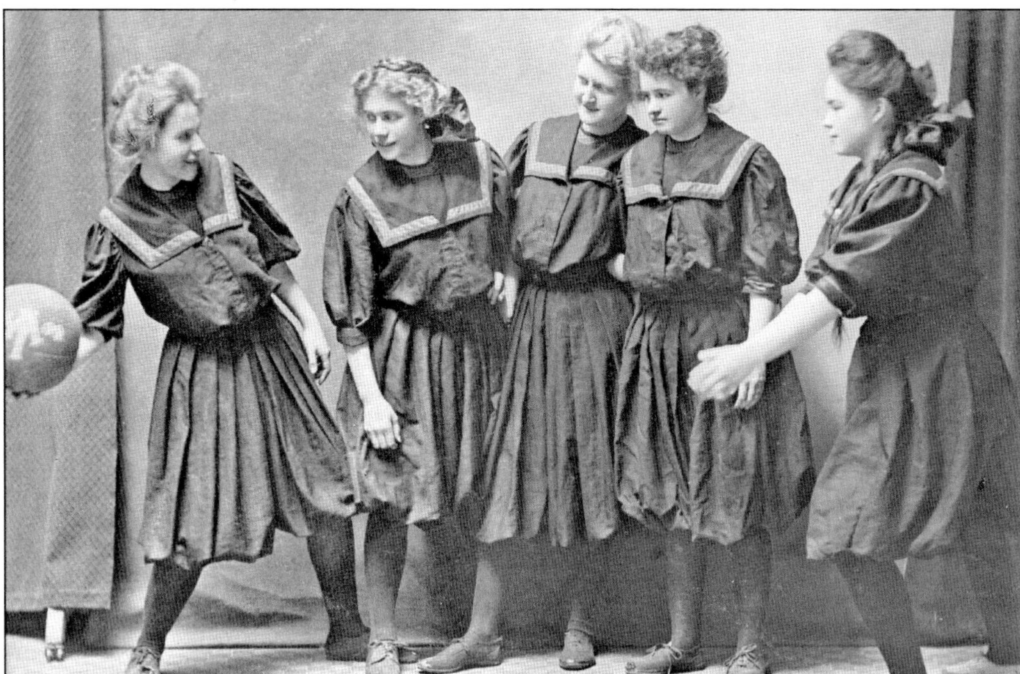

By 1908, the men's basketball team (right) had finally taken off, and by 1909, athletics had already become permanently engrained and well established at the Academy of Idaho. Intramurals quickly gained popularity; track and field events, as well as field tennis, were popular early sports. The Academy of Idaho unofficially started using the orange and black colors, and the first reference to the "Tigers" as the school mascot appeared. The athletics department had grown to encompass men's basketball and men's baseball teams as well. In 1912, the budding baseball team took home its first state championship (below).

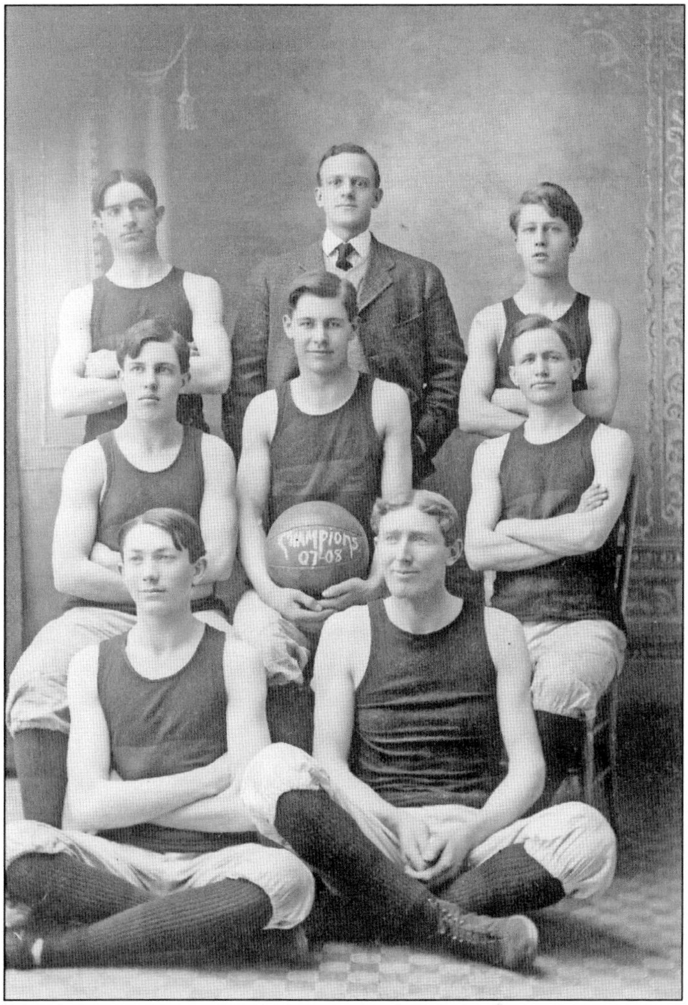

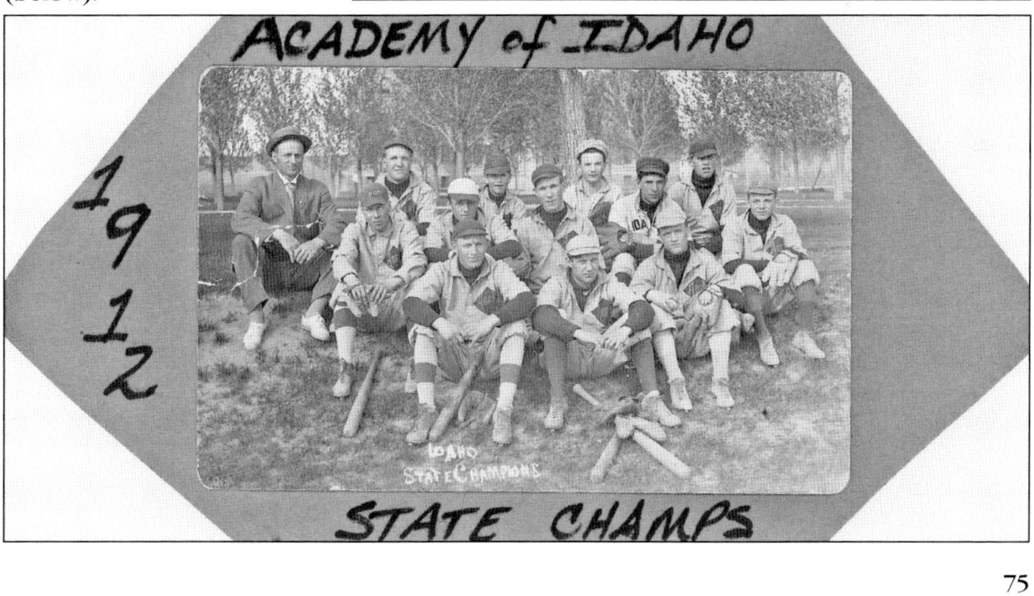

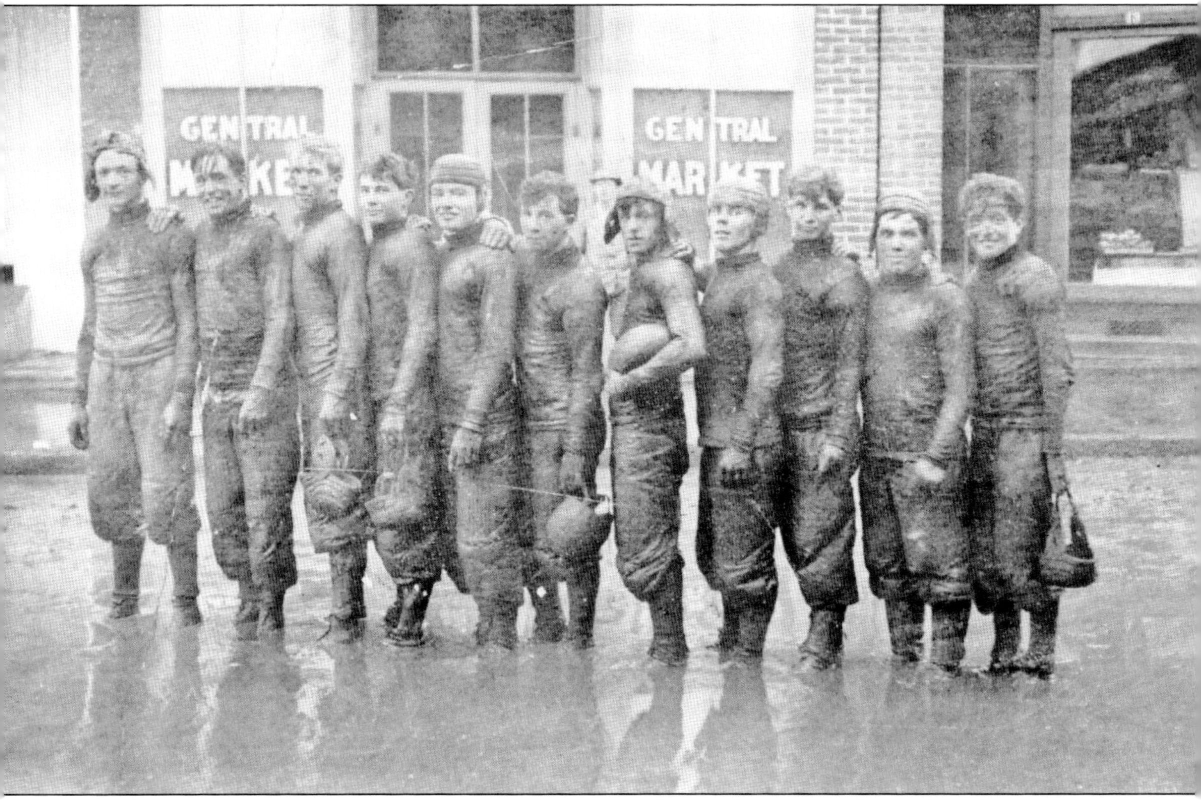

The Interscholastic League was created to help facilitate early football games among colleges and club teams in their geographical region, but the Academy of Idaho would quickly grow too large to participate in it. After the Academy of Idaho won the league by a wide margin in 1910, it was excluded from it for being "too advanced," instead focusing on playing other local colleges. Pictured is the 1910 championship football team.

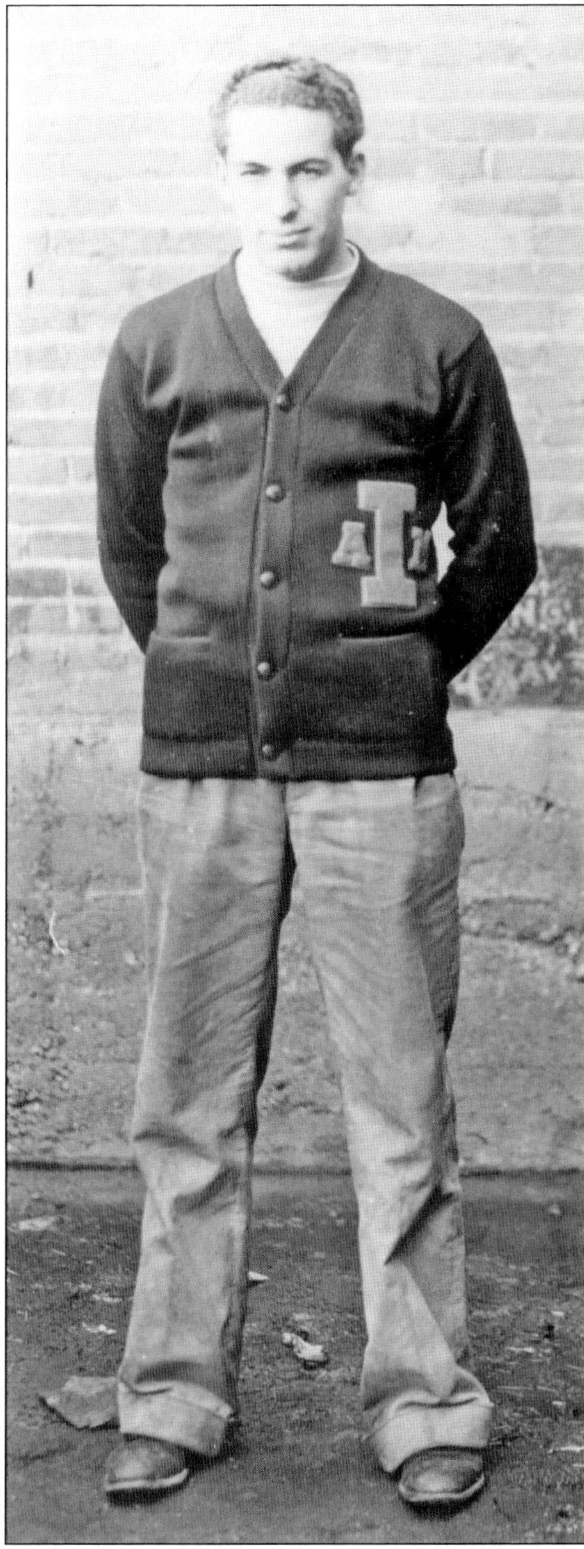

Football players were among the first to receive academic letters at the Academy of Idaho. In 1911, football players could earn and wear the Academy of Idaho letters—a large "A" with a stylistic "I" inset into it, although styles differed slightly from team to team. Pictured is a young football player with some of the original Academy of Idaho lettering.

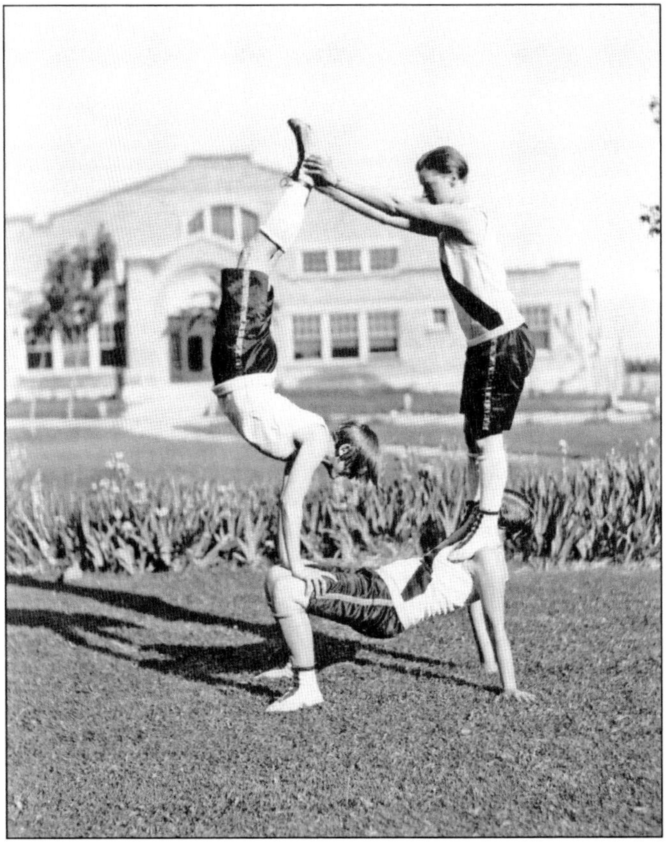

The onset of American involvement in World War I resulted in the athletic programs taking a hit—most able-bodied men had enlisted in the war effort. A particularly concerning government statistic showed that 45 percent of men between the ages of 21 and 30 were physically unfit for service, and as a result, greater emphasis was placed on physical education classes, which became an official part of the curriculum. Gymnastics was one such popular course that both men and women could receive credit for. Although ISU no longer has a tumbling team, in the early 1900s, the tumbling team at Idaho Technical Institute was both very popular and incredibly photogenic. Seen here are two photographs of the men's tumbling team.

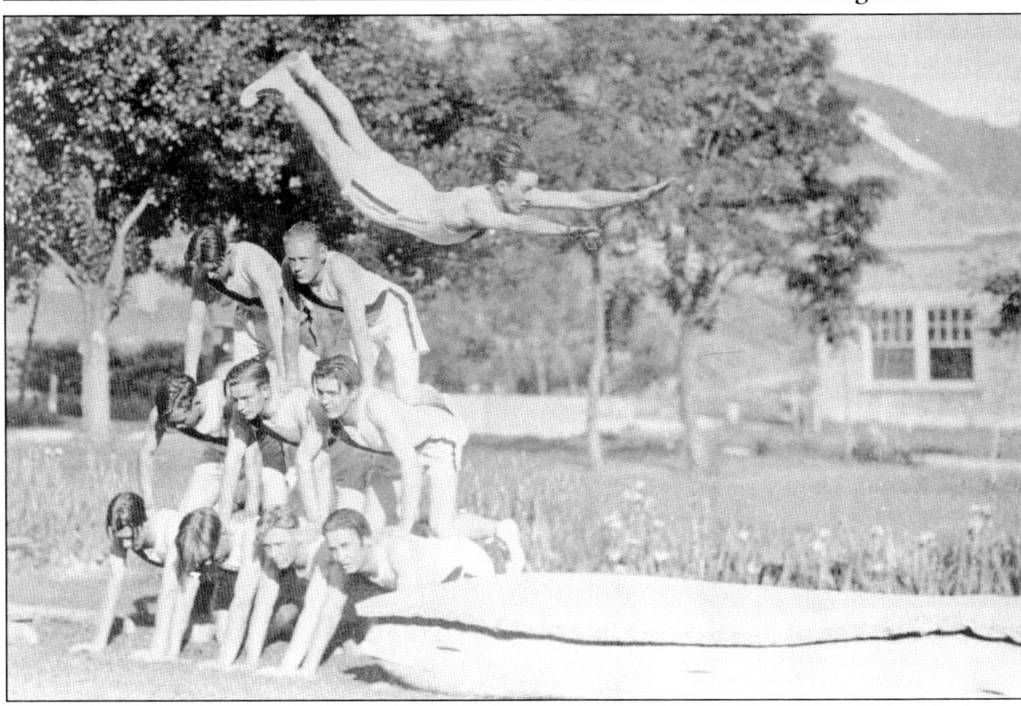

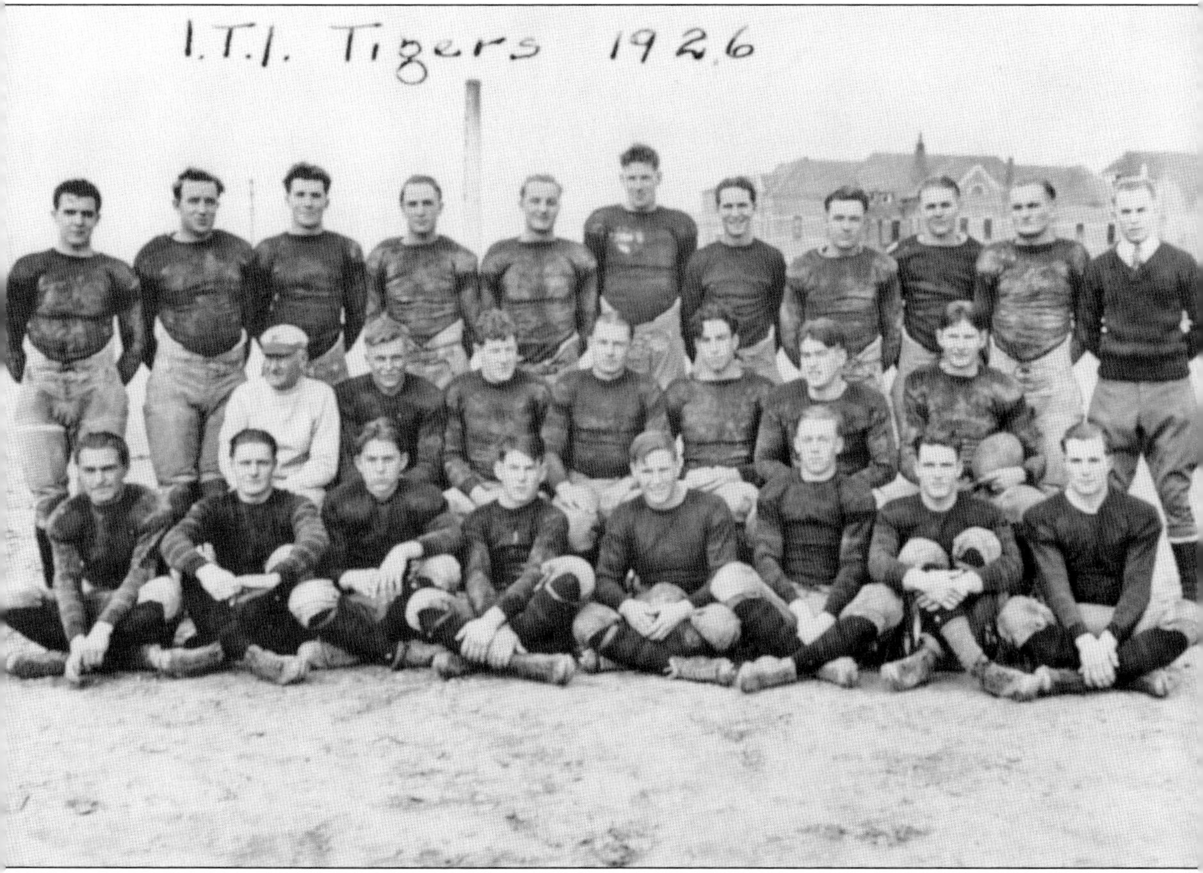

After World War I, athletics had a rough restart. In the first season, as the re-branded Idaho Technical Institute, the school suffered its largest defeat ever at the hands of the Utah State Aggies, 137-0. To turn things around, Idaho Tech brought in a new athletic director and football coach, Ralph "Hutch" Hutchinson. A former Princeton student-athlete, Hutchinson transported Princeton's orange-and-black color scheme and Tigers (later Bengals) mascot to Idaho Tech. Hutchinson was an accomplished athlete himself, competing and excelling in football, baseball, and track at Princeton, as well as qualifying for the 1900 Olympics in the 120-yard dash. Pictured is the 1926 football team with Coach Hutchinson.

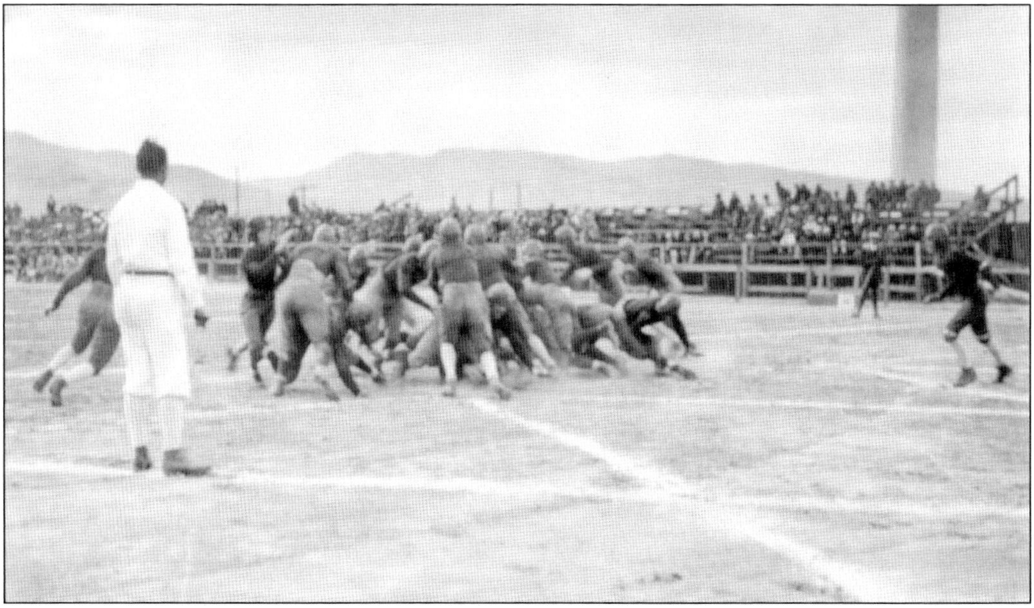

Hutchinson transformed the athletic department. Idaho Tech primarily began to play other universities and traveled greater distances, and the football, basketball, baseball, and swimming programs all expanded greatly under his watch. Hutchinson did not just care about the athletes, but also the spectators. He personally raised money to build a new field, which both improved the seating availability and conditions at athletic events. As a testament to his dedication to the school, the Hutchinson Quadrangle in the middle of lower campus was dedicated and named after him, and out of respect, no buildings have ever been erected on it.

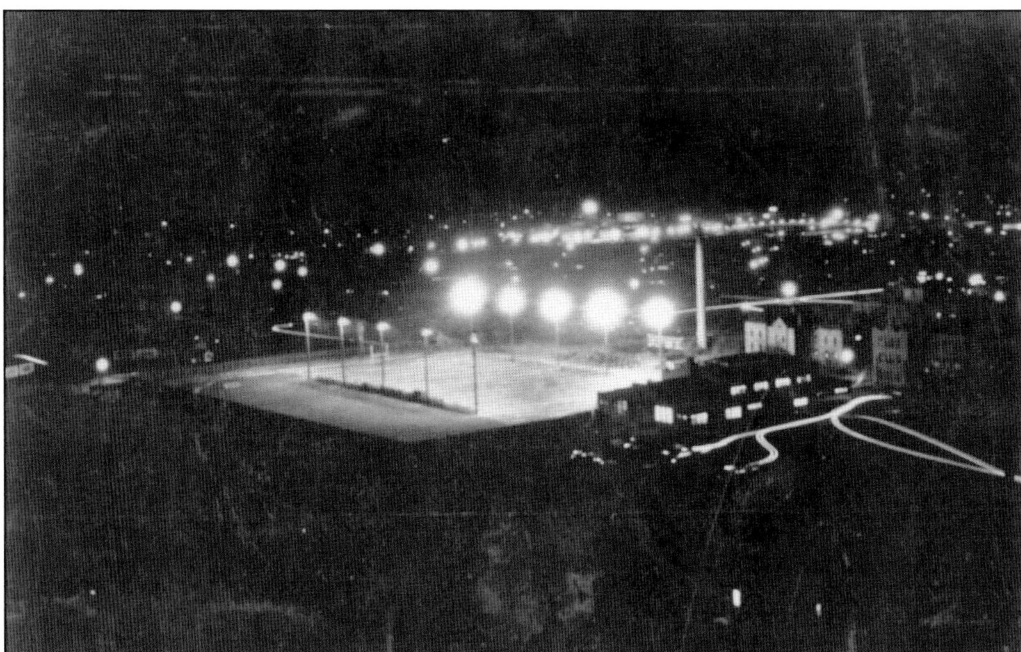

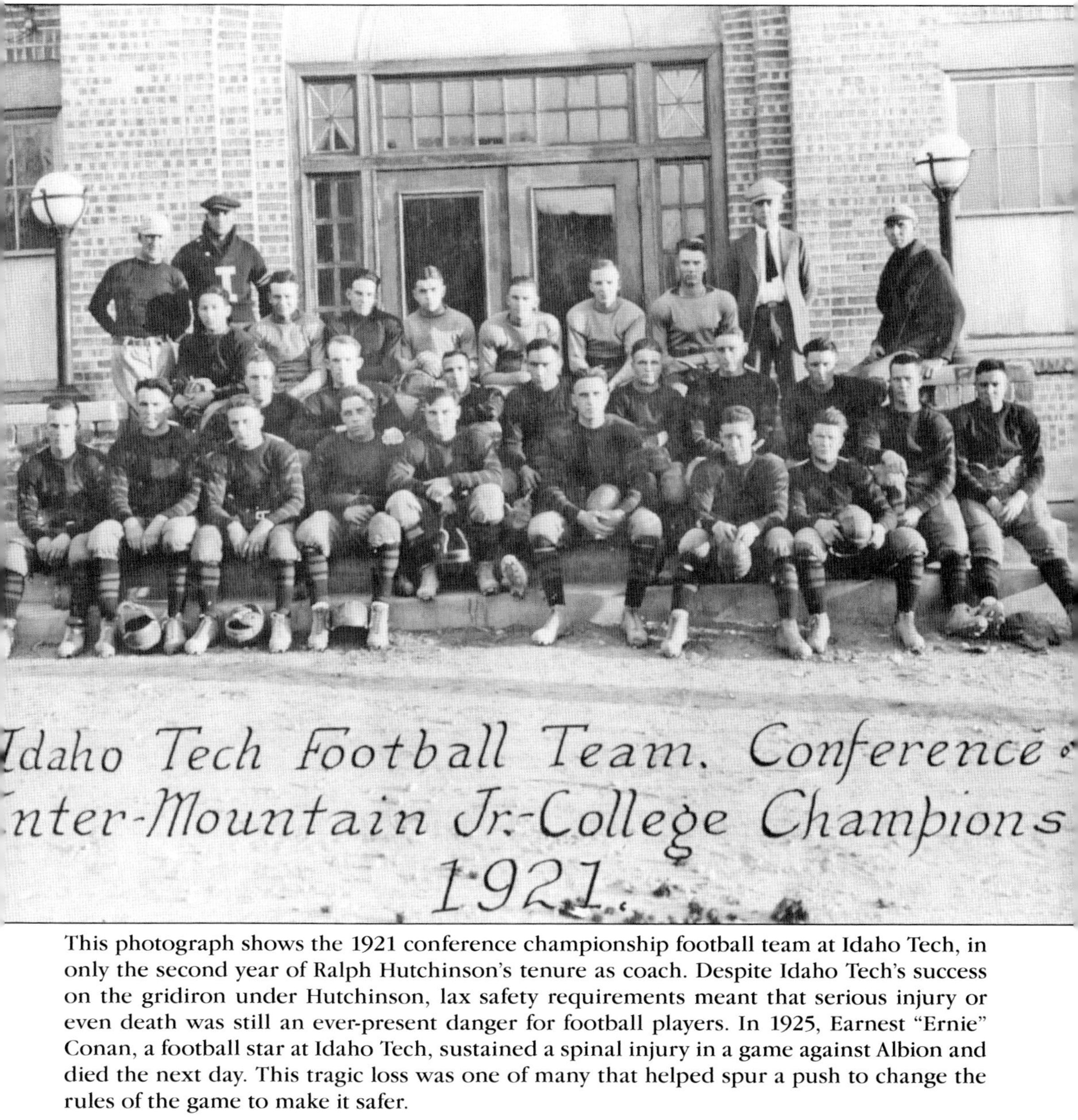

This photograph shows the 1921 conference championship football team at Idaho Tech, in only the second year of Ralph Hutchinson's tenure as coach. Despite Idaho Tech's success on the gridiron under Hutchinson, lax safety requirements meant that serious injury or even death was still an ever-present danger for football players. In 1925, Earnest "Ernie" Conan, a football star at Idaho Tech, sustained a spinal injury in a game against Albion and died the next day. This tragic loss was one of many that helped spur a push to change the rules of the game to make it safer.

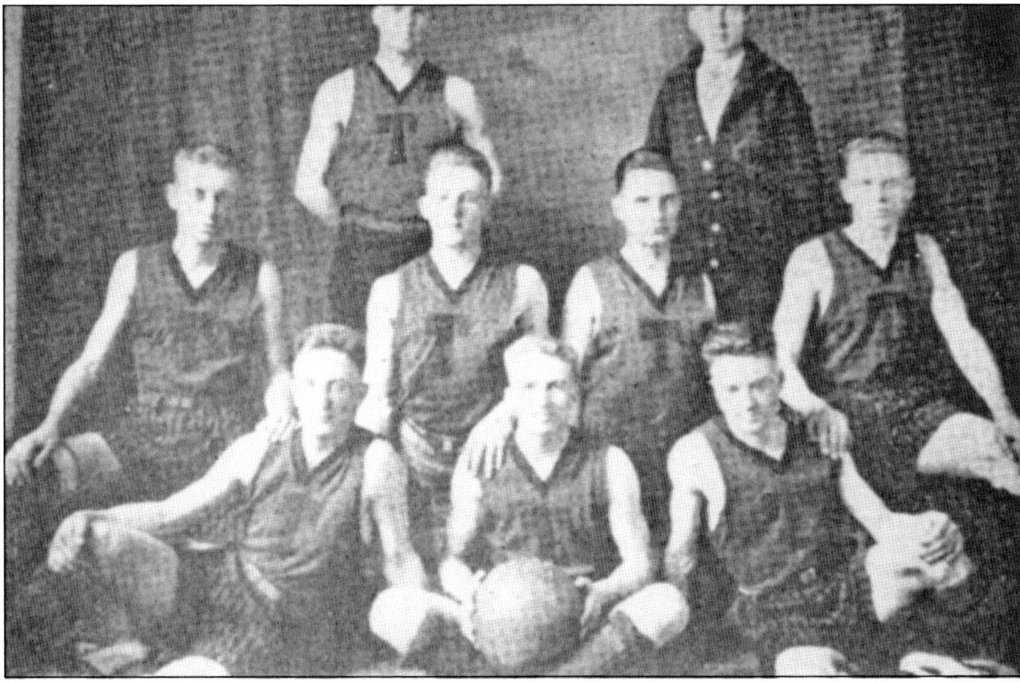

Men's basketball finally started to blossom under Hutchinson's direction, and in 1926, the basketball team won the Southern Idaho Conference championship. Hutchinson also brought his expertise as a sprinter to Idaho Tech's track program. Pictured below are hurdlers competing on the original Idaho Tech cinder track, situated on the edge of Tech's main campus.

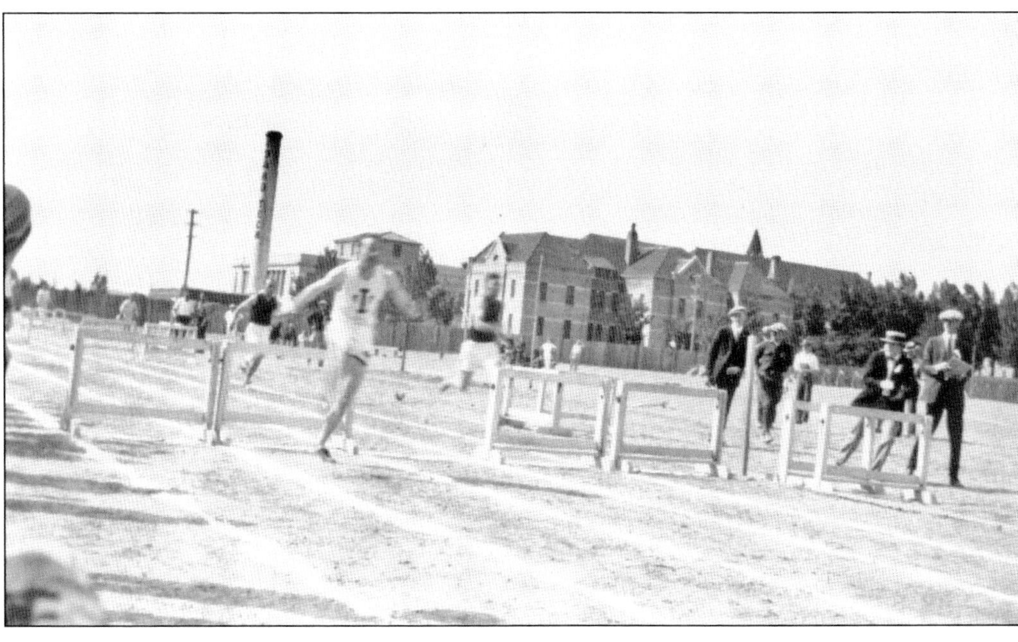

The school began to attract significant attention in athletics outside of basketball and football as well. In 1925, Idaho Tech was selected to hold the State High School Track and Field meet over Moscow for the first time in history, and in 1926, it hosted the first Southern Idaho Conference tennis tournament. In addition to attracting outside interest in the school's facilities, both the track and tennis teams were becoming very successful. Soon after, in 1927, the school became the University of Idaho Southern Branch, which sparked significant debate over whether Idaho Tech should remain the orange-and-black tigers or adopt the black-and-gold theme of the University of Idaho Vandals. Pictured at right is a pole vaulter, and below is the tennis team from 1929.

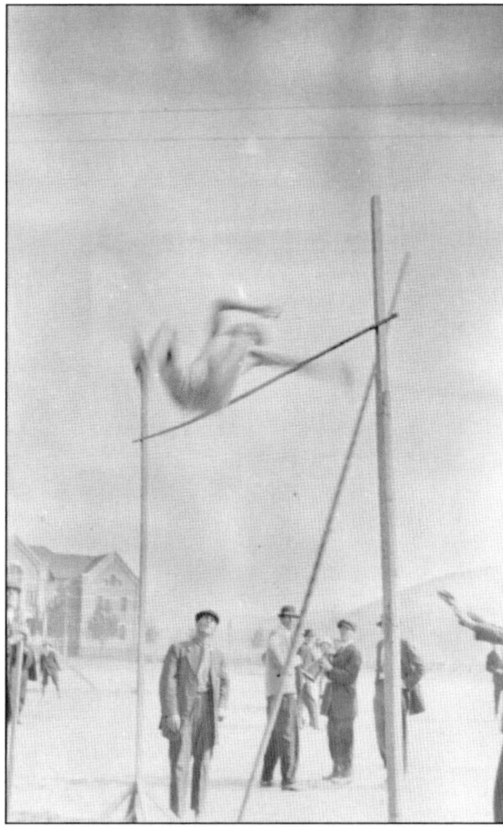

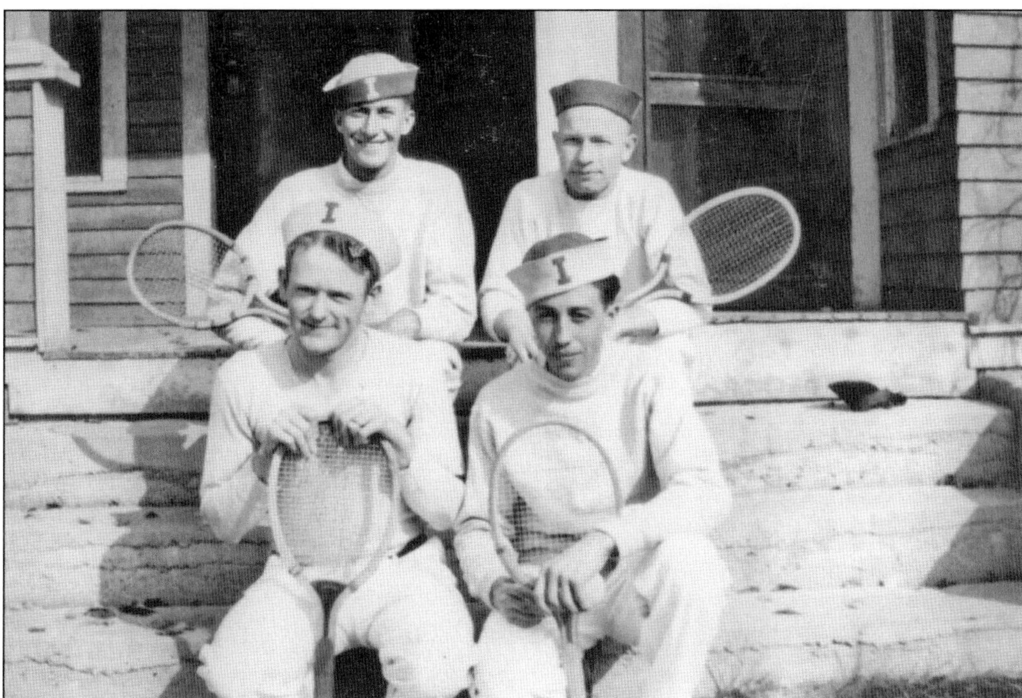

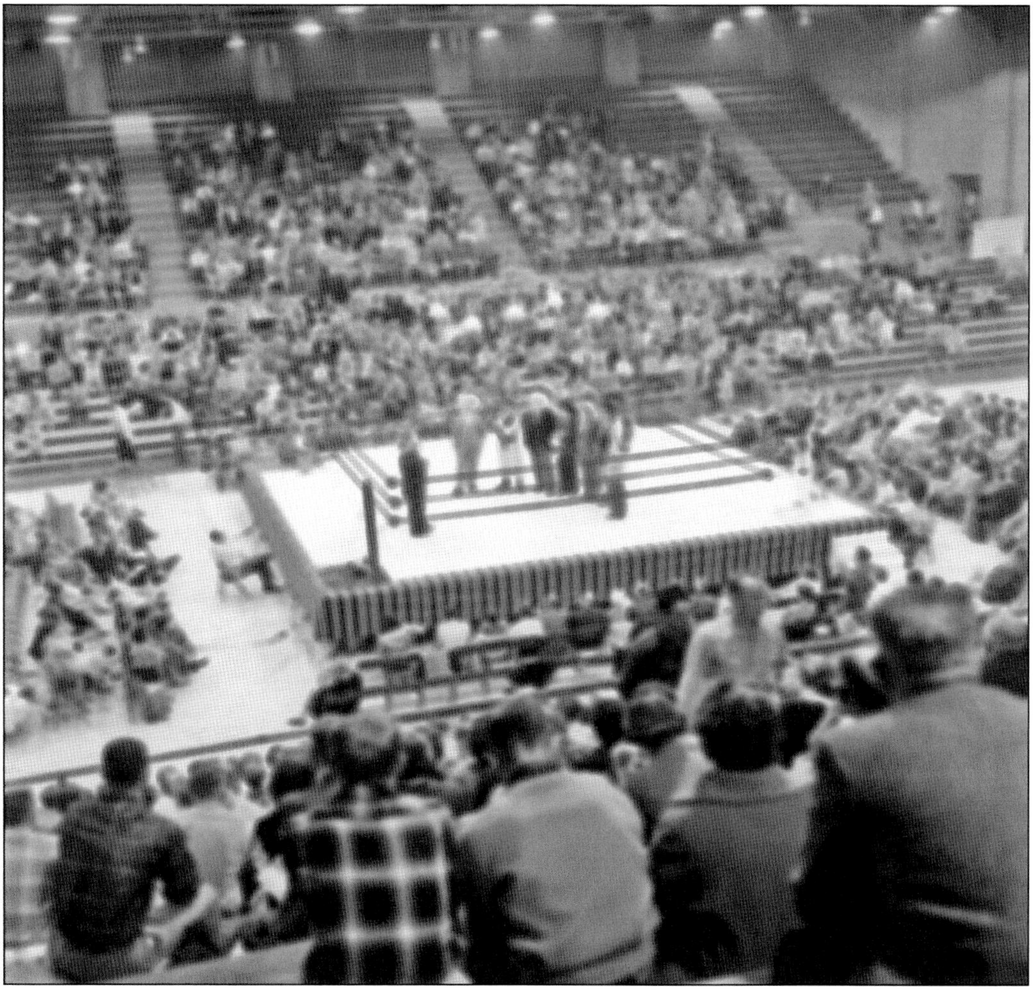

The annual Hulme Fight was a tradition that began in the 1920s and continued up until around World War II, in which freshmen were forced to wear green caps—as a symbol of their verdancy—for most of the school year. Each year, the freshmen class would battle the sophomore class in various athletic events, including boxing (as pictured here), tug of war, track and field, and many others. If the freshmen prevailed, they would receive a reduced sentence, but if the sophomores prevailed, the freshmen would be stuck with the caps all year. Although it started as a tradition among male athletes, the women began participating in the mid-1930s.

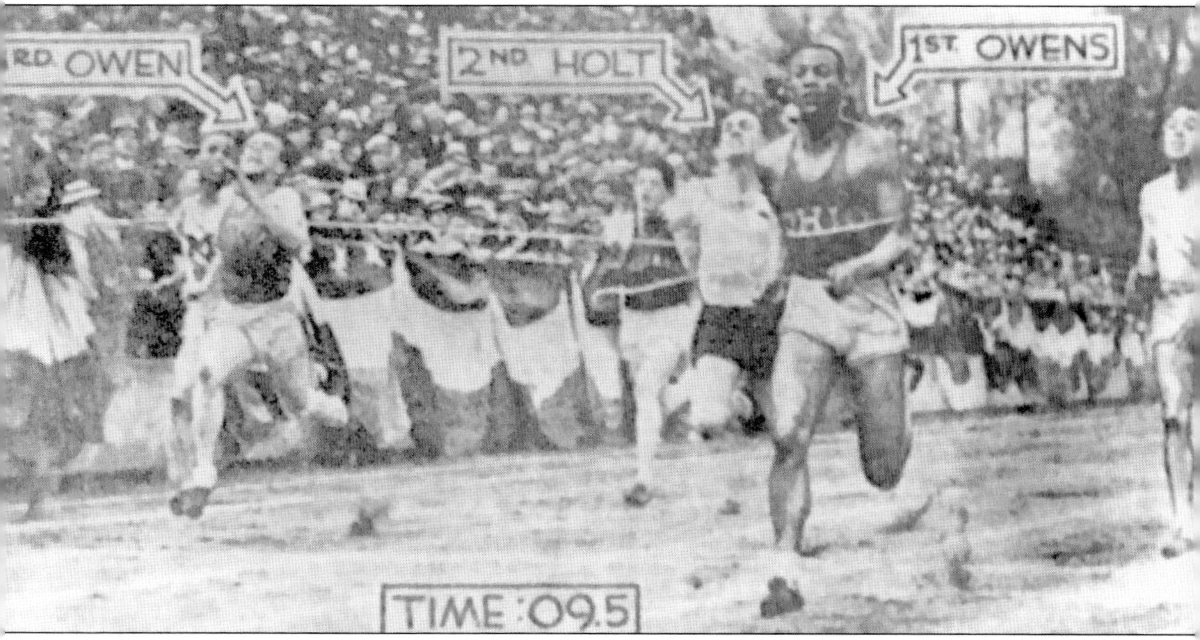

Milton "Dubby" Holt was a student athlete and later a coach of 34 years, significantly impacting the success of ISU's athletic programs throughout the years. As a student at Idaho Tech, he was an accomplished track and football star, setting a school record in 1937 with an 88-yard punt return, which still stands today, and competing in track against the famed Jesse Owens. Although Owens bested holt in this picture, Holt had beaten Owens in a national meet prior to the Olympic trials. Later, he returned to ISU as athletic director and coach of both the boxing and swim teams. Lincoln Yamashita, who was on the swim team Holt coached, recalls that during a meet, Holt said to him, "When we win the meet, throw me in the shallow end of the pool," since he did not know how to swim. His memory lives on in the incredible impact he had on both Bengal athletes and the athletic department, and Holt Arena is named in his honor.

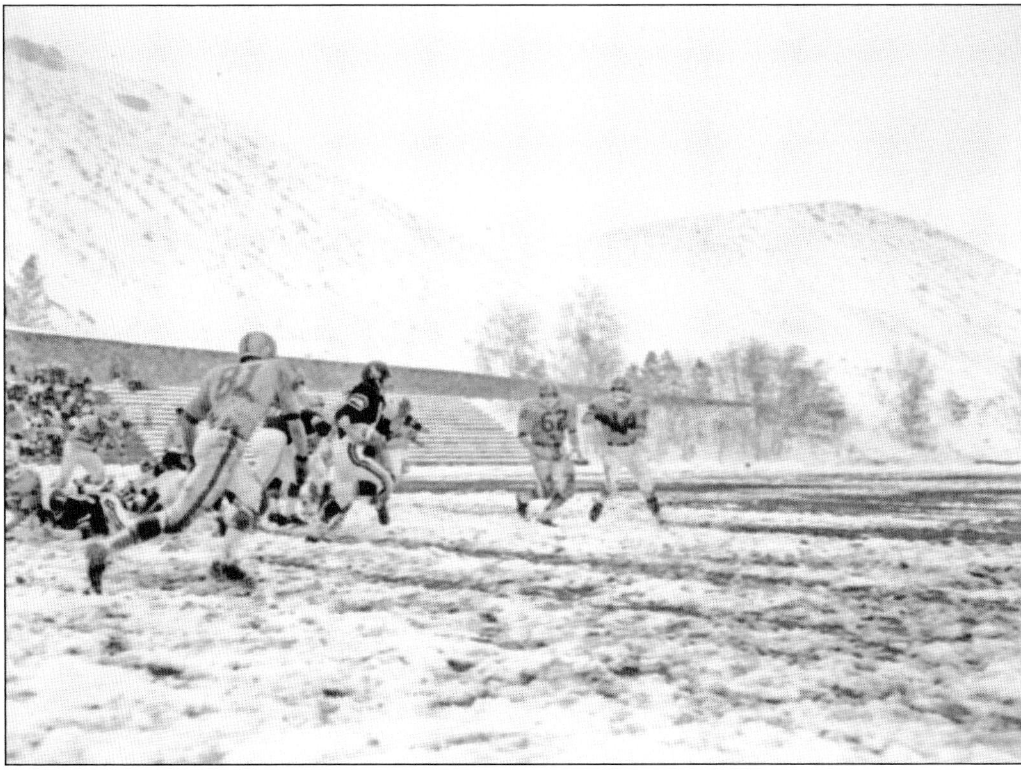

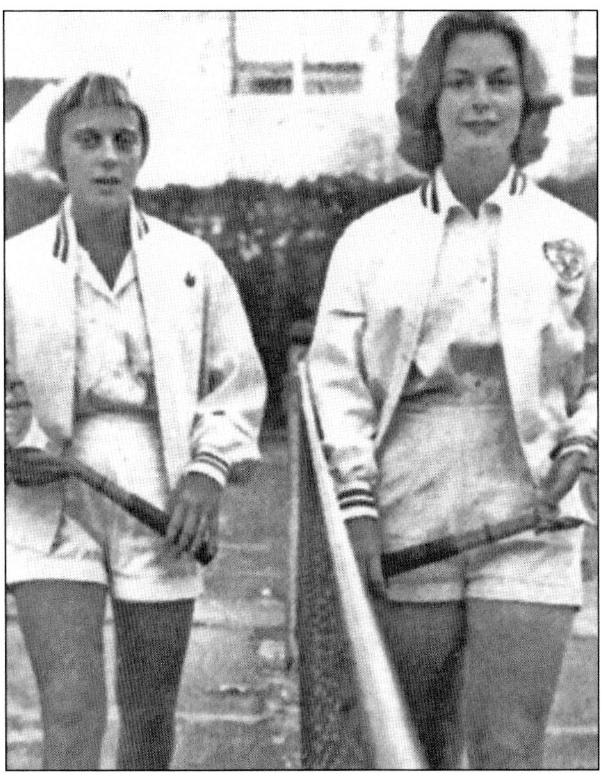

While the men's teams continued to expand and compete against larger schools, women's sports struggled and came under increased and often frivolous criticism. One sports column in 1939 exemplified an extreme example of this, saying that the only dignified women's sports were "swimming and diving. Swimming because it is underwater so that they can't be seen, and diving because it is so fast it is hard to notice anything but the good points." At one point, the funding disparity between men's and women's sports was so large that the average male athlete received more than 400 times the support a female athlete might receive. Despite these hardships, women athletes bravely shook off this criticism and continued to excel. Pictured above is a football practice in the winter, and at left are the women's tennis doubles champs from 1959.

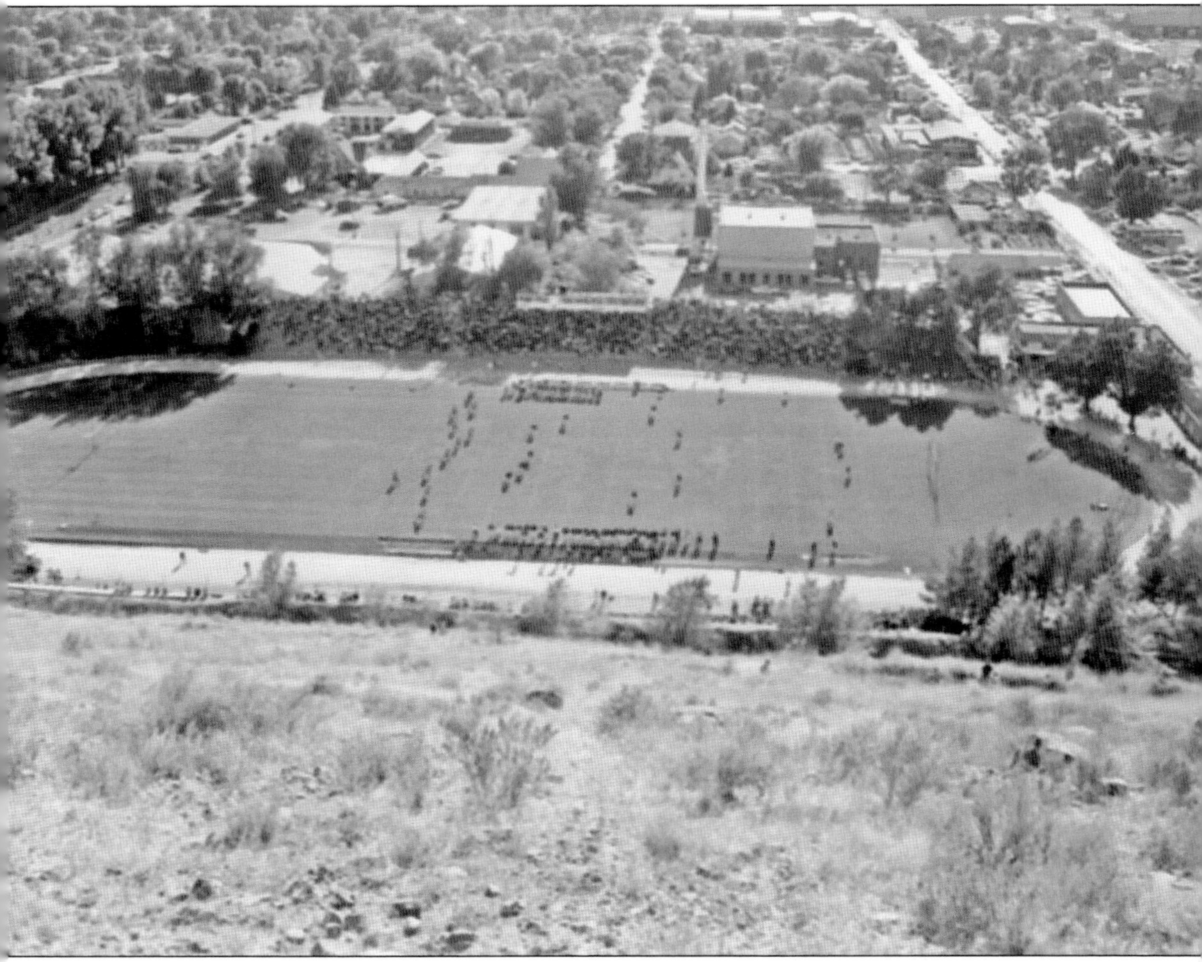

When the United States entered World War II in December 1941, enrollment dropped drastically, nearly closing the school again. After the war, the school was re-branded as Idaho State College (ISC), and a new era of athletics was born. Pictured is an image taken from Red Hill of the football team practicing just after the war.

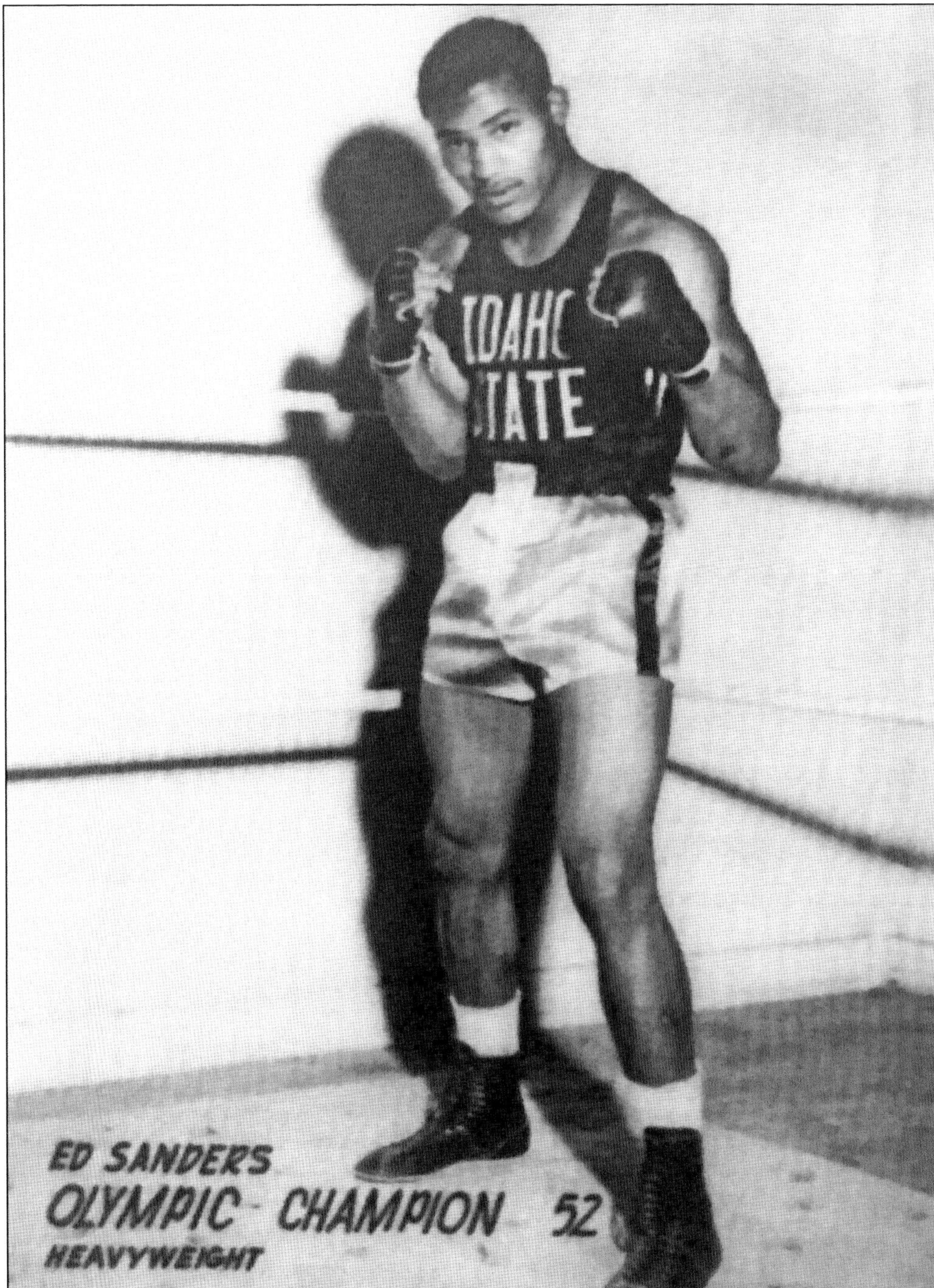

In 1952, ISC boxer Ed Sanders won gold at the Helsinki Olympics. Sanders had been recruited by former athlete-turned-coach Dubby Holt in 1950 to box and play football at ISC. Sanders thrived, setting a record for never losing a collegiate match. In addition to his impressive collegiate record, Sanders was drafted in 1951 and joined the Navy boxing team, where he collected wins around the globe. He inspired a resurgence in popularity in boxing at ISC and is pictured here shortly after his 1952 win.

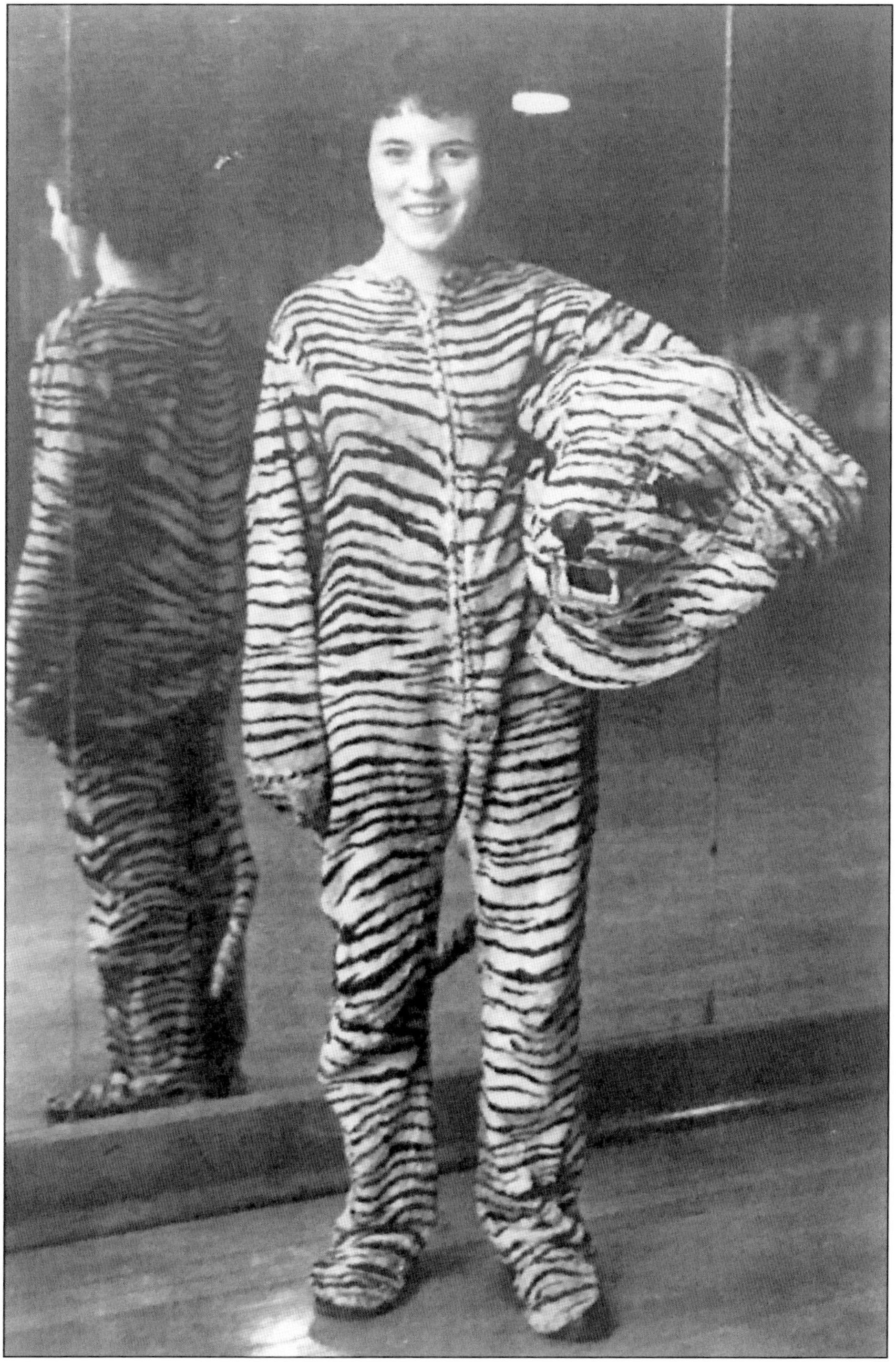

This photograph from the 1950s shows Benjie, Idaho State College's first precursor to Benny the Bengal—the mascot today. With the mascot in place, the transition to the Bengals was solidified, and Ralph Hutchinson's decision to rename Idaho Tech in honor of Princeton's Tiger mascot has endured.

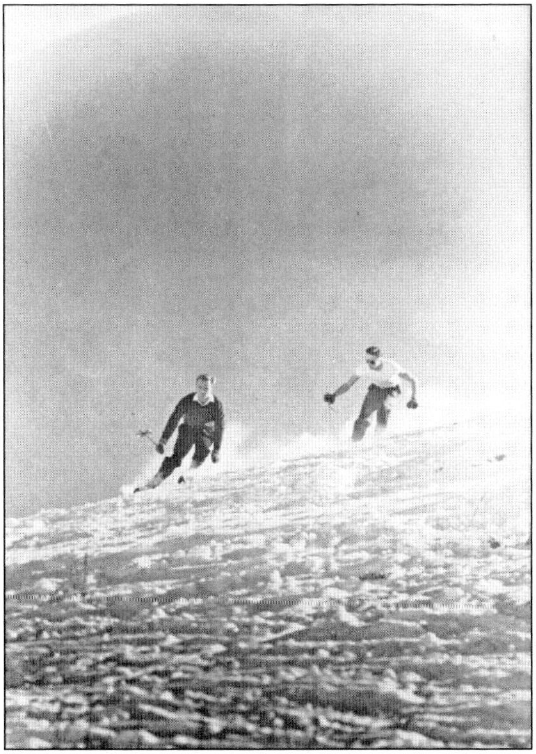

While the most popular sports at Idaho State College continued to be basketball and football, there were a wide variety of other teams in the athletic department. While many of the sports in Idaho State's storied history are no longer played today, at one time there was a ski team (pictured at left), bowling, ice hockey (pictured below), and even a water polo team.

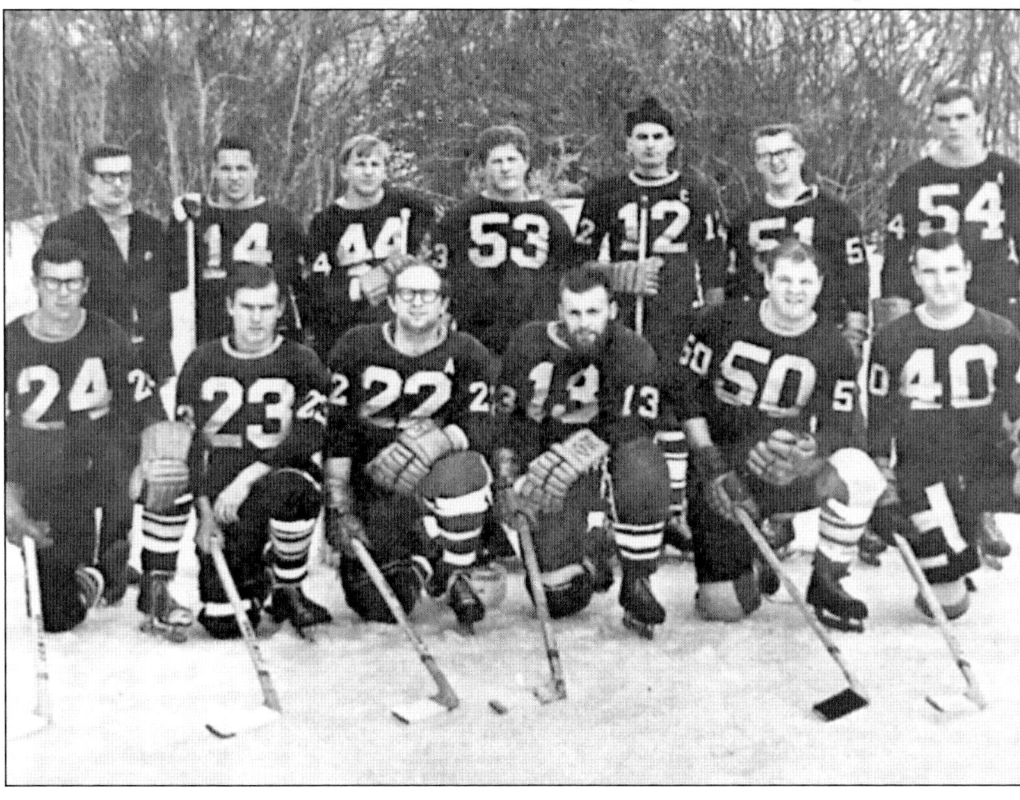

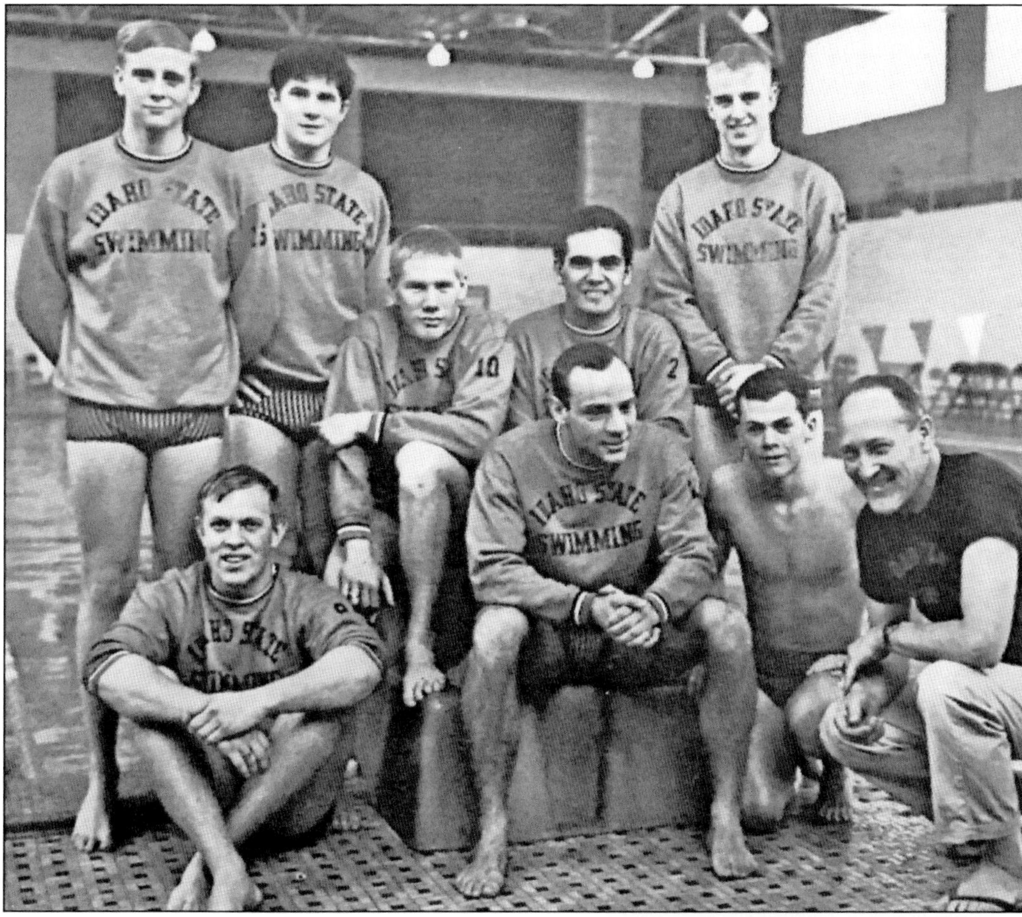

After the completion of the new (and current) Reed Gym in 1952, for the first time, student athletes had access to an indoor lap pool. When ISC decided to join the Big Sky Conference, the school needed to add another official varsity sport to qualify, so a swim team was put together. The school already had the facilities, swimming cost very little to sponsor, and athletes on the team helped to pay for their scholarships by working as lifeguards. Many athletes are distinguished alumni, and all share a universal respect for the school and the opportunities it gave them. Lincoln Yamashita (right), a hall-of-fame swimmer under coach Dubby Holt, reflected on why he continues to be involved with ISU, saying "In Hawaii, we have a culture of reciprocity. Acceptance of a gift obliges the recipient to reciprocate or bring dishonor if he doesn't. They gave me a gift of an education, and after all these years, I still feel I need to give back." (Right, courtesy of Lincoln Yamashita.)

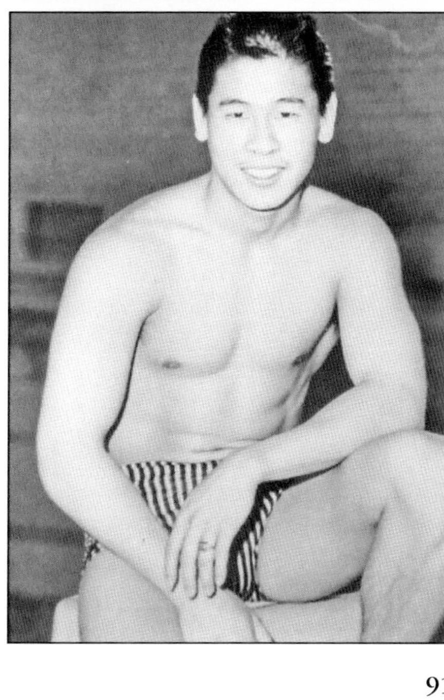

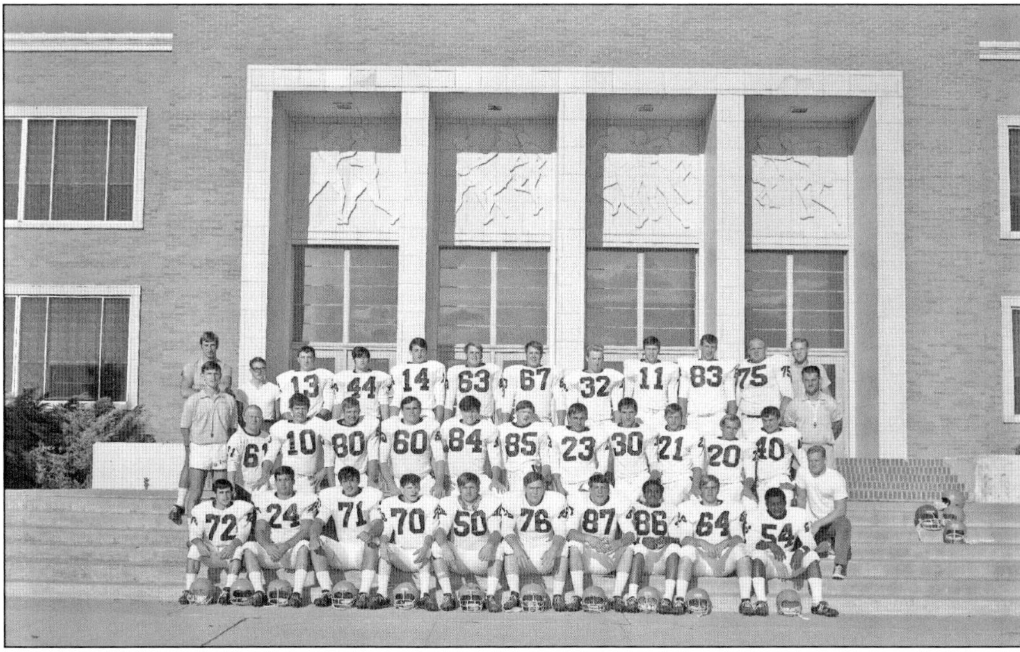

In the 1960s, Bengal athletics began to come into their own. In 1969, shortly after Americans landed on the moon, the Bengals accomplished what was likewise a previously unheard-of achievement: they finally beat their old parent school, the University of Idaho, in a gripping game that finished 47-42. Pictured above is the 1969 football team in front of Reed Gym. The Bengals also experienced success in men's cross-country, winning the Big Sky championship in 1964, 1966, and 1968. The 1964 team included Phil Luckey, who served as an athletic trainer at ISU for over 40 years, and Bruce Nelson, the former CEO of Office Depot.

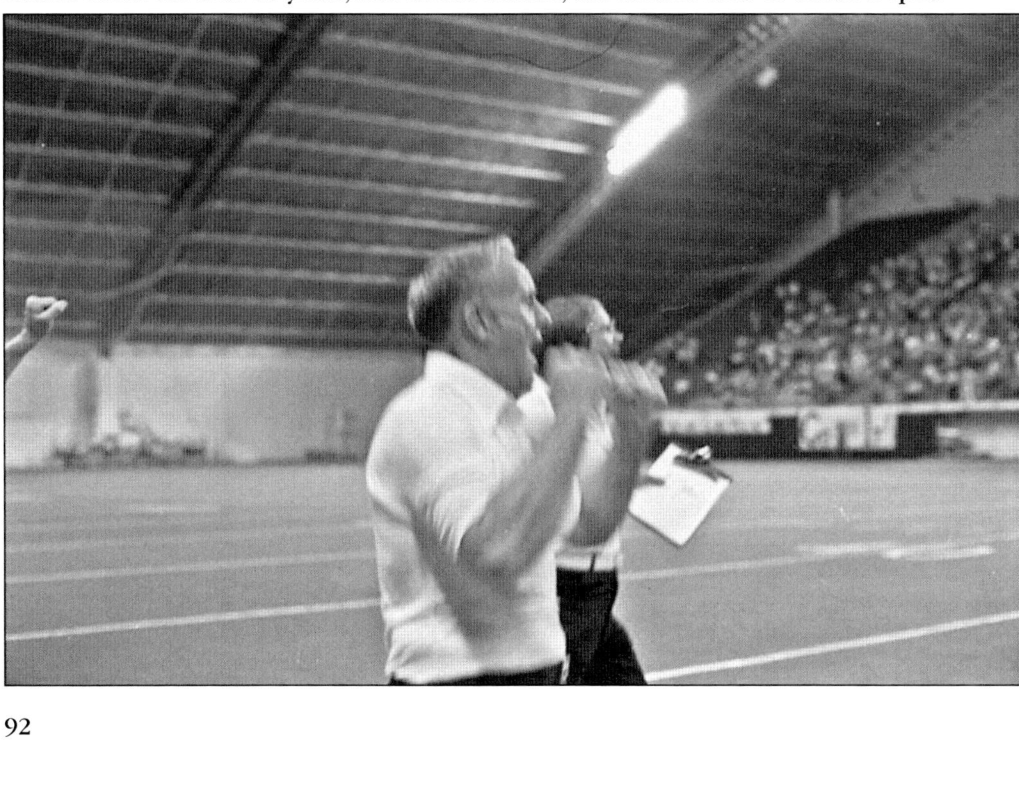

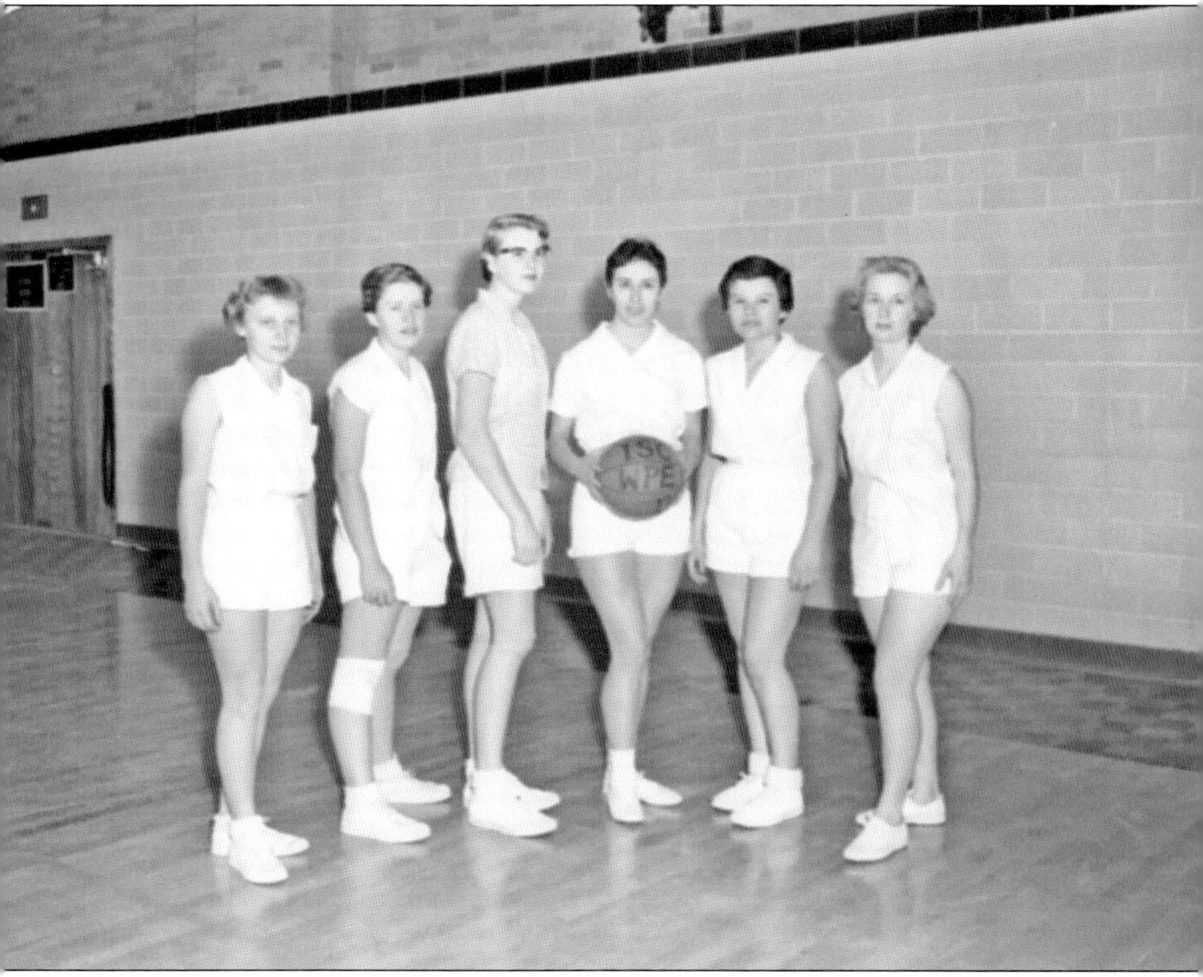

By the 1970s, the disparity in funding between men's and women's sports had grown to untenable levels, with athletic scholarships for women disappearing at an astonishing rate. The US Justice Department stepped in to enforce funding and opportunity equality between the genders with the introduction of Title IX in 1975, and women's sports, such as basketball, blossomed in this new era.

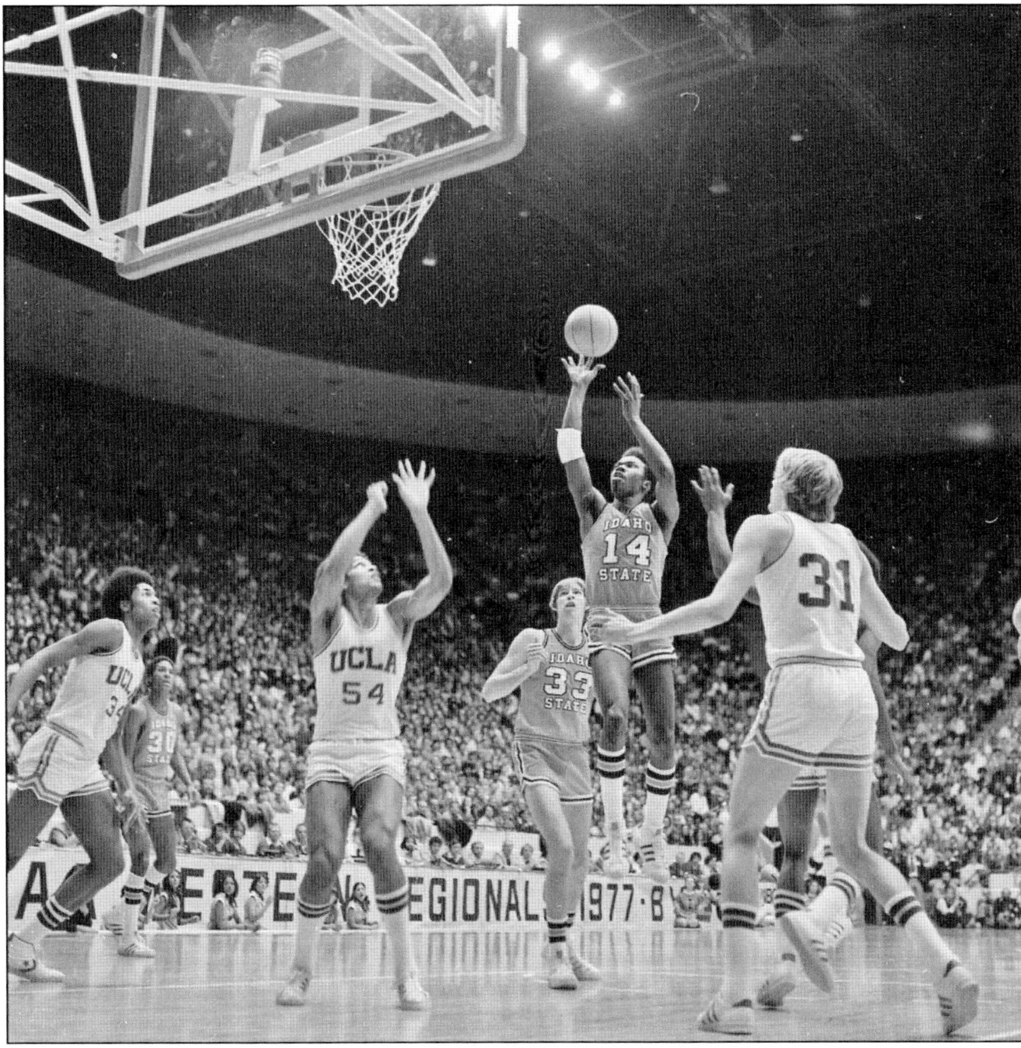

The 1970s and early 1980s were arguably the golden age of sports at Idaho State University. In 1977, the men's basketball team went on to a surprise victory in the Sweet Sixteen of the NCAA Tournament (the school's first and only), where the team handed basketball giants UCLA their third-ever defeat in the playoffs.

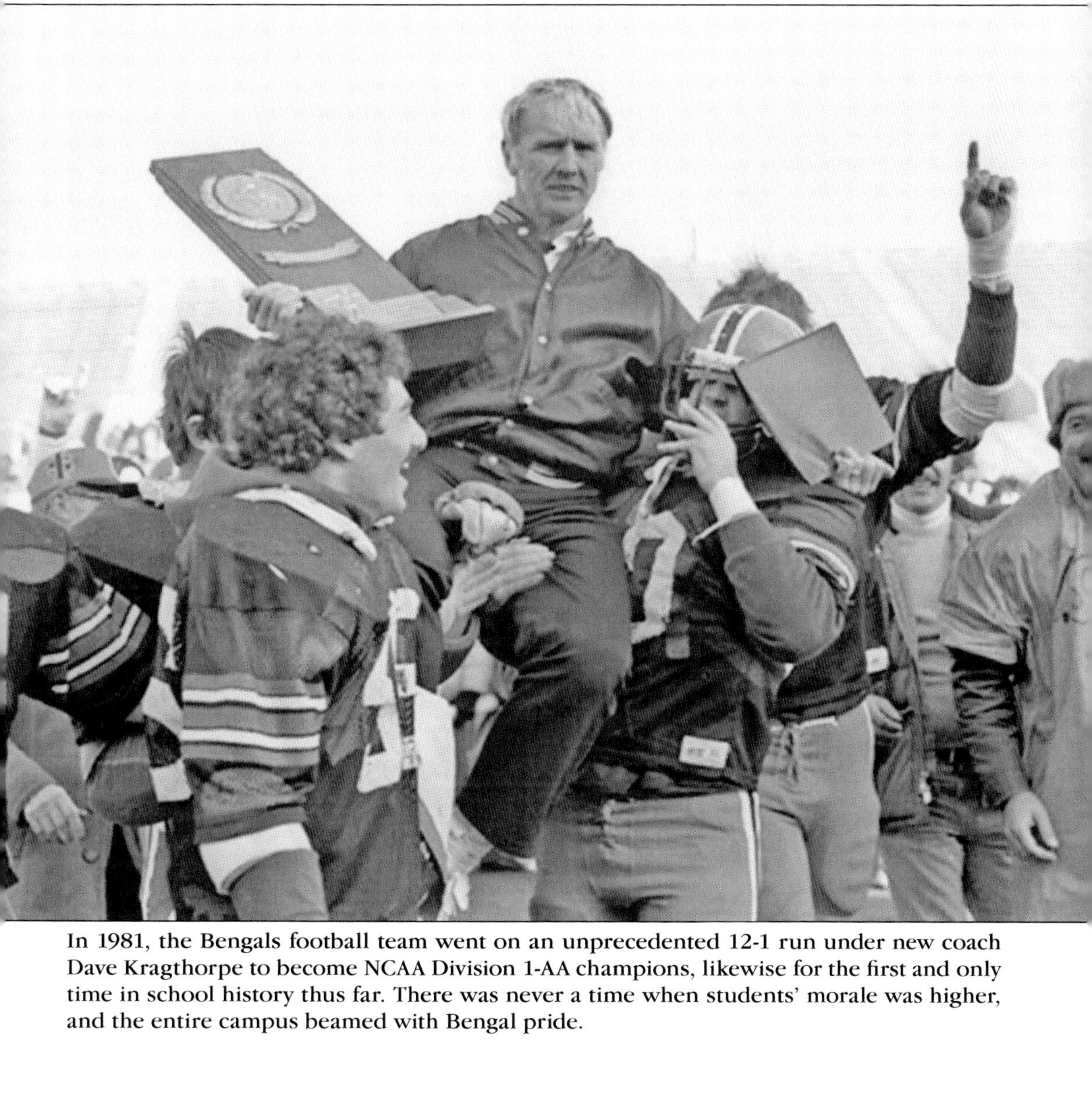

In 1981, the Bengals football team went on an unprecedented 12-1 run under new coach Dave Kragthorpe to become NCAA Division 1-AA champions, likewise for the first and only time in school history thus far. There was never a time when students' morale was higher, and the entire campus beamed with Bengal pride.

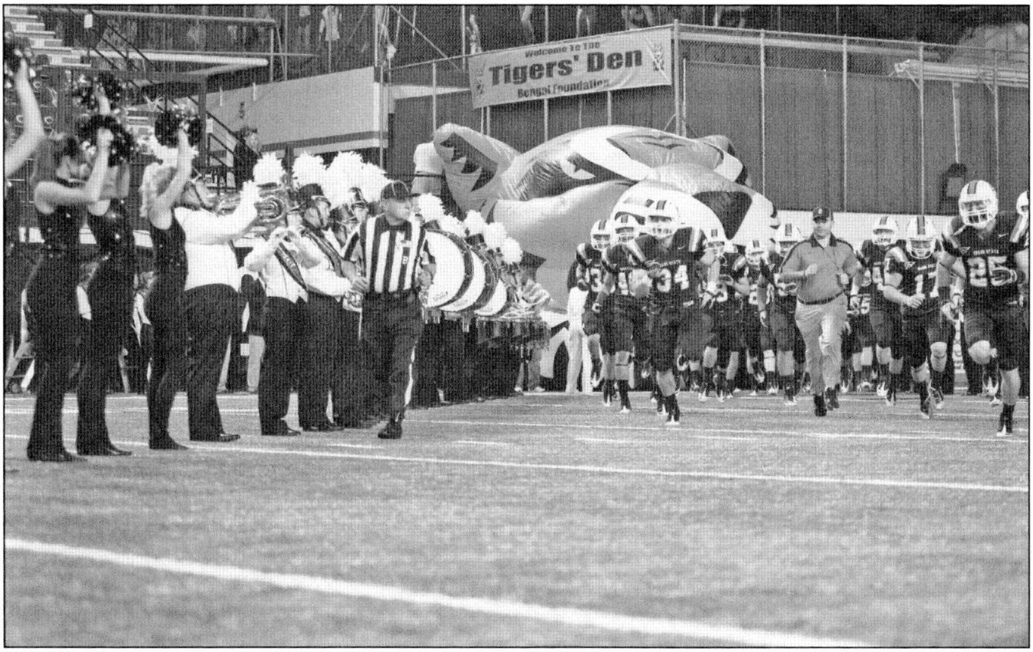

Since the 1980s, the Bengals have continued their tradition of both academic and athletic excellence. Students, alumni, and community members enjoy watching football (as pictured above), indoor track, and men's basketball in Holt Arena, women's basketball, volleyball, and tennis in Reed Gym, soccer and outdoor track and field at Davis Field, and softball in the new Miller Ranch Stadium on Bartz Field. Although the sports, rules, and traditions have changed over time, the Bengal spirit lives on in every athlete, supporter, and student at Idaho State University.

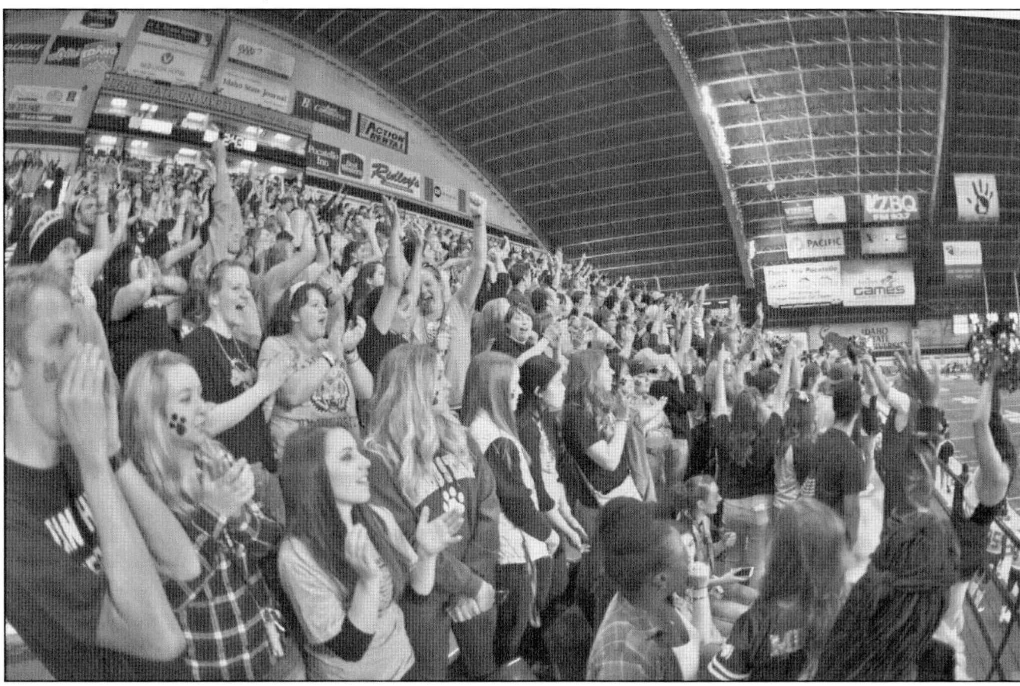

Five

BUILDINGS

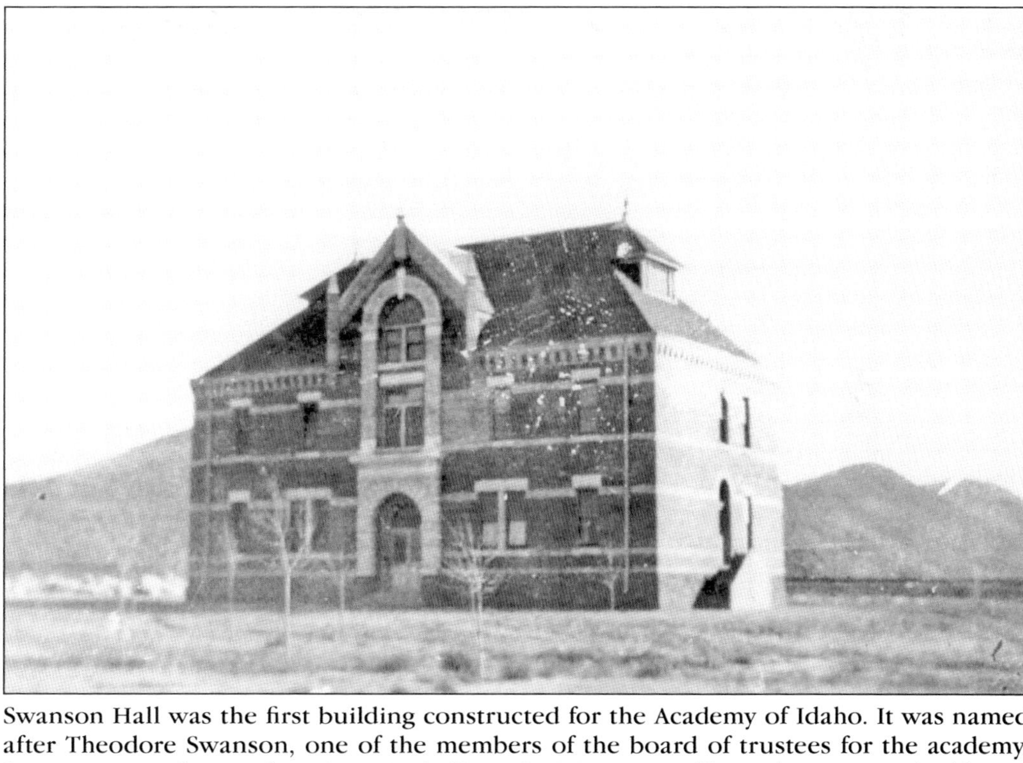

Swanson Hall was the first building constructed for the Academy of Idaho. It was named after Theodore Swanson, one of the members of the board of trustees for the academy. Swanson served many functions, including administrative offices, classrooms, the library, and focal point for the school's first football field. Swanson was central for the school until it fell into disrepair, being demolished in 1973 due to safety concerns. This building was so admired by students and alumni that they exhausted every measure to save part of it. As a result, the original arch of Swanson was left standing, and now students march through the arch before starting their first semester at Idaho State University, to signify becoming a Bengal.

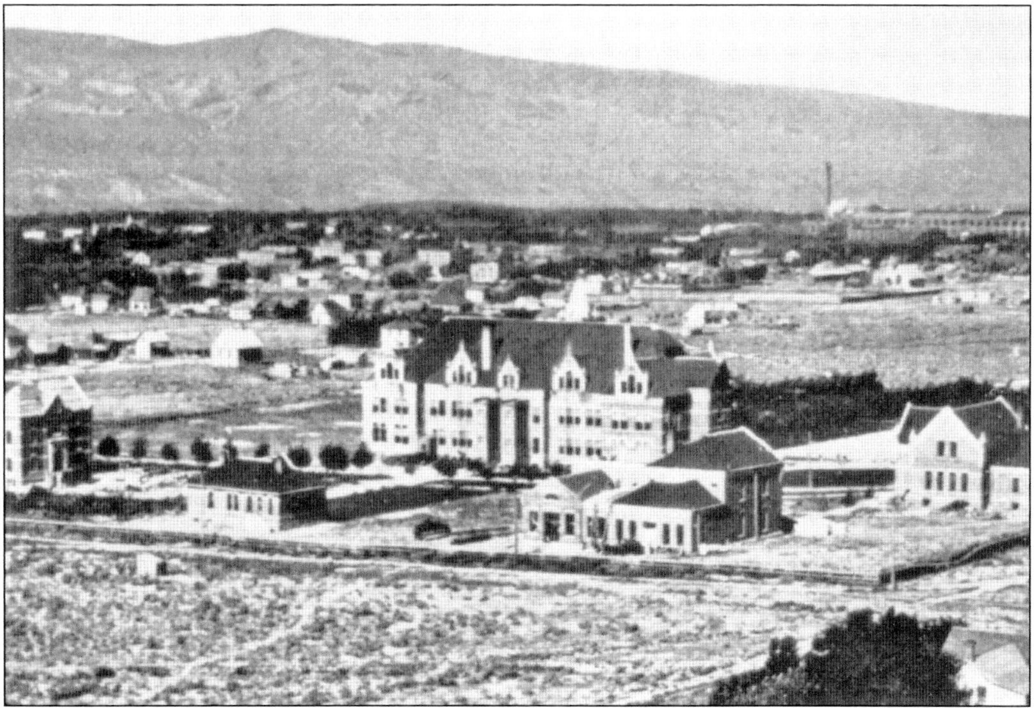

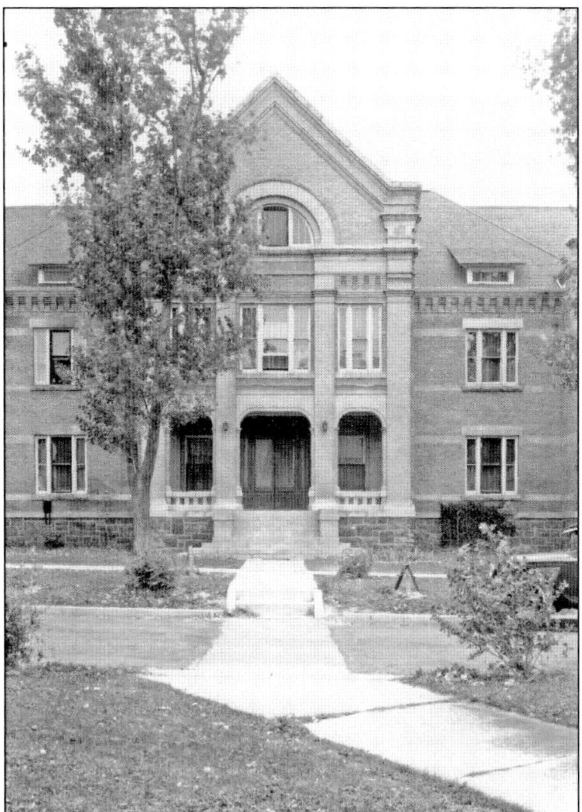

Faris Hall, the "Premier Men's Dormitory," was named after the first administrator and principal of the Academy of Idaho, John W. Faris. Built in 1903, Faris Hall was the second building on campus and also housed the pharmacy program in the basement. It was torn down in 1959 due to safety concerns.

Built in 1902, Girl's Dormitory was the first hall for women on campus. In 1921, in honor of Sen. Theodore Turner who helped found the Academy of Idaho, the hall was renamed Turner Hall. The building stood close to Swanson Hall, illustrating the development of campus and student life. Turner Hall was converted into a men's dormitory in 1948 and then housed women from 1957 until it was torn down.

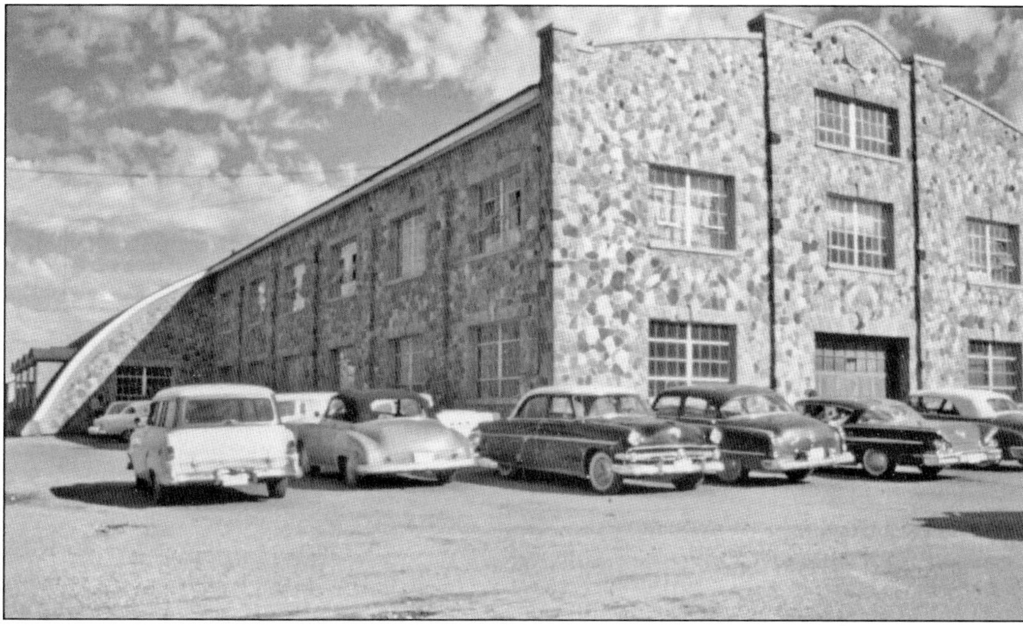

Also known as the "plane hangar building," the Vocational Arts Building is truly unique to ISU. Built to accommodate and train military recruits, the building held airplanes that would land on the strip of land where Holt Arena stands today. The building's exterior was built using rocks from Red Hill, and are said to have a series of hearts carved into them since the building's architect was so in love at the time of its construction.

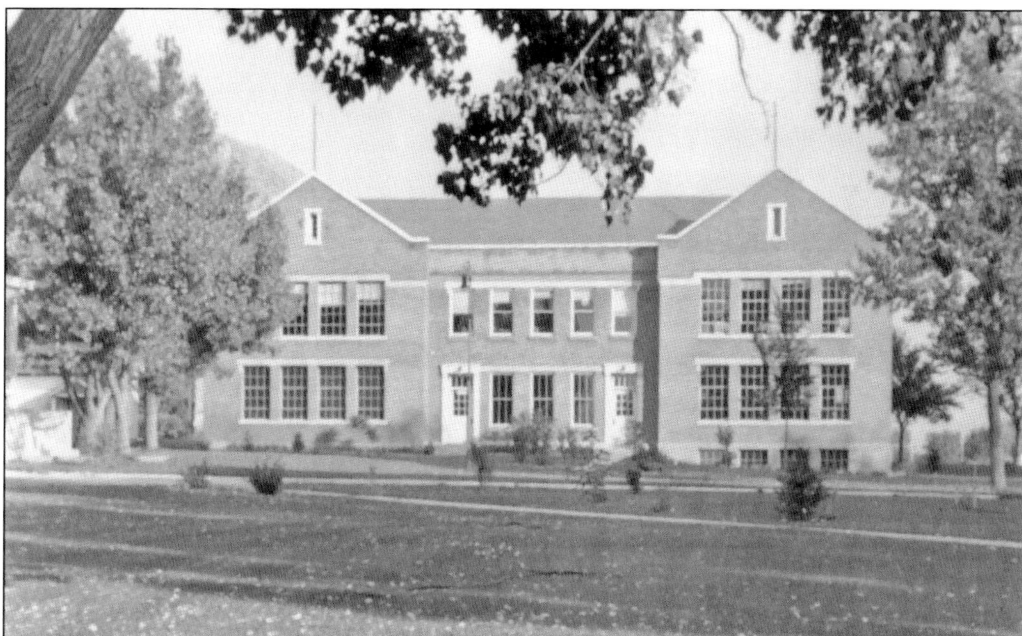

Although it was started in 1903, Engineering Hall was not fully completed until 1925. Some of the original programs included farm machinery and automobile mechanics. The building was torn down in 1971, and engineering coursework is now housed in the Lillibridge Engineering Building.

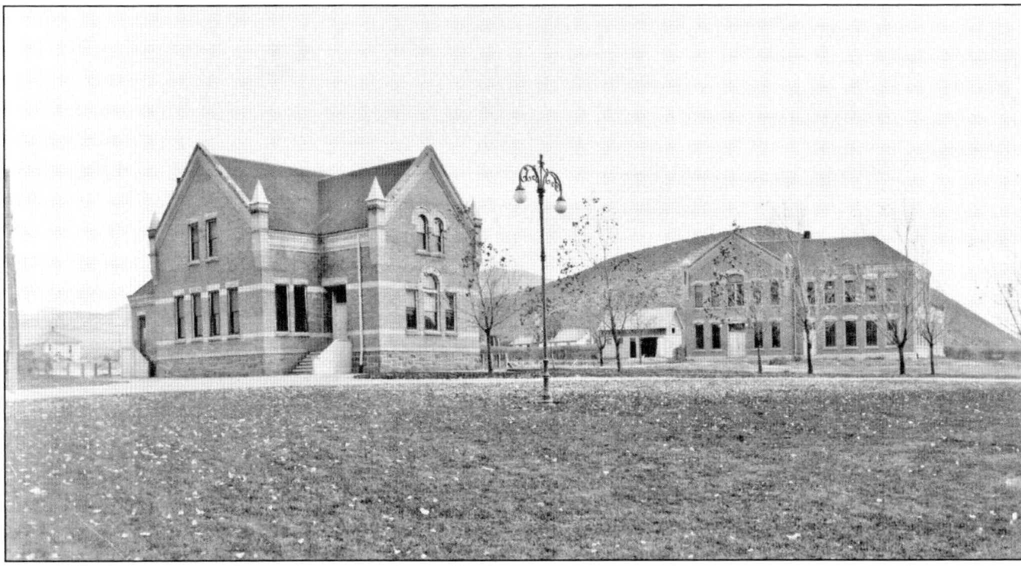

Built in 1903, the dining hall served as the main center for food services on campus. Also known as "the Cafeteria" and "the Beanery," the building stood as a main focal point for students and the surrounding Pocatello community for the next 50 years, until it closed its food services in 1959. After its 61 years of service, the dining hall was demolished in 1964.

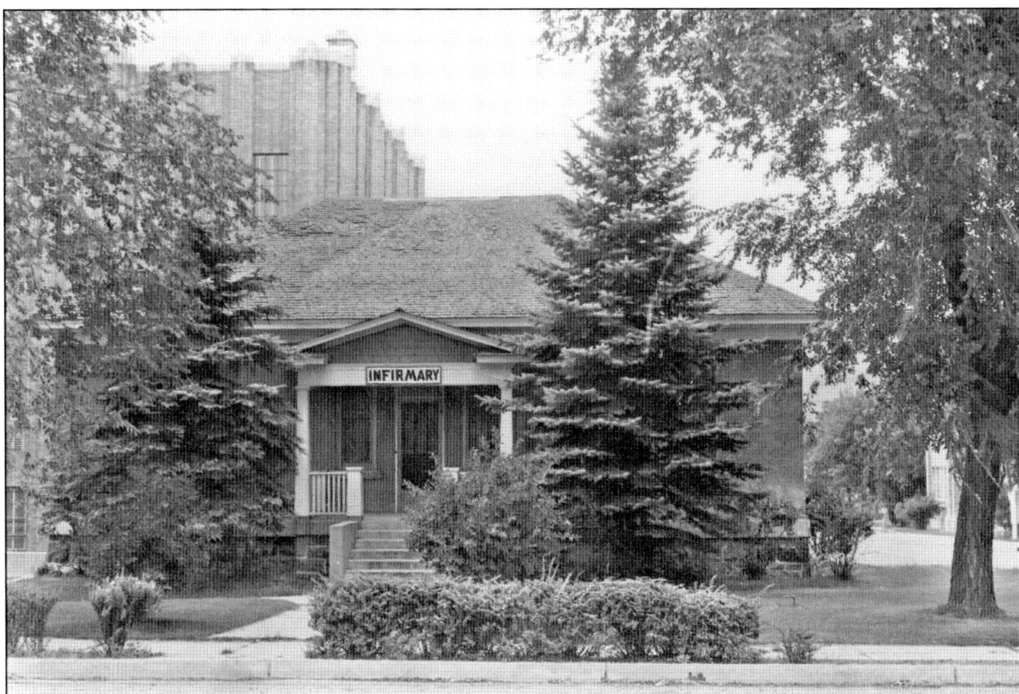

Built in 1907, this building originally served as the office of the principal of the Academy of Idaho; however, in order to improve student services, it was converted to the infirmary in the late 1920s. The building's main level served as a health center, while the basement was the nurse's living quarters. It stood on campus in front of the administration building for decades until it was destroyed by a fire.

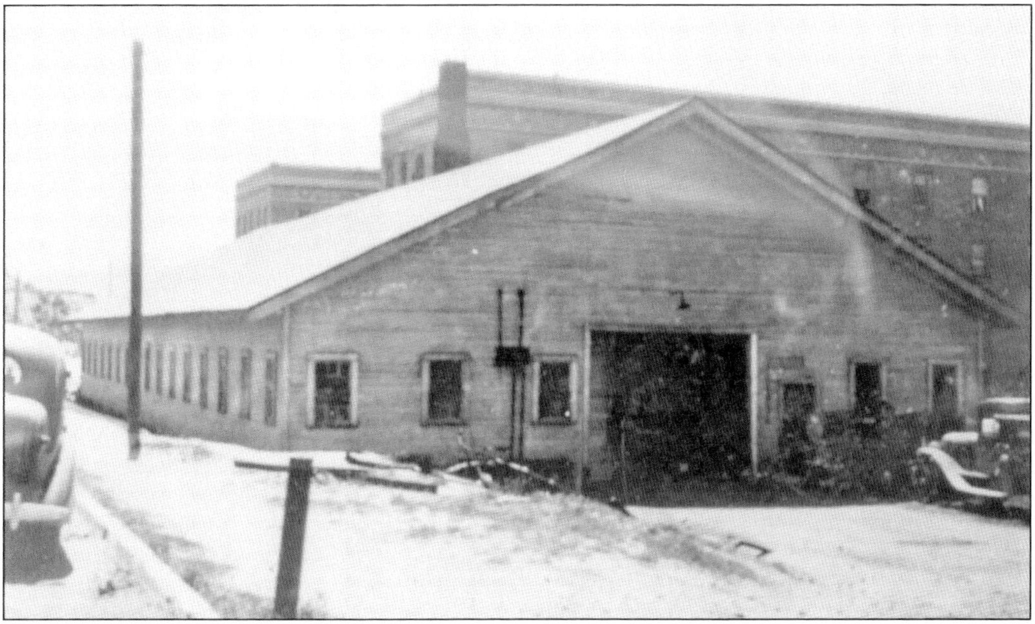

Horse stables seemed like a ridiculous idea for the Academy of Idaho but ended up being one of the institution's biggest assets. At the onset of World War I, the Academy of Idaho was struggling with enrollment and saw a rapid drop in numbers as young men were called away to battle. However, because the academy had the infrastructure to house horses, the US Cavalry moved in and kept the institution afloat. After the war, the stable was donated to the Idaho Technical Institute and was used as a maintenance shed.

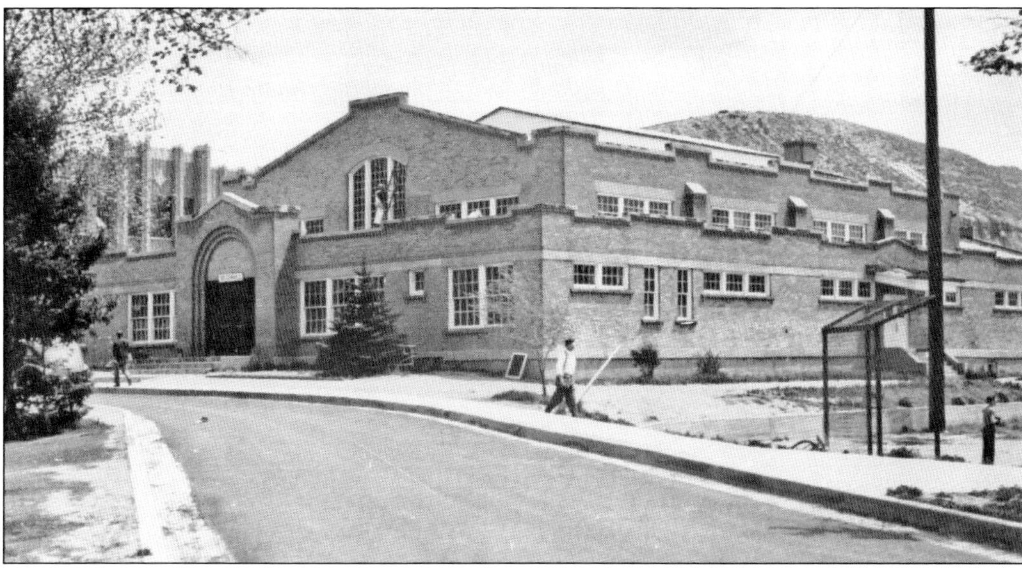

Reed Hall, built in 1917, served as the university's first athletic facility. The building served both the athletic needs of students as well as housing for several athletes. At the time that Reed Hall was built, it was known as the nicest athletic complex in the state. The building was condemned in 1947 and replaced with the current recreational facility. Prior to its condemnation, Dubby Holt, the athletic director at the time, once made athletes swim to their lockers to retrieve equipment after a large water pipe broke in the building.

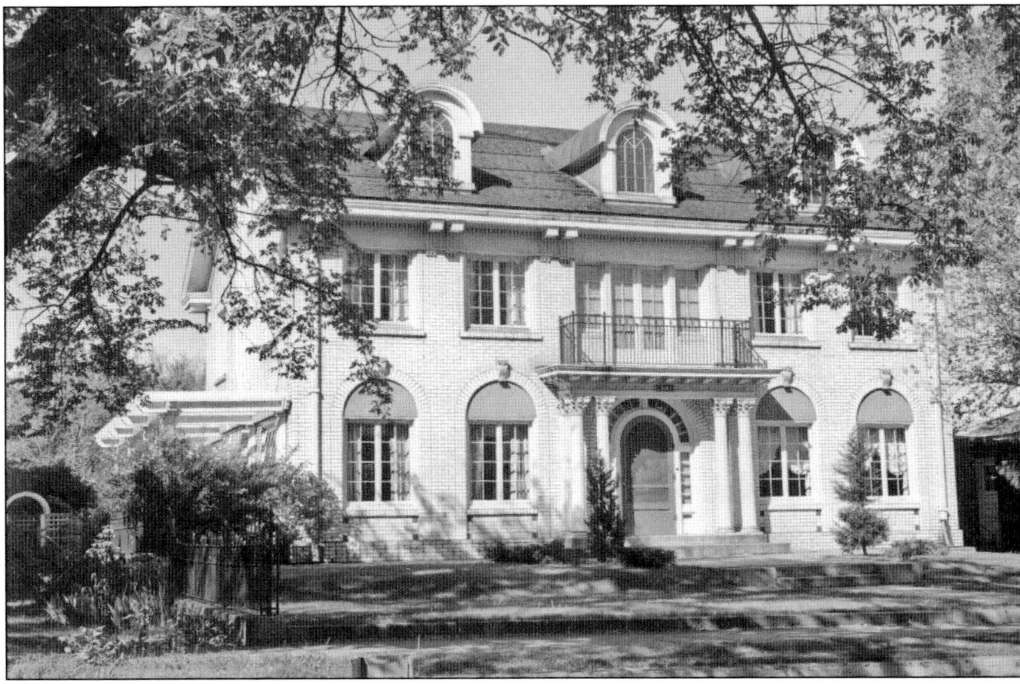

Built in 1917 and purchased by the Idaho State Board of Education in 1951, the Servel Home serves as the official president's residence. Originally built for a wealthy sheep man, the house was a marvel of its time, with electricity, a centralized vacuum cleaning system, and handcrafted mantle pieces. Through the years, the house underwent renovations and served several different functions, ranging from a quaint family home to a cooperative for underprivileged girls. Today, the house is host to the university president and a wide range of social functions.

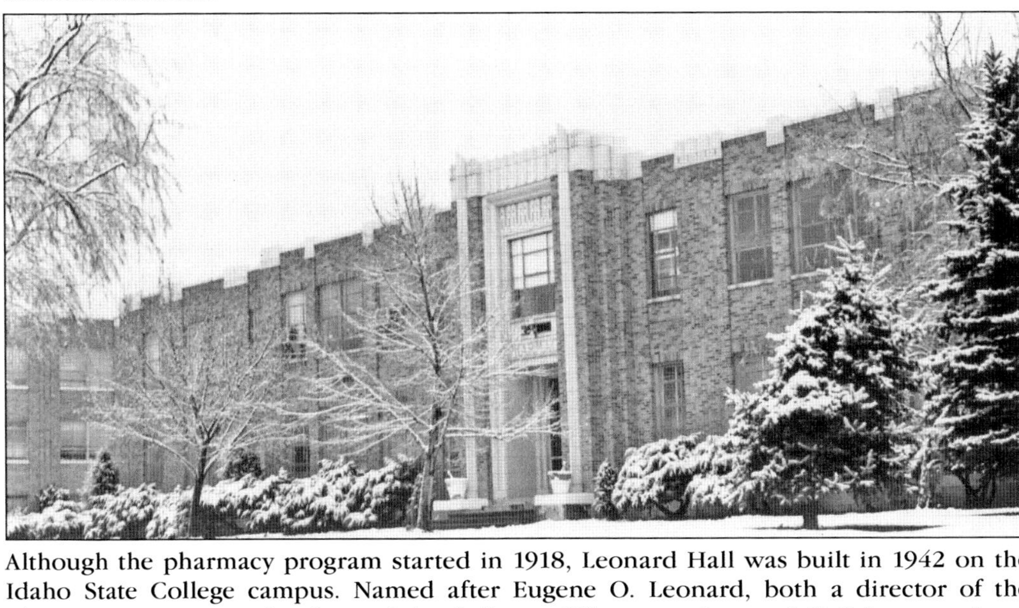

Although the pharmacy program started in 1918, Leonard Hall was built in 1942 on the Idaho State College campus. Named after Eugene O. Leonard, both a director of the pharmacy program and a dean of the College of Pharmacy, Leonard Hall houses a large collection of items from the Idaho Museum of Pharmacy.

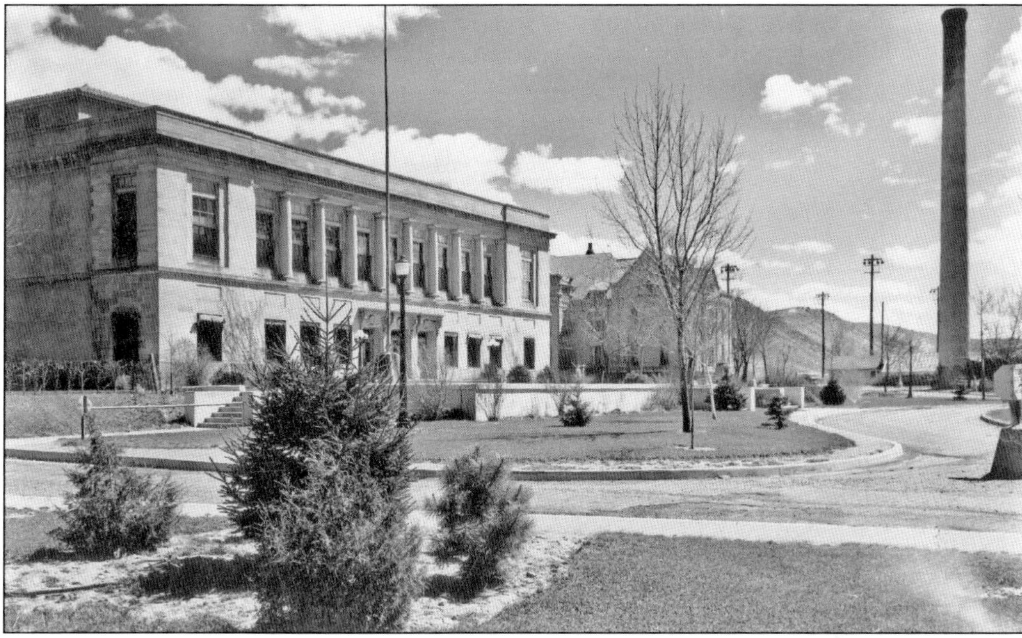

Frazier Hall, built in 1924, was the first building of "collegiate status" in the state of Idaho. Frazier Hall served as the Idaho Technical Institute's performance hall, while the top floor of the building served as the library. Out front, the American Legion sundial was a memorial to the four students who attended Idaho Technical Institute and were killed during World War I. Frazier Hall is now the oldest building still standing on campus and houses the communication, media, and persuasion program. Frazier Hall is even the center of paranormal activity on campus, with several reports of strange whispers and movements throughout the performance hall.

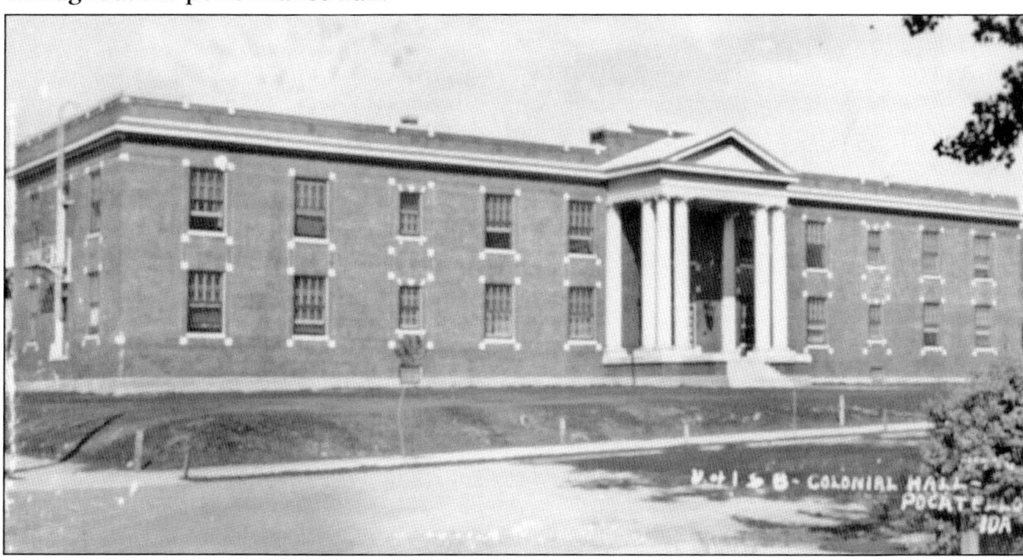

Built in 1925, Colonial Hall served as a women's only dormitory. It was converted to a men's dormitory in 1945 following the end of World War II and now serves as the administration building for the engineering department. The building's majestic design makes it a substantial addition to the campus's architecture.

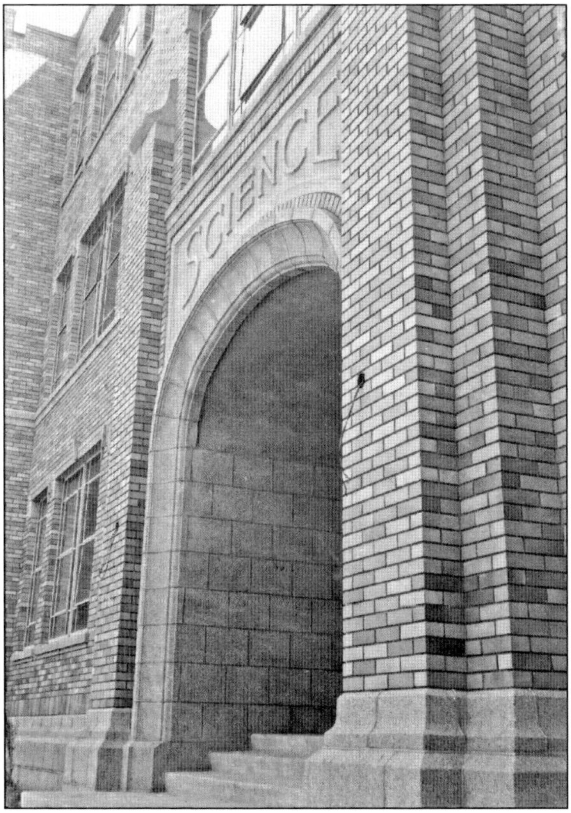

Built in 1927, Science Hall was the home to many of the physical and biological sciences along with the pharmacy program. It was renamed Baldwin Hall in 1960 after Dr. Ernest J Baldwin, who served as the dean of the University of Idaho Southern Branch. Baldwin Hall was torn down in 1992 due to safety concerns.

A poignant example of the Great Depression, Hooverville, or the Shanty Town, was a prominent presence on campus during the 1930s. Located south of Graveley Hall at the base of Red Hill, this area served as a temporary home for students. The building materials ranged from cardboard boxes to tents and even milk delivery wagons. The students who called this area home personified the fighting spirit of campus and dedication to the institution's success.

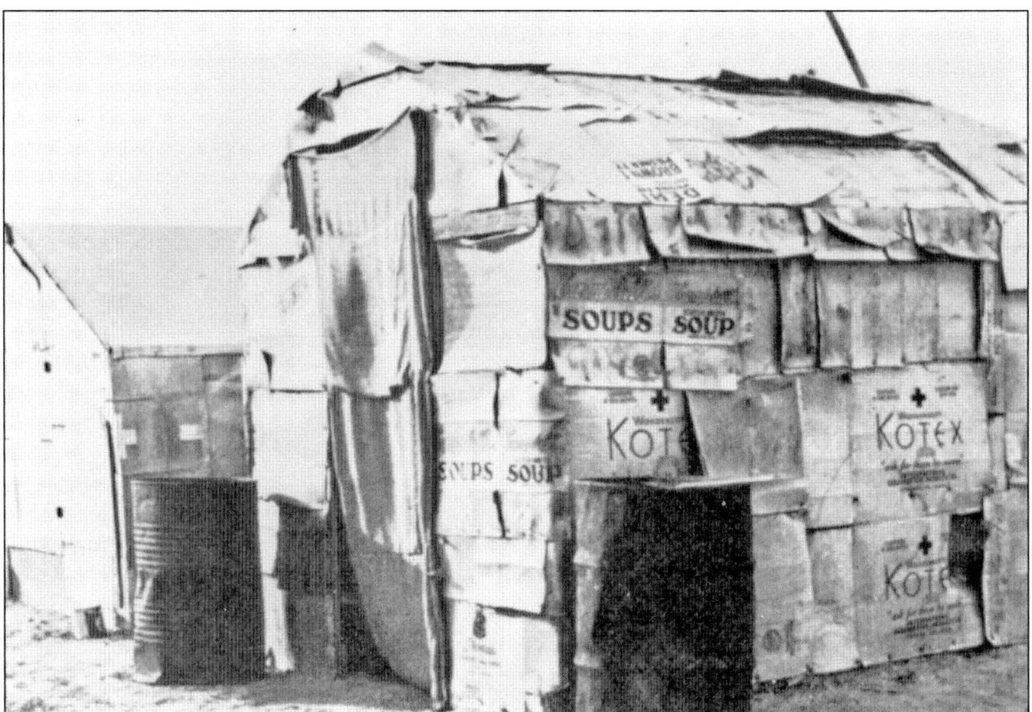

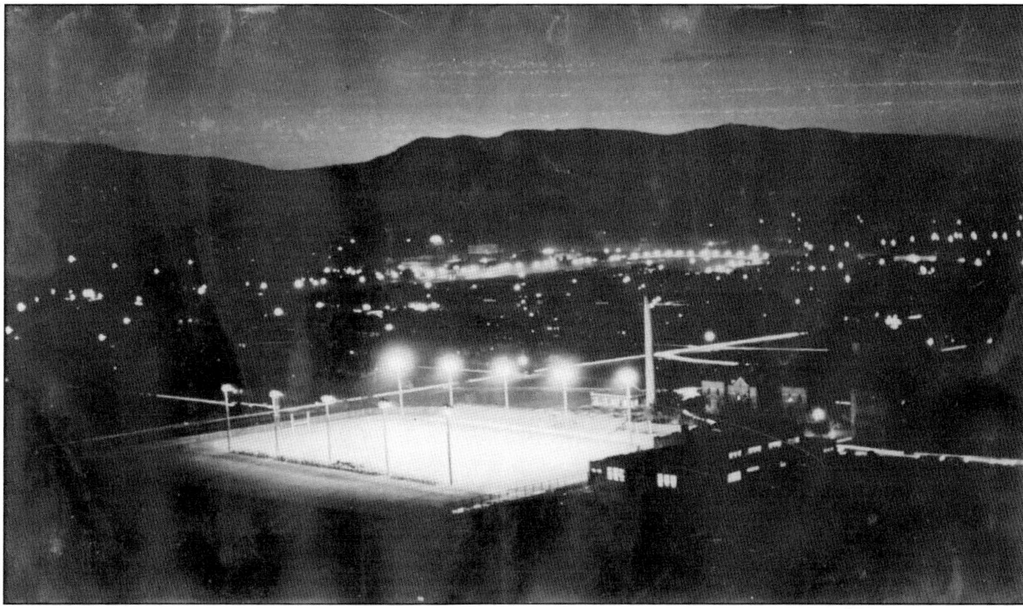

The Spud Bowl, one of the first federally funded projects on campus, served as the school's football field. This immense project was completed using only manual labor of men and horses. The rocks, taken from Red Hill, were one of the only resources used to construct the project. When completed, the field was proposed to be named Dyer Stadium; however, due to Idaho's association with potatoes, it was called the Spud Bowl instead.

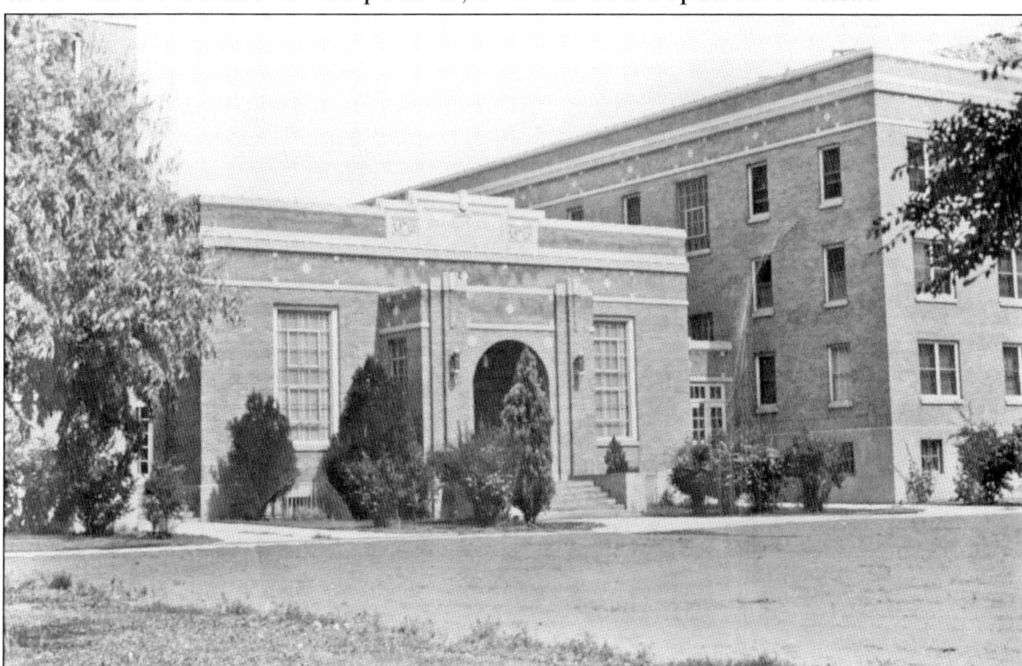

Graveley Hall, built in 1939 as a women's only dormitory, stands as one of the first buildings of the Hutchinson Quad. The hall was named after Lottie Graveley, the first female member of the Idaho State Board of Education.

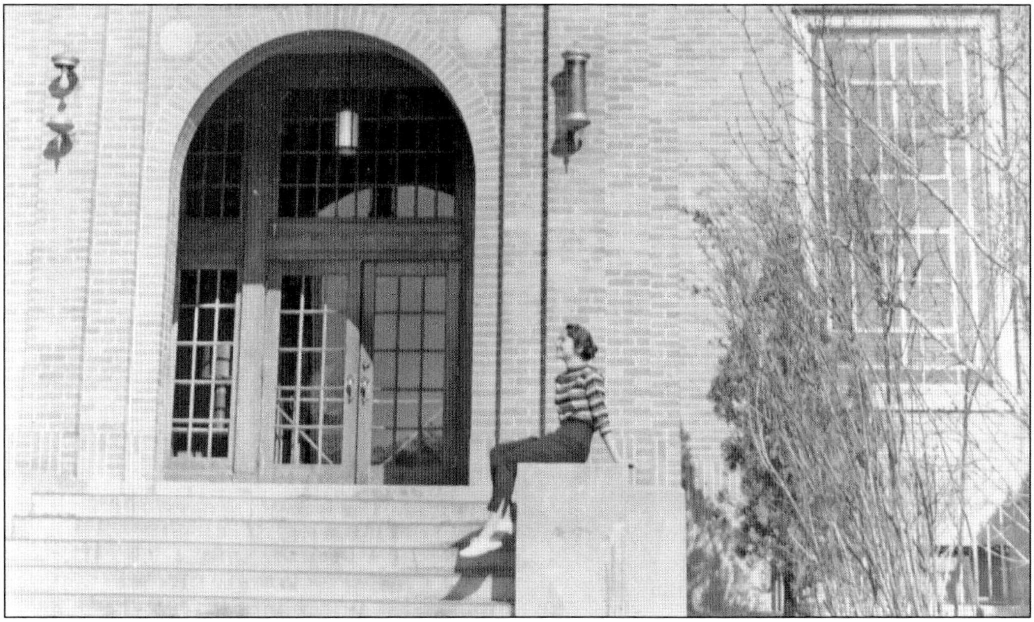

Graveley was an iconic building for student life, frequently being used for activities such as roof sunbathing. Gravely housed only women until 1942, when it was remodeled into a mock ship to assist in training Navy officers and aviation specialists in Idaho State University's V-12 program, a special program for training a variety of servicemen. Rumors have it that men would even frequent the underground service tunnels to enter the building after curfew.

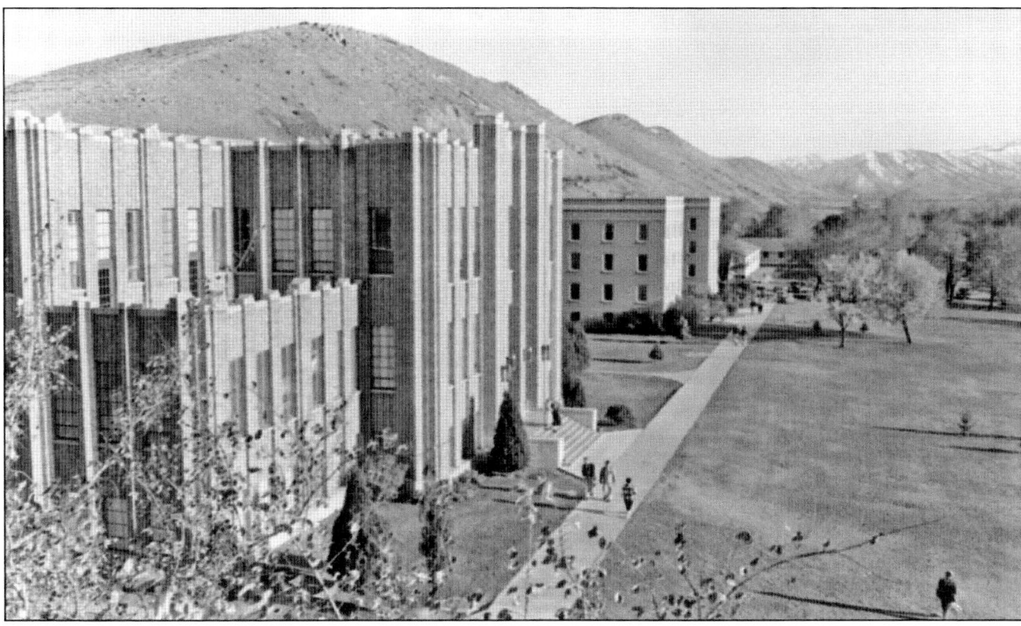

Originally finished in 1939, the current Administration Building stood as one of the first student union buildings in the Intermountain West. Built as a Public Works Administration project, the building astonished people with its complexity and beauty. Its elegant design follows the same concept as Pocatello's oldest high school, Pocatello High. It served as the student union building (SUB) for the next 20 years, until a new SUB was built.

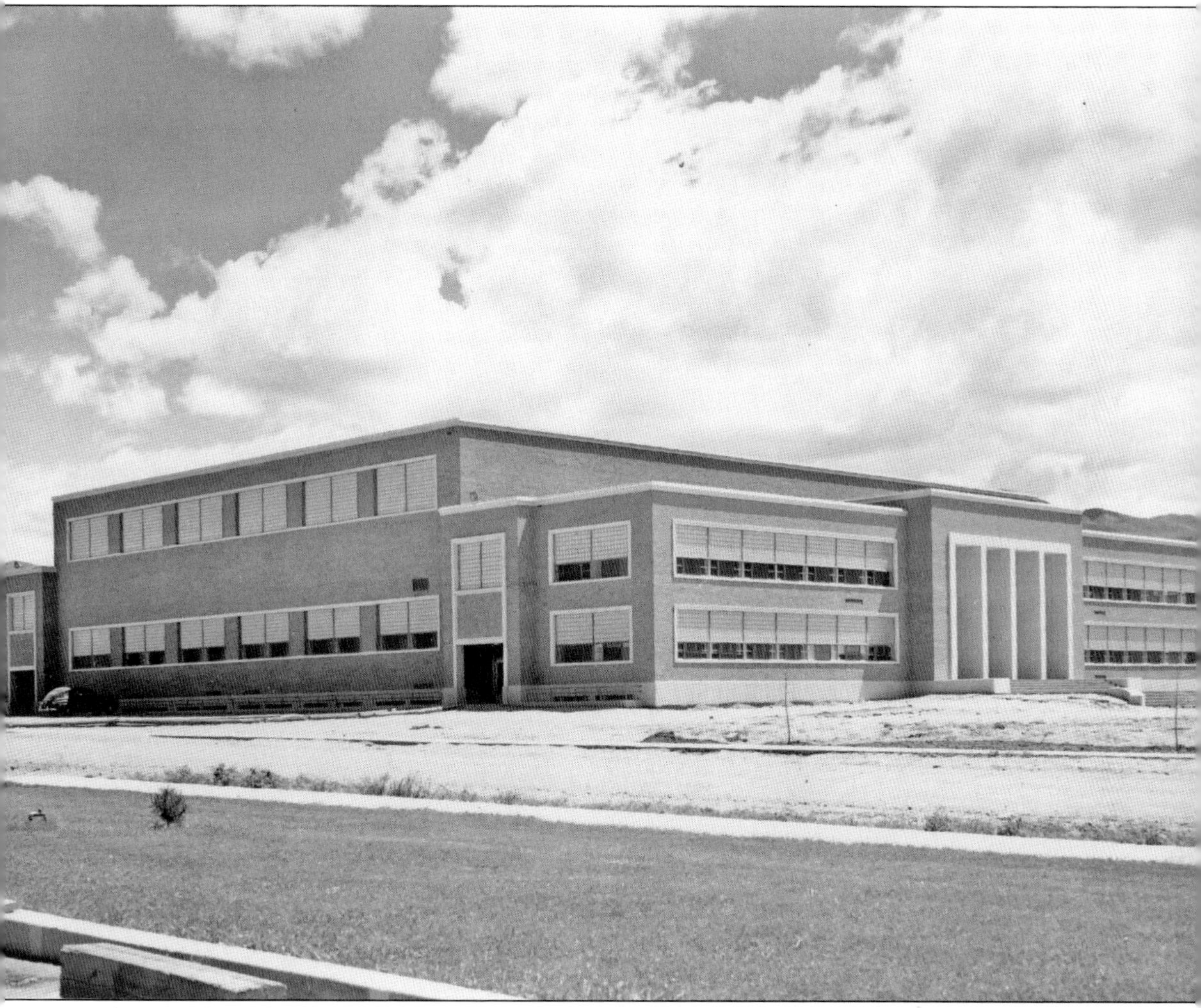

Built to replace the condemned Reed Hall, Reed Gym was constructed to be the premiere athletic facility on campus. Basketball, volleyball, and many other sports have been hosted in the Reed Gym, and today, it is a focal point for student life. Housing a state-of-the-art exercise facility, swimming pool, and human performance lab, Reed Gym is a staple on ISU's campus.

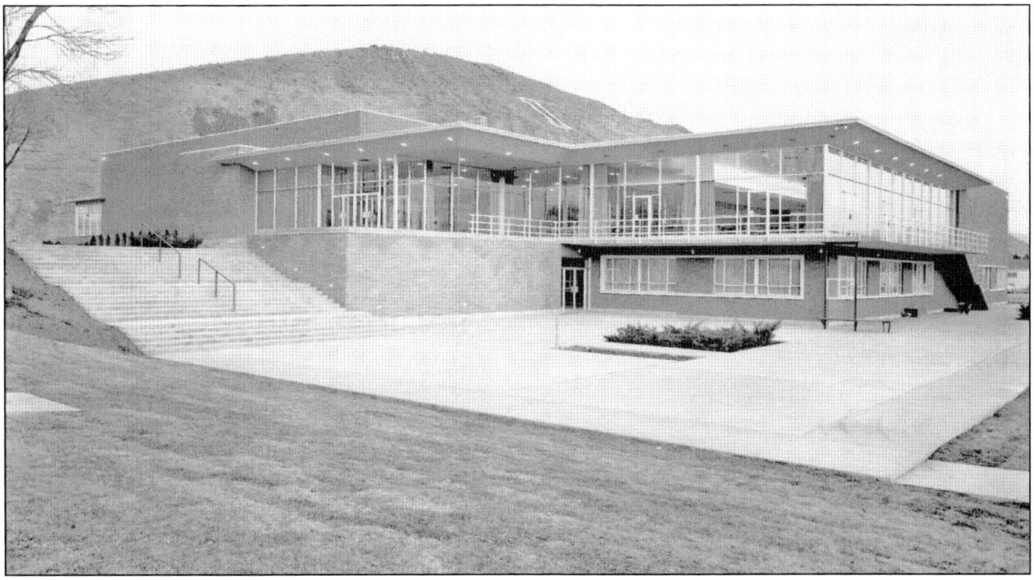

Built in 1956, the student union building was a designated space for students, staff, and faculty to eat, study, socialize, or do whatever else they wished. In 1985, the SUB was renamed the Earl R. Pond Student Union Building after the real "Mr. ISU" himself, Earl Pond, who served as the SUB general manager for over 23 years. This picture shows the building's original design, constructed with a full balcony patio before the addition of the hypostyle. The hypostyle, built to connect the SUB to the Museum of Natural History building, connects on the right side of the photograph and provides better access to critical services on campus, such as Central Academic Advising and the Scholarship Office.

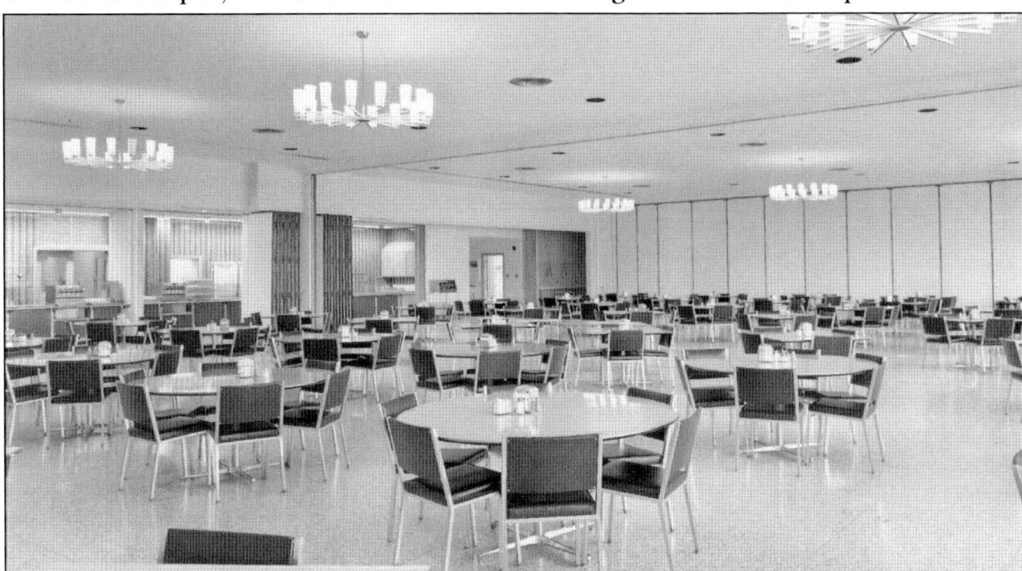

The SUB offers a variety of activities to the university, ranging from a full-size movie theater to a bowling alley and even an arcade. It is said that the SUB is the source of school spirit, having both the school's bookstore as well as the clock tower that sings the university's fight song. Though the SUB has undergone a series of renovations from its original layout (as seen here), the SUB still maintains its legacy of being student-centered.

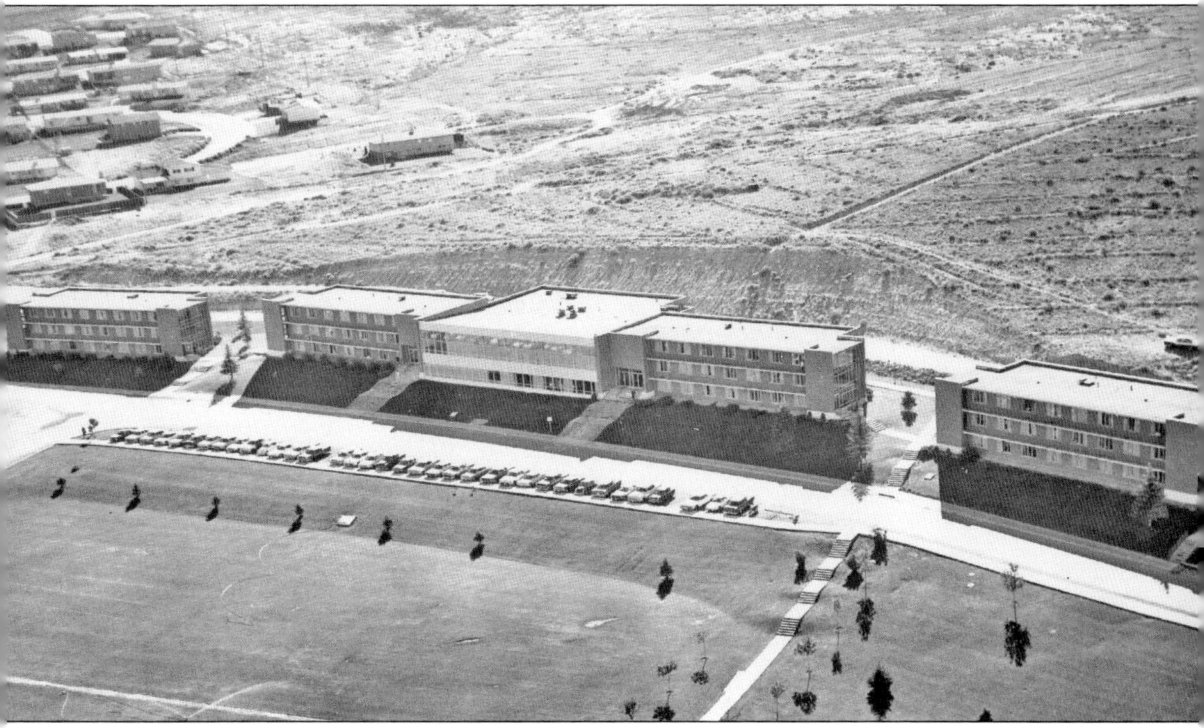

Completed in the 1960s, South Complex was built to combat the housing crisis the school was facing. The complex, composed of four separate buildings, was built with a little over a $1 million budget. Each building—Owen, Nichols, Redfield, and Dyer—is named after the school's esteemed presidents or other notable individuals whose efforts substantially improved the school. The grand opening of this complex was well-attended, including Pocatello's mayor, several state politicians, and even the governor.

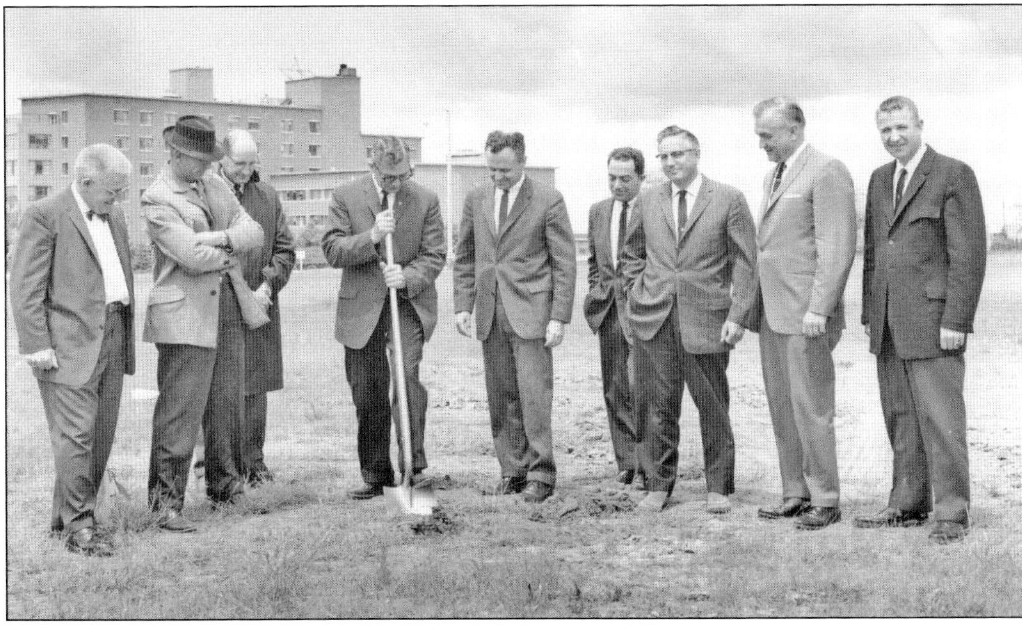

This picture shows the ground breaking for the Turner-Garrison Complex. After years of severe housing shortages, this complex was approved by the Idaho State Board of Education and was one-of-a-kind due to its eight stories. In order to build the complex, construction crews had to pour cement at ground level and hydraulically raise each floor. Through the innovative efforts of both Cedric Allen and Brent Ballif, the architect and engineer, the towers were completed on time and under budget.

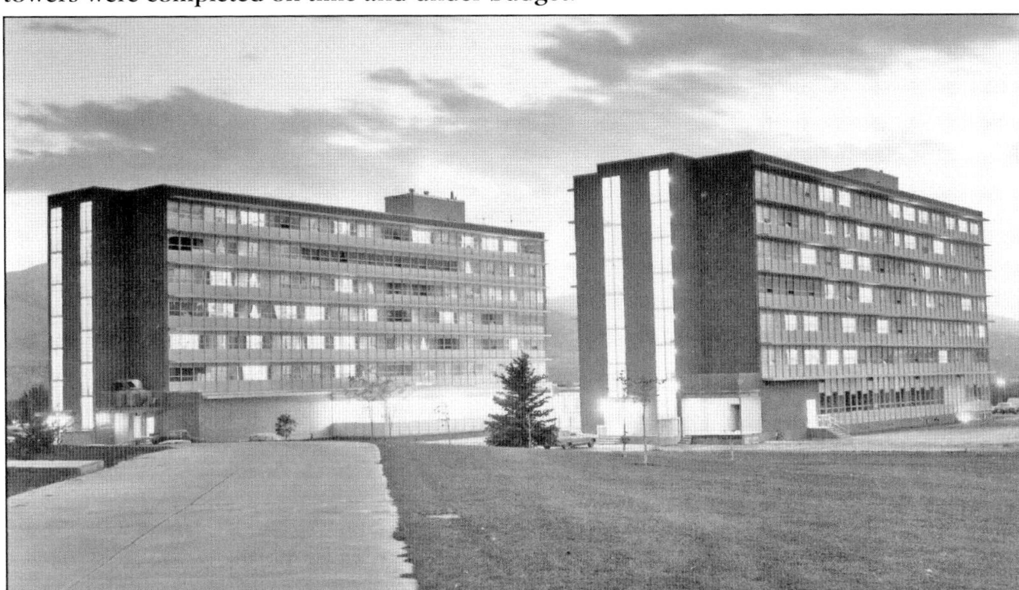

This is the completed Turner-Garrison Complex. Turner, originally built for women, is on the right, while Garrison, the male dormitory, is on the left. Connecting the two buildings is the campus cafeteria. This cafeteria underwent a major remodel in the summer of 2016, its first since the construction half a century ago, to become state-of-the-art.

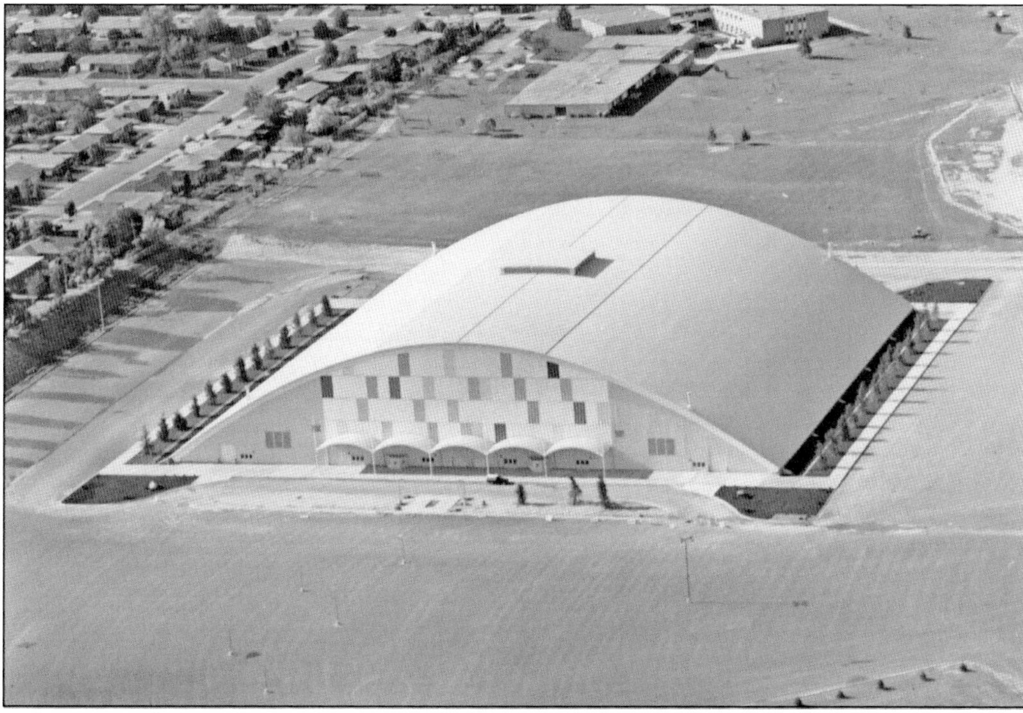

In the late 1960s, Idaho State University undertook one of the most impressive endeavors seen on campus: building a covered football stadium. The dream of assistant athletic director Milton "Dubby" Holt, the stadium was to be modeled after the Houston Astrodome and was the first enclosed stadium on a college campus in the United States. The ASISU Minidome was finished in 1970 and now is the oldest covered stadium in the nation.

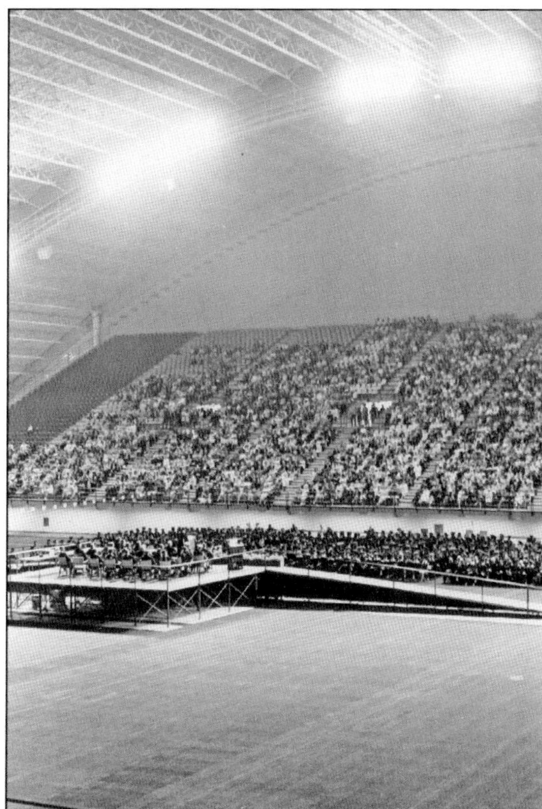

With a price tag of just over $2.8 million, gathering the funds for the new stadium was a daunting task. In a historic decision, ISU students voted in favor of a $12 tuition increase to fund the project, and the ASISU Minidome became a reality. In 1988, it was renamed the ASISU Holt Arena in honor of Dubby Holt and his contributions to athletics at ISU. Today, the ASISU Holt Arena is the home of football and men's basketball and is considered the home of the Bengals.

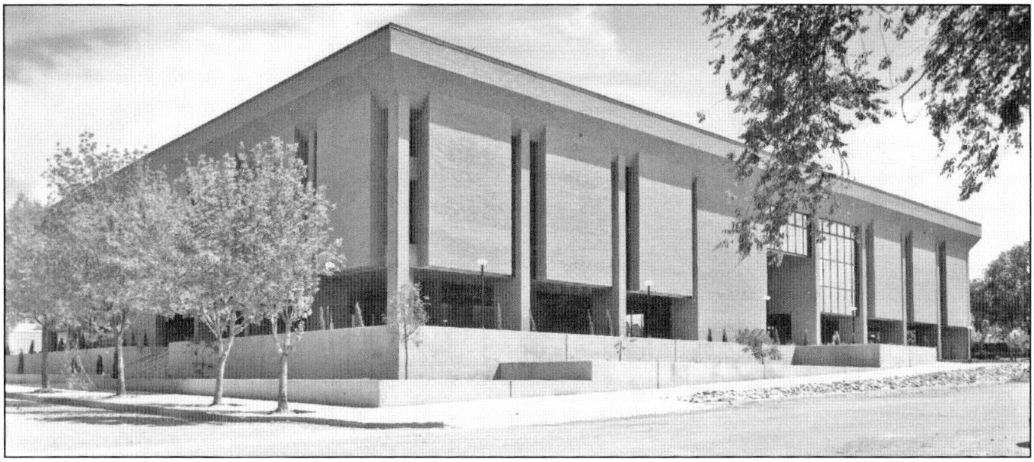

In 1971, the Idaho State Board of Education made a library building at Idaho State University its number-one priority. But by 1972 the project had been halted, taking a backseat to other projects at other universities. The library was finally built in 1977, and the construction went so smoothly, John Korbis, the former director of the physical plant, stated that the process was "unreal." When the building was finished, four moving companies and an assortment of faculty, staff, and students moved 13 miles of books to the new library. Finally, during homecoming week 1977, the $5 million building was opened to the public.

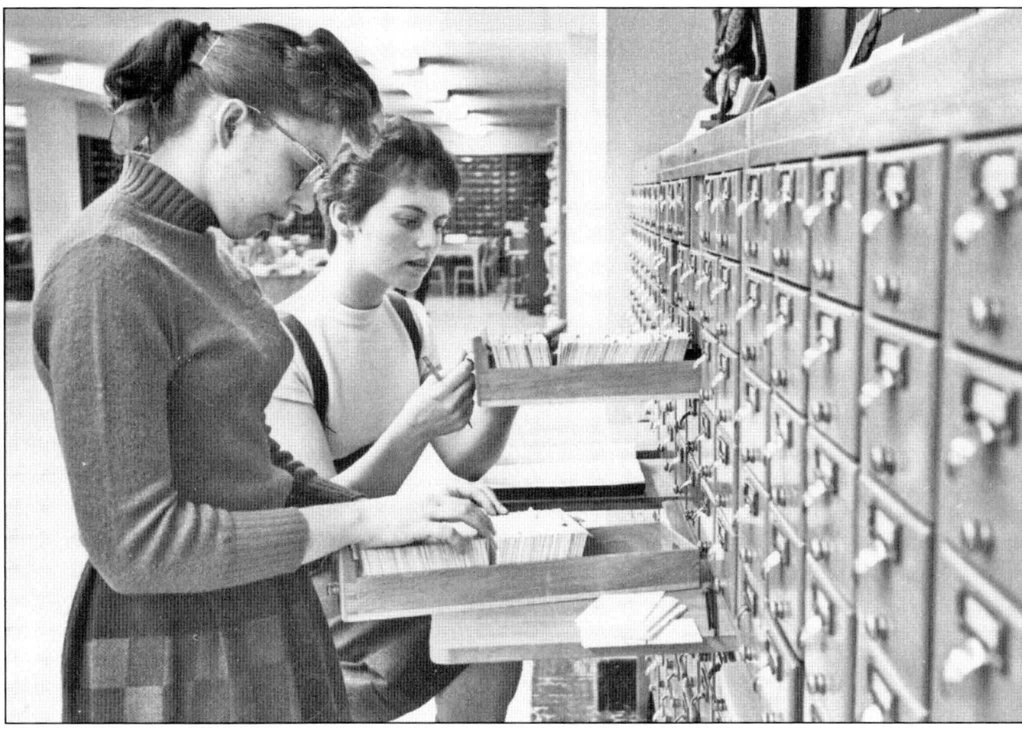

At the time, the library building was the largest building in Idaho dedicated entirely to education and was eventually named after longtime librarian Eli M. Oboler. Today, the Eli M. Oboler Library serves students with an expansive online collection. It is also home to the Idaho Health Sciences Library, which houses cutting-edge health science research and information for the State of Idaho.

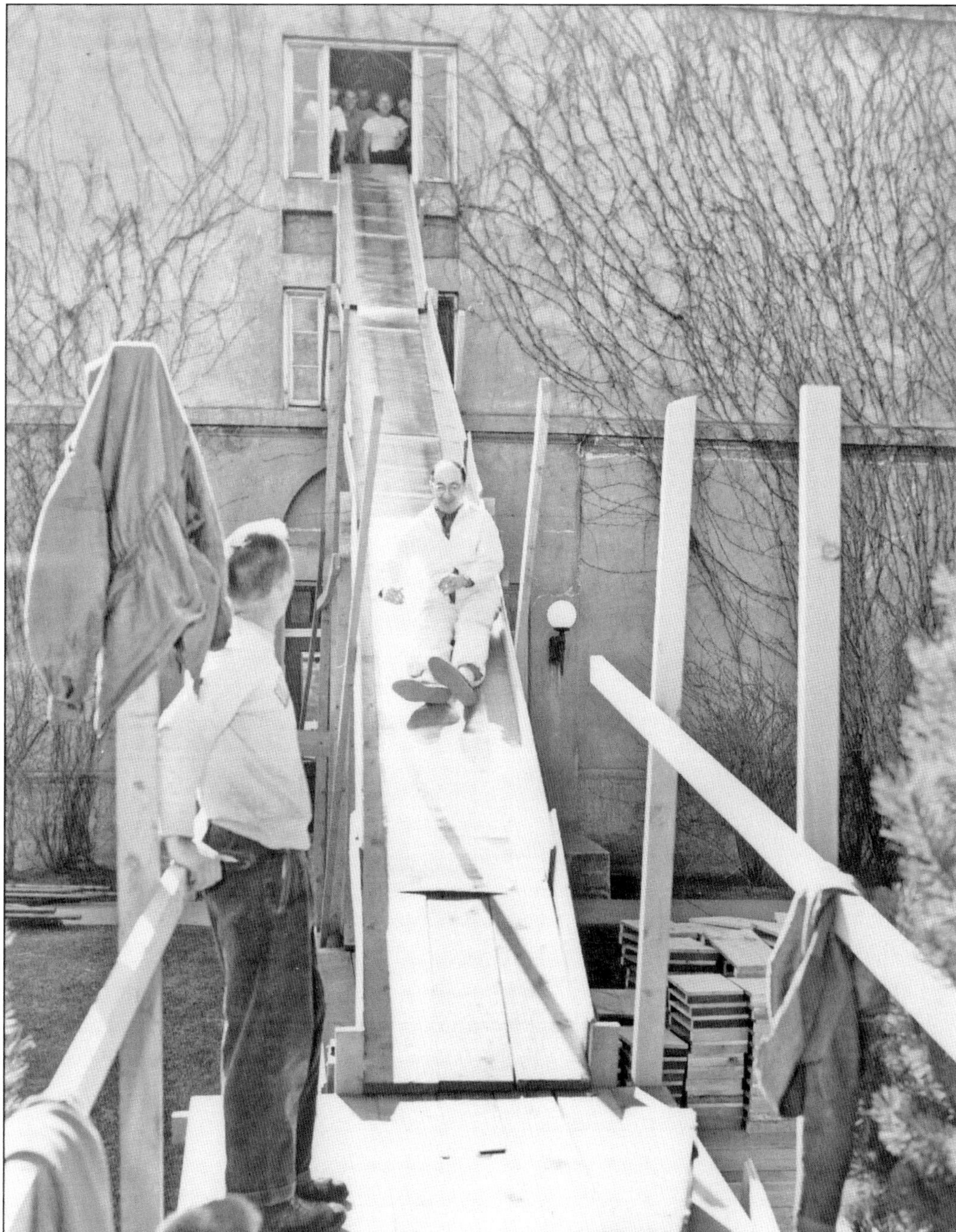

This photograph illustrates the innovative and fun methods in which books were moved across campus. Since the safety of the books was a top priority, Eli Oboler, the man on the slide, decided to test it for himself. Throughout the school's history, the library has grown alongside it. Originally a small room in Swanson Hall, the library found itself moving to the top floor of Frasier, then to what is the present-day museum building, and eventually to the present library.

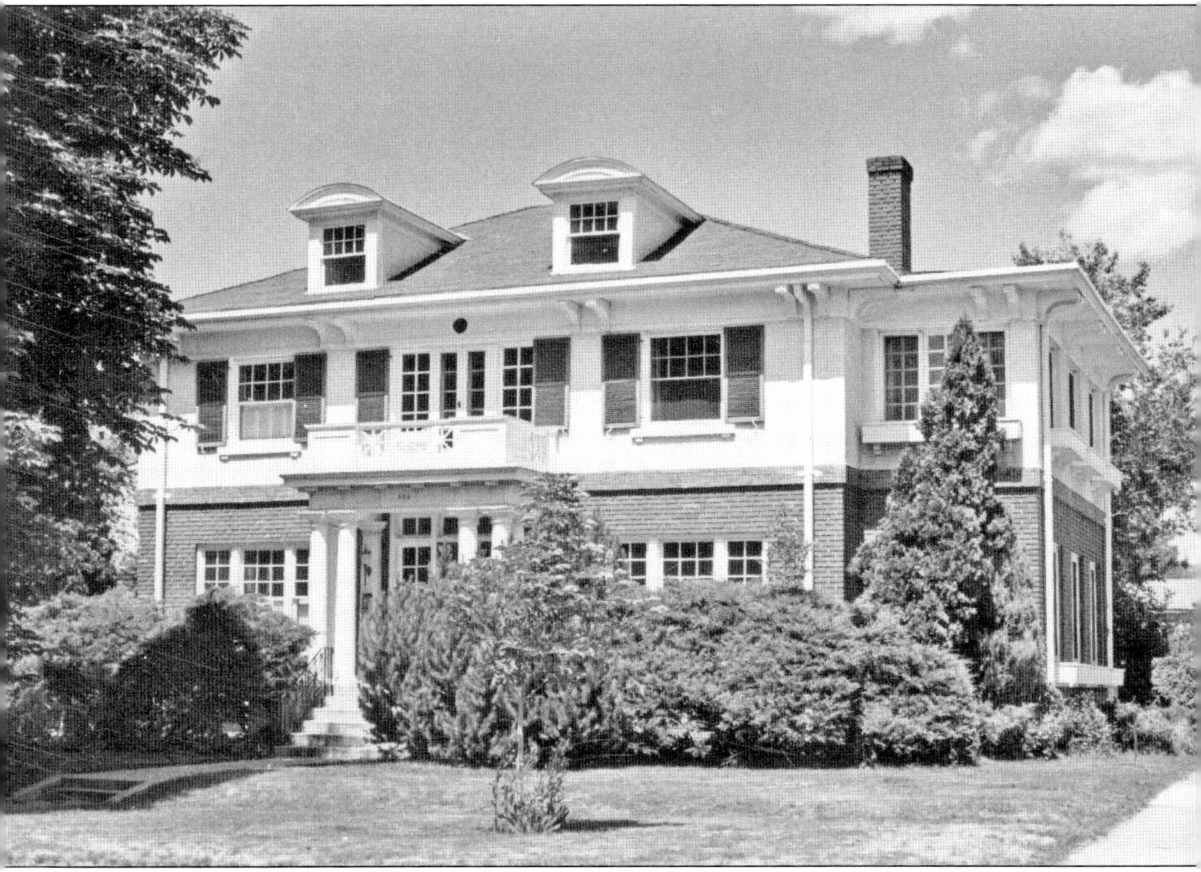

The Magnuson House, built in 1916 and purchased in 1972, serves as the central office for the alumni association and hosts many of its events. Originally built by John Hood, a former coworker of J.C. Penney, the house was a meeting place for celebrations, including graduation parties, homecoming, and even the occasional baptism. Though often host to these uplifting events, there are rumors that a spirit also haunts the hallways.

Six

The Later Years

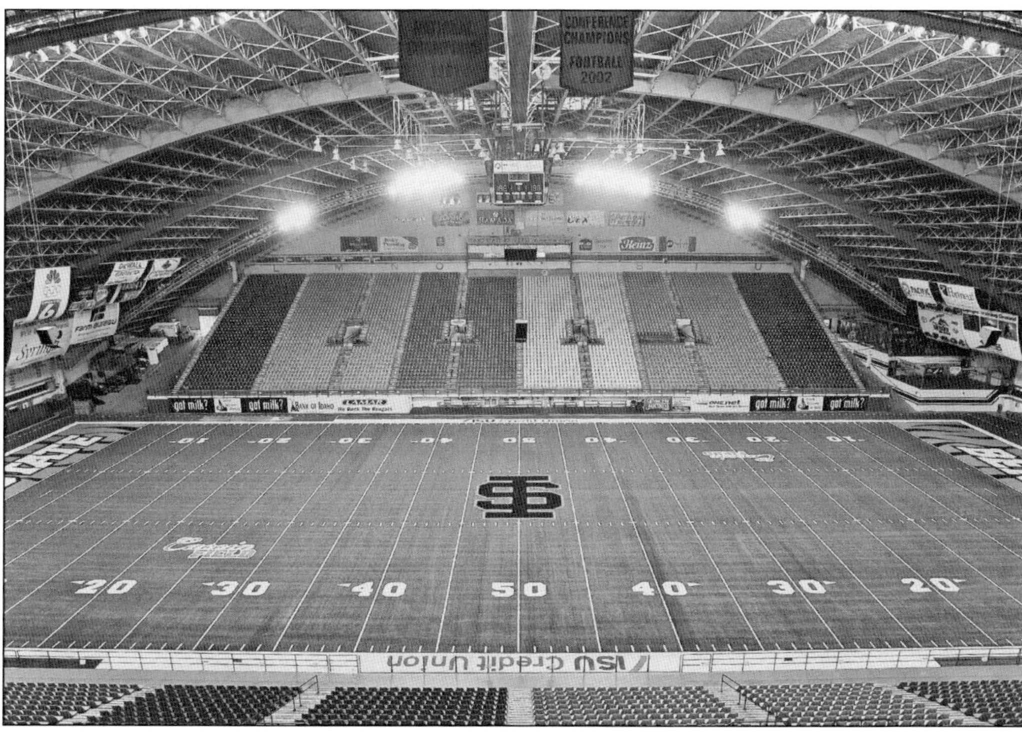

In the years following 1980, Idaho State University and its students have started new traditions and led ISU to success. Shown here is the interior of ASISU Holt Arena, the "students' building," where sporting events and other campus and community activities are held regularly. (Courtesy of Idaho State University.)

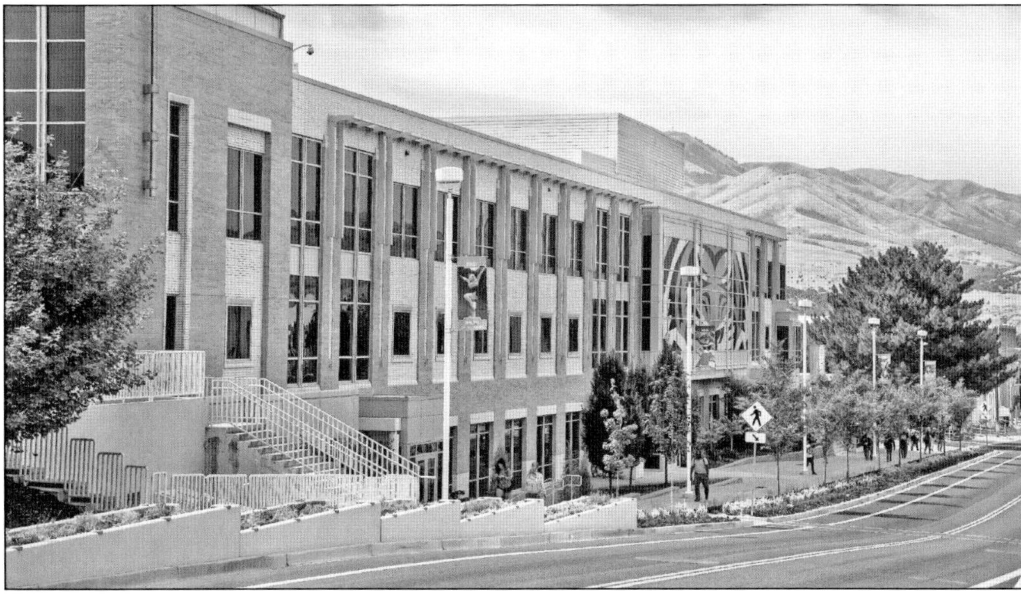

On April 9, 2001, Idaho governor Dirk Kempthorne signed a bill that provided funding for state capital projects after he visited the Idaho State University campus. On July 15, 2003, the governor himself attended the ground breaking ceremony for the Rendezvous Complex. Completed in 2007, the Rendezvous provides housing for 301 students and has classrooms with sizes ranging from 15 seats to the 250-seat lecture hall with a domed planetarium. Today, the Rendezvous Complex is a popular meeting place for students and faculty alike who can meet in the computer labs, the dining area, or the formal meeting rooms. There is always a steady flow of activity in this complex. (Courtesy of Idaho State University.)

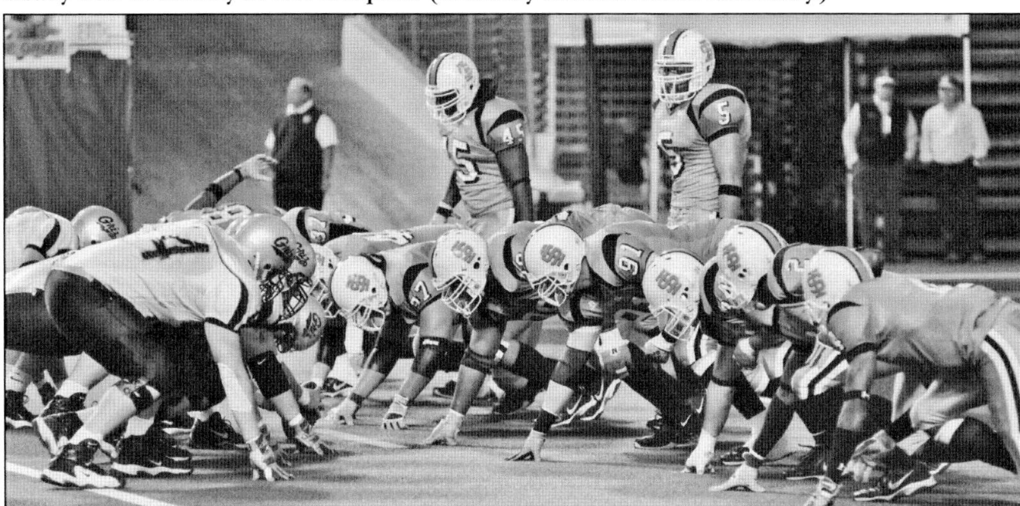

In the years since 1980, Idaho State University has continued to show its athletic prowess in basketball, soccer, cross-country, track and field, tennis, and more. In 2002, ISU won the Big Sky Conference championship for football. Players on the team credited their coach and their synergy as a team. Working together and helping each other grow led them to victory. Pictured here are members of the ISU football team in the Holt Arena facing off against longtime rivals from the University of Montana in 2009. (Courtesy of Idaho State University.)

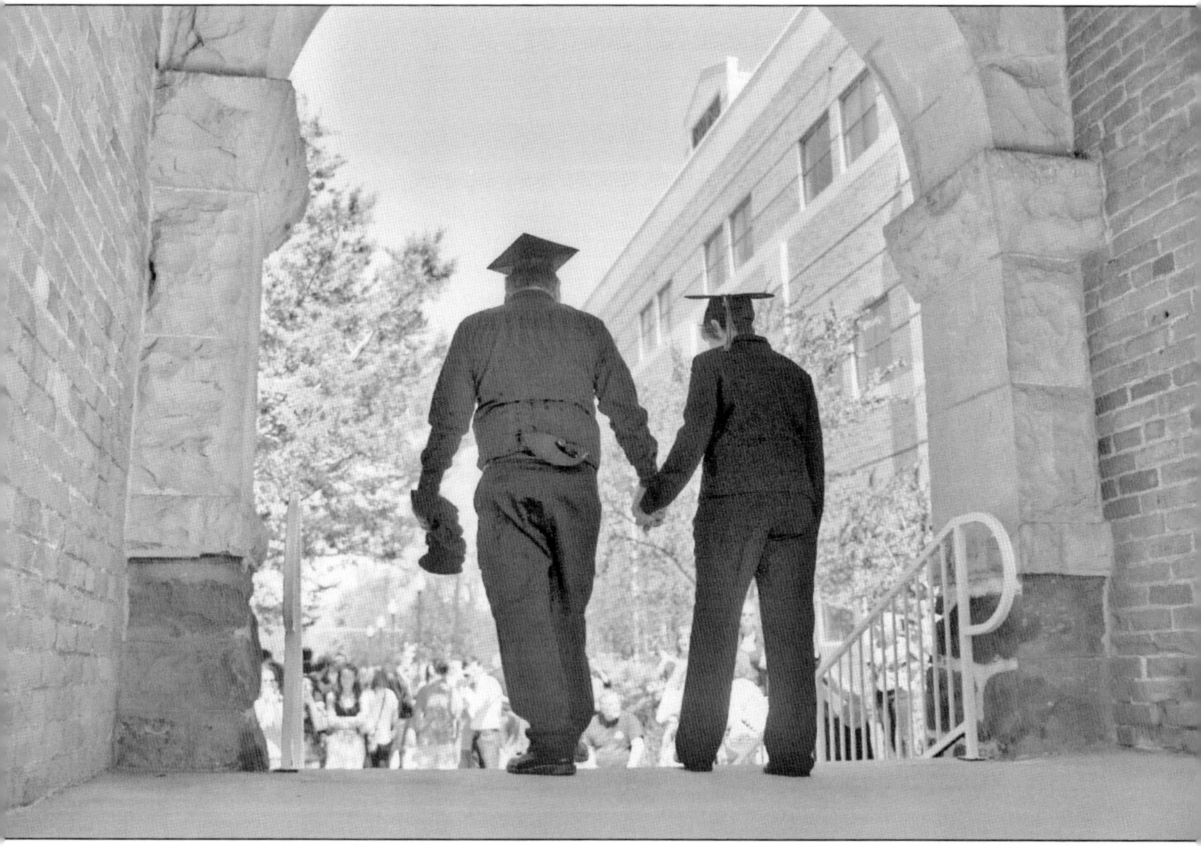

After Swanson Hall was demolished in 1973, it was decided that the main entrance of the very first building at Idaho State University was to be left standing. In 2000, alumni director Valerie Watkins started the March Through the Arch tradition. At the beginning of every fall semester, the incoming students participate in marching through the arch of the old Swanson Hall to be welcomed into the ISU family. During the spring semester, just before graduation, graduating seniors march back through the arch to commemorate their time at ISU. (Courtesy of Idaho State University.)

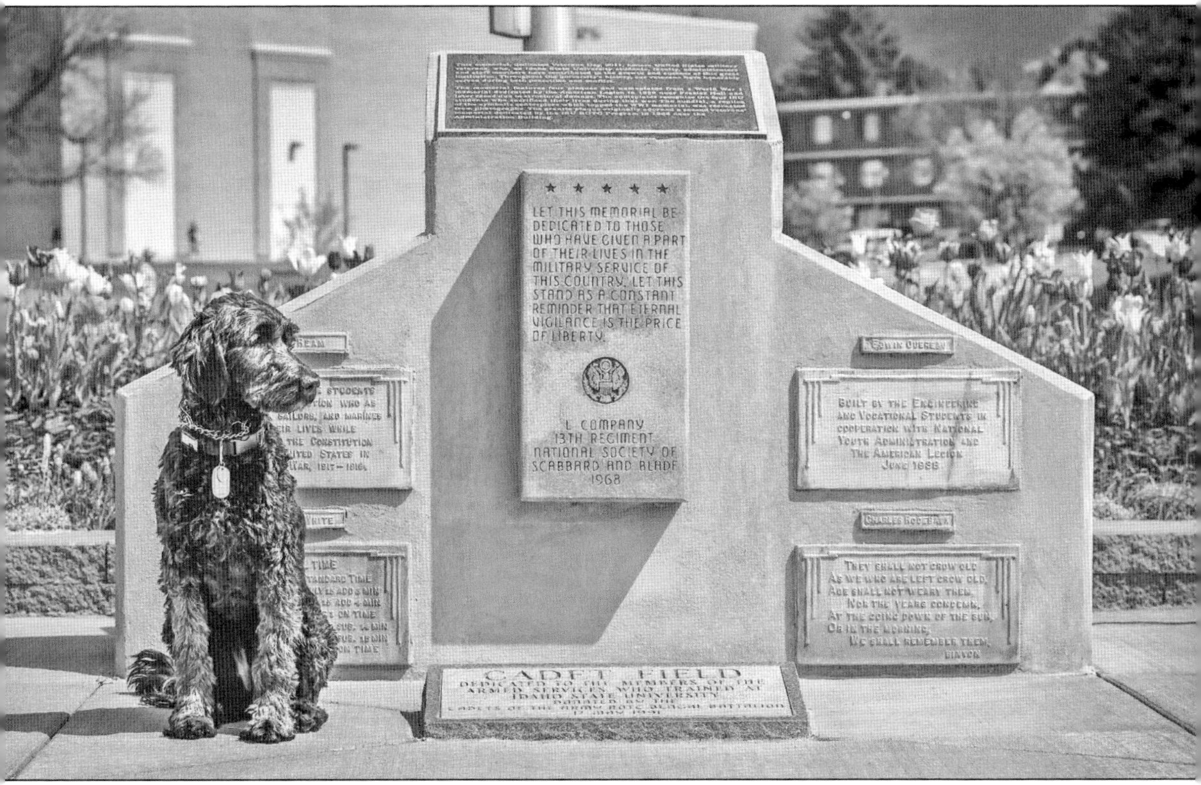

The military has long been an important part of Idaho State University's history. In keeping with that, ISU's Veteran Student Services Center helps veterans, current service members, and their dependents transition into university life at ISU. They provide a variety of student services, including academic advising, benefit assistance, and more. Hero, pictured here at the Cadet Field Memorial, is the Veteran Student Service emotional support dog. She is known around campus for providing stress relief not just to patrons of the Veteran Student Services center, but also to any student who meets her. (Courtesy of Idaho State University.)

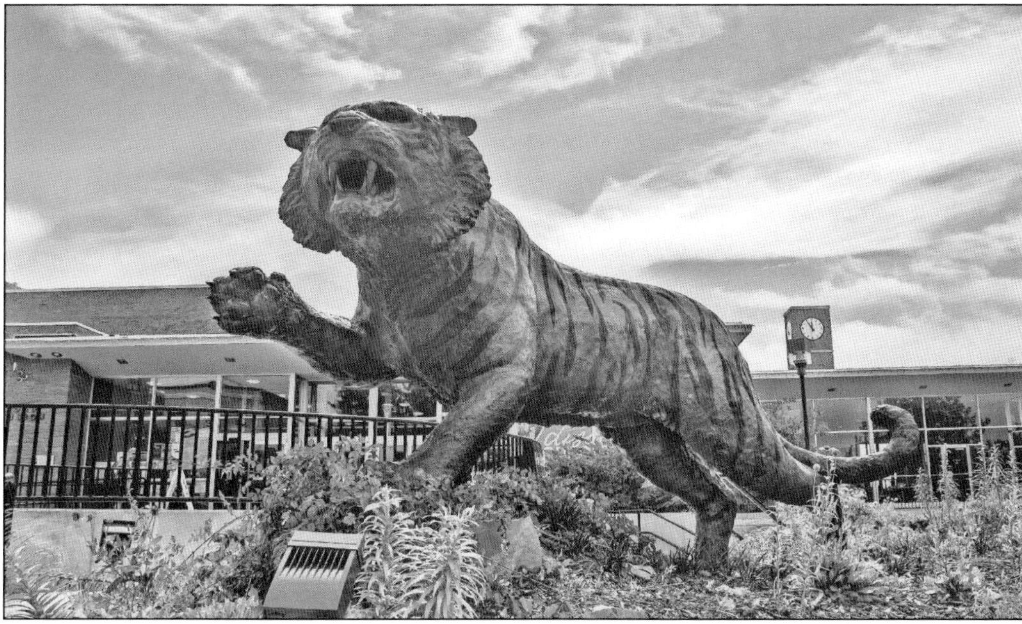

Fraternities and sororities were a big part of life for many years at Idaho State University. In the early 1950s, Phi Sigma Kappa (specifically, ISU athlete Chuck Koval, an art major) built a float for the homecoming parade that included a large Bengal tiger to represent the ISU mascot, Benny the Bengal. It became a regular part of events for the next several years and was eventually placed permanently outside Reed Gym. Due to upkeep issues, the tiger was removed from this spot in 2013. A new Bengal tiger statue now stands in front of the Earl R. Pond Student Union Building. This tiger was designed by local artist Malynda Cooper and was unveiled on October 24, 2012. It is now considered good luck to touch the paw of the Bengal. Pictured below is mascot Benny the Bengal raising spirits at a men's basketball game. (Both, courtesy of Idaho State University.)

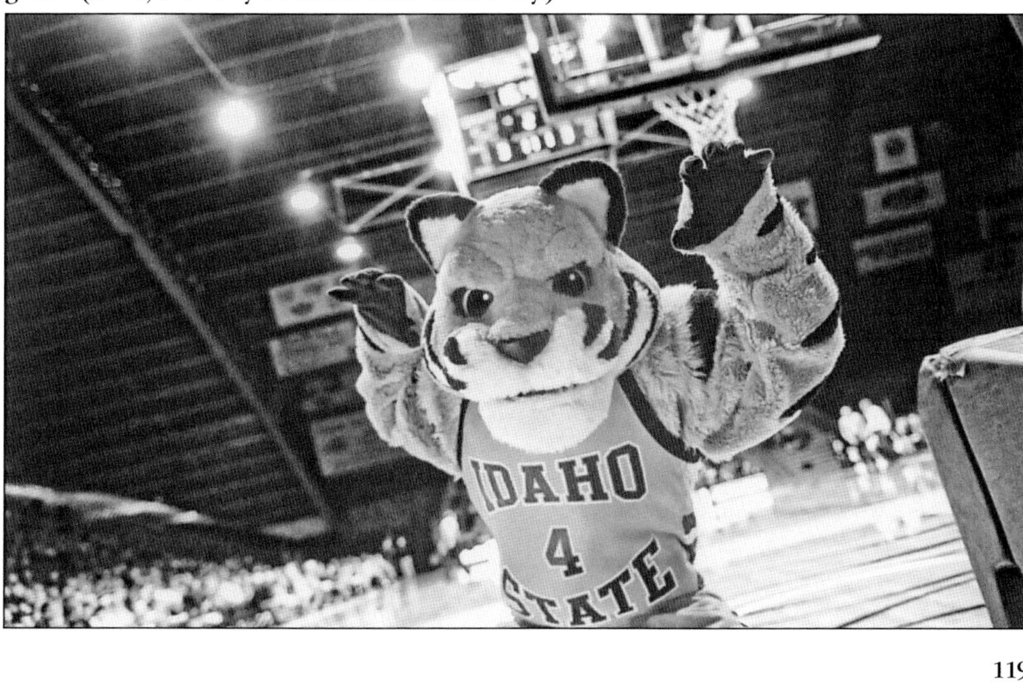

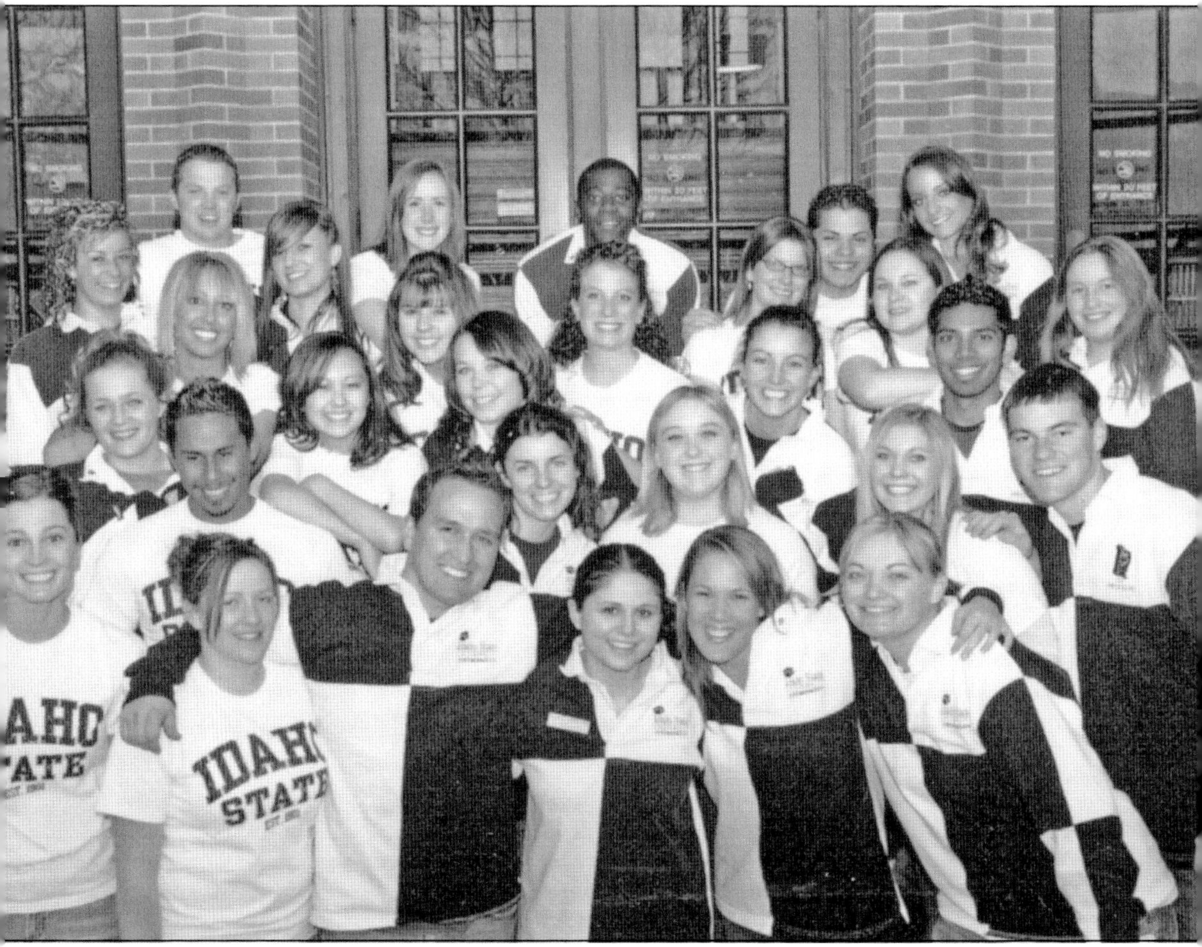

The ISU Ambassador program has persisted since 1980, now existing as a scholarship program in which a group of elite students provide information to prospective students and help with events on campus. These students attend a three-day camp designed to train and prepare them to work with future Bengals. The group is easily identifiable with their black-and-orange jackets leading groups of students around campus throughout the year. Pictured here is the 2006-2007 group of ambassadors—the uniforms may have changed, but the mission and spirit of the group has remained the same. (Courtesy of Mark Bolinger.)

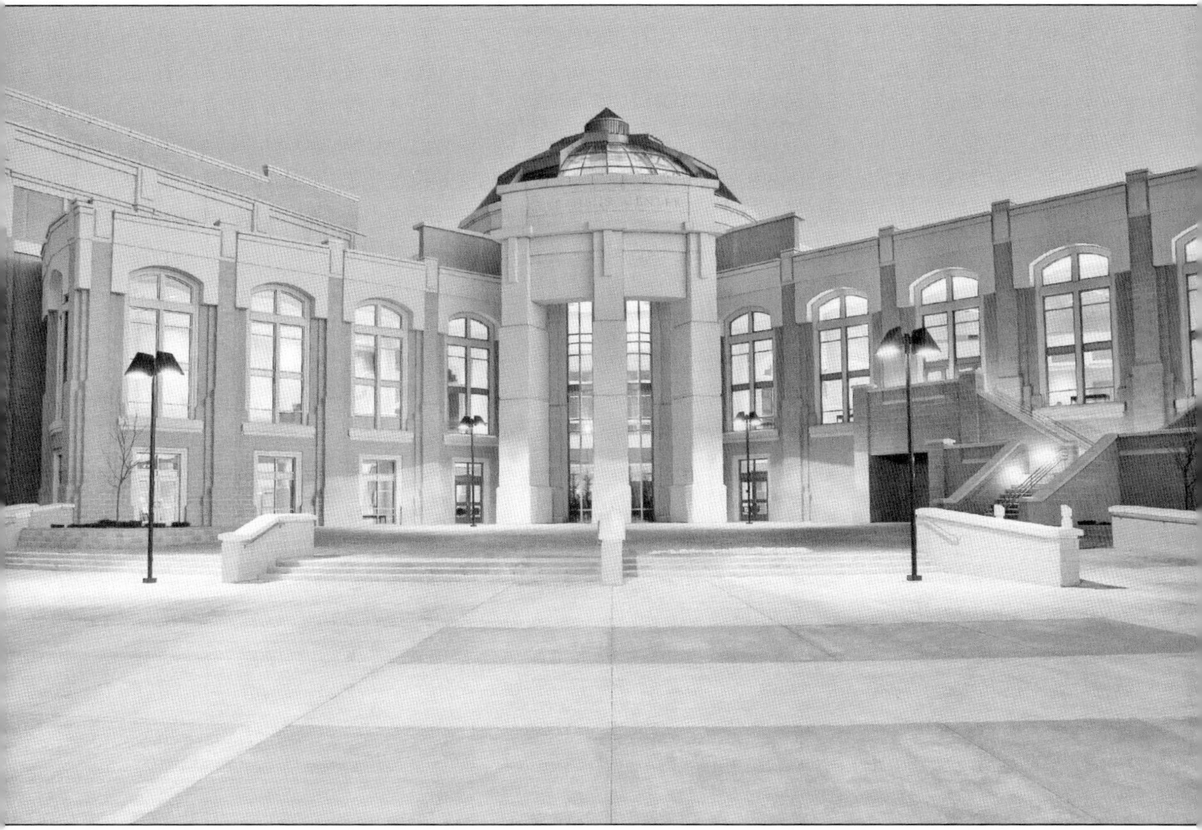

The Stephens Performing Arts Center (SPAC), located on the top of Bartz Hill on the Idaho State University campus, was funded by donations from hundreds of supporters. Thelma E. Stephens was a great supporter, providing $10 million to support the project. After completion of the SPAC, the center held its first performance, *Man of LaMancha*, in 2004. The SPAC is a facility like no other, and performers from around the world have appeared in the center. (Courtesy of Idaho State University.)

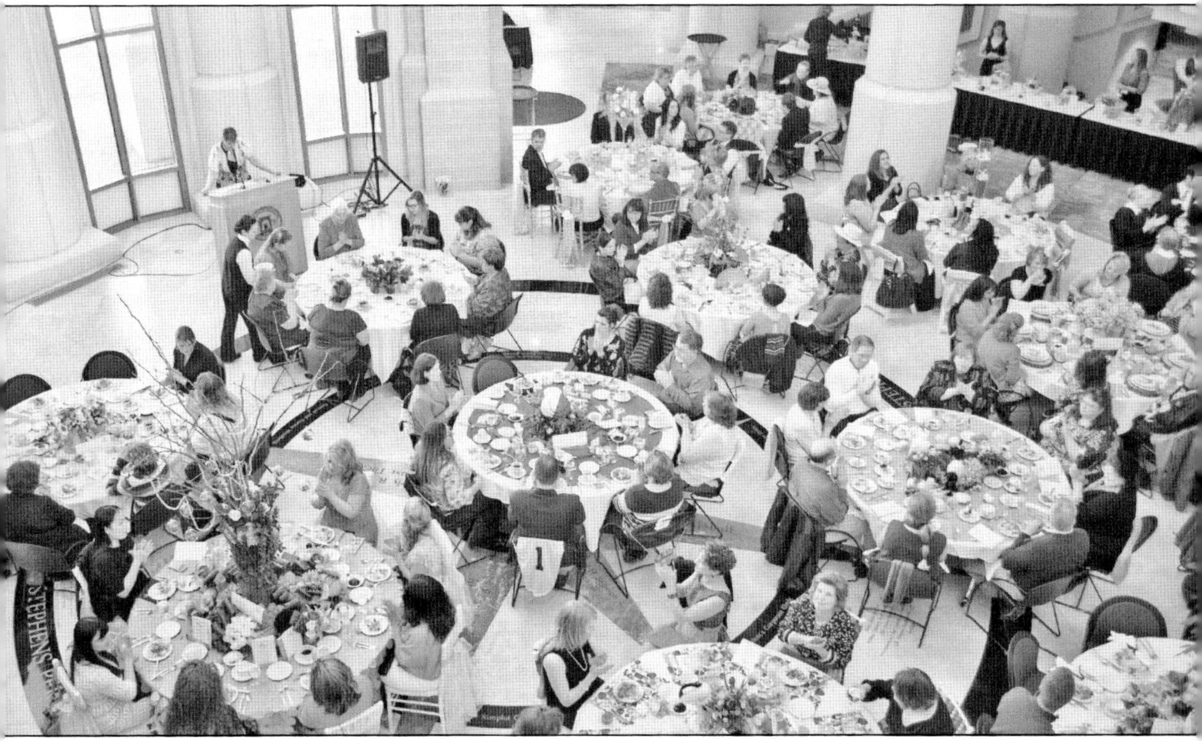

The University Honors Program (UHP), established in its current form in 2007 with a large expansion in 2014, offers a one-of-a-kind cohort experience to students. With an interdisciplinary program and small class sizes, students in the UHP are able to have the experience of a small liberal arts college while enjoying access to the resources of a large research university. Students in the UHP can earn an honors degree noted on their diploma—the only such designation in the state. Honors students perform research, publish articles, and serve as leaders in the community. Pictured here is the Opportuni-Tea, the annual fundraising event for UHP students. (Courtesy of Idaho State University.)

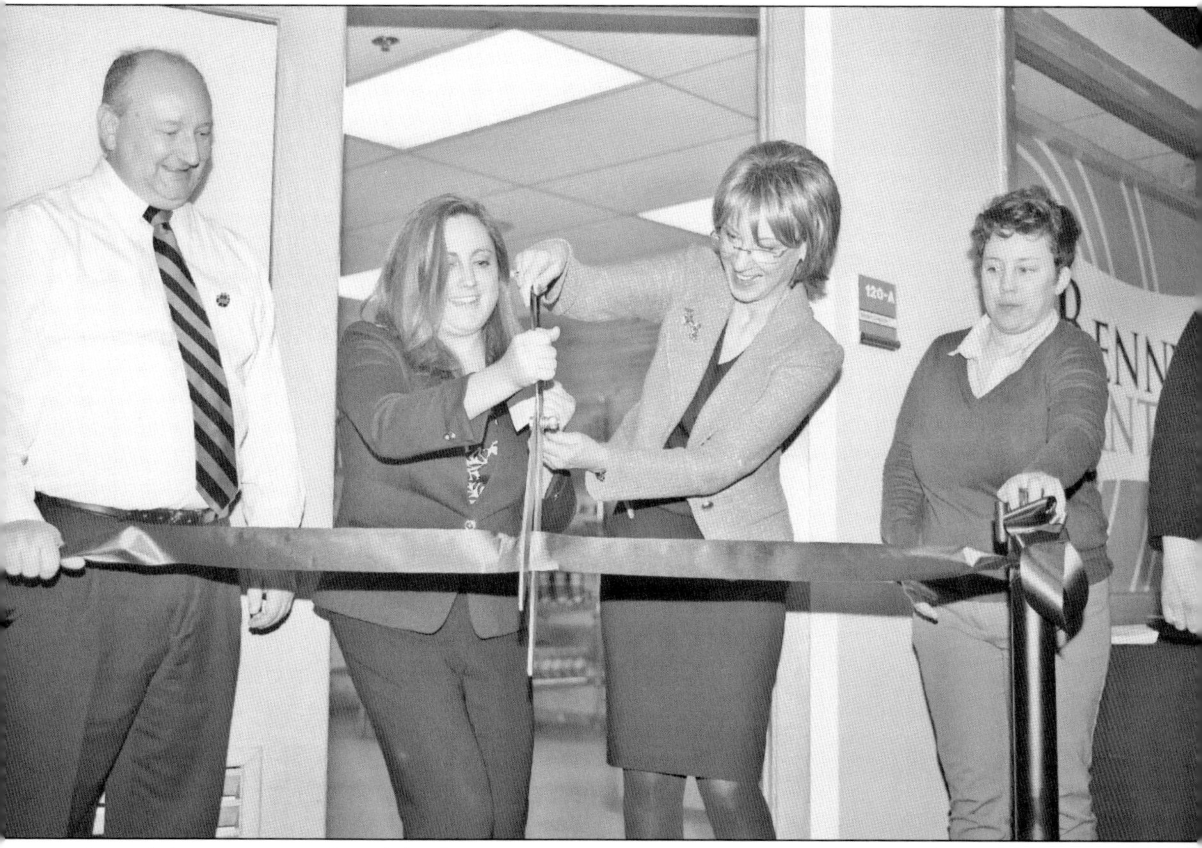

Benny's Pantry opened at Idaho State University on January 20, 2014, in an effort to alleviate food insecurity for the ISU student community. The pantry is staffed by ISU employees and student volunteers. Pictured here are Brooke Barber, director of the LEAD Center, and ISU first lady Dr. Laura Vailas at the ribbon cutting in 2014. (Courtesy of Idaho State University.)

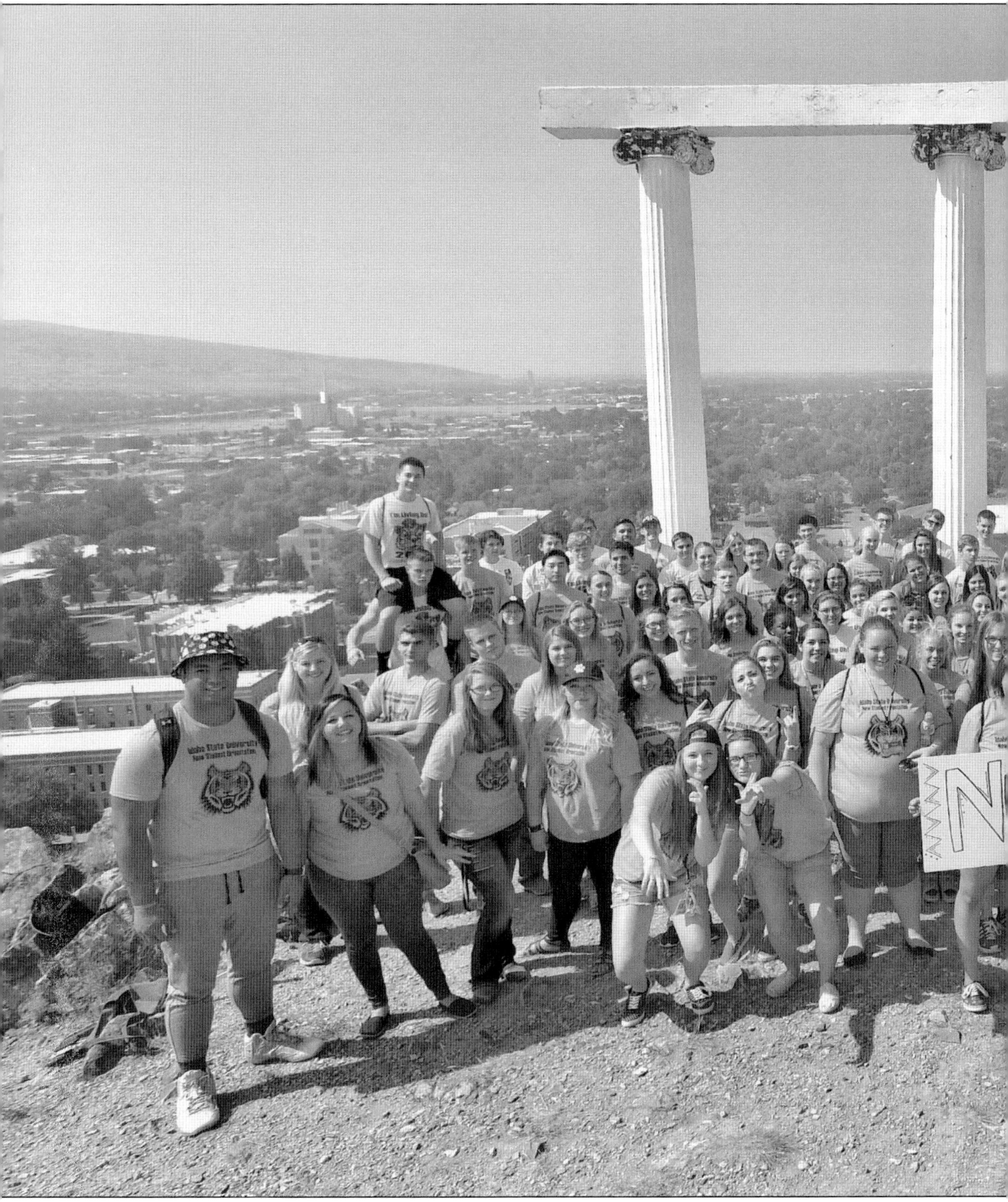

New Student Orientation (NSO) provides incoming freshmen and transfer students the opportunity to get to know the Idaho State University community, meet their peers, and become familiar with a variety of campus resources. During NSO, they meet with their major departments, participate in social activities, and learn more about campus

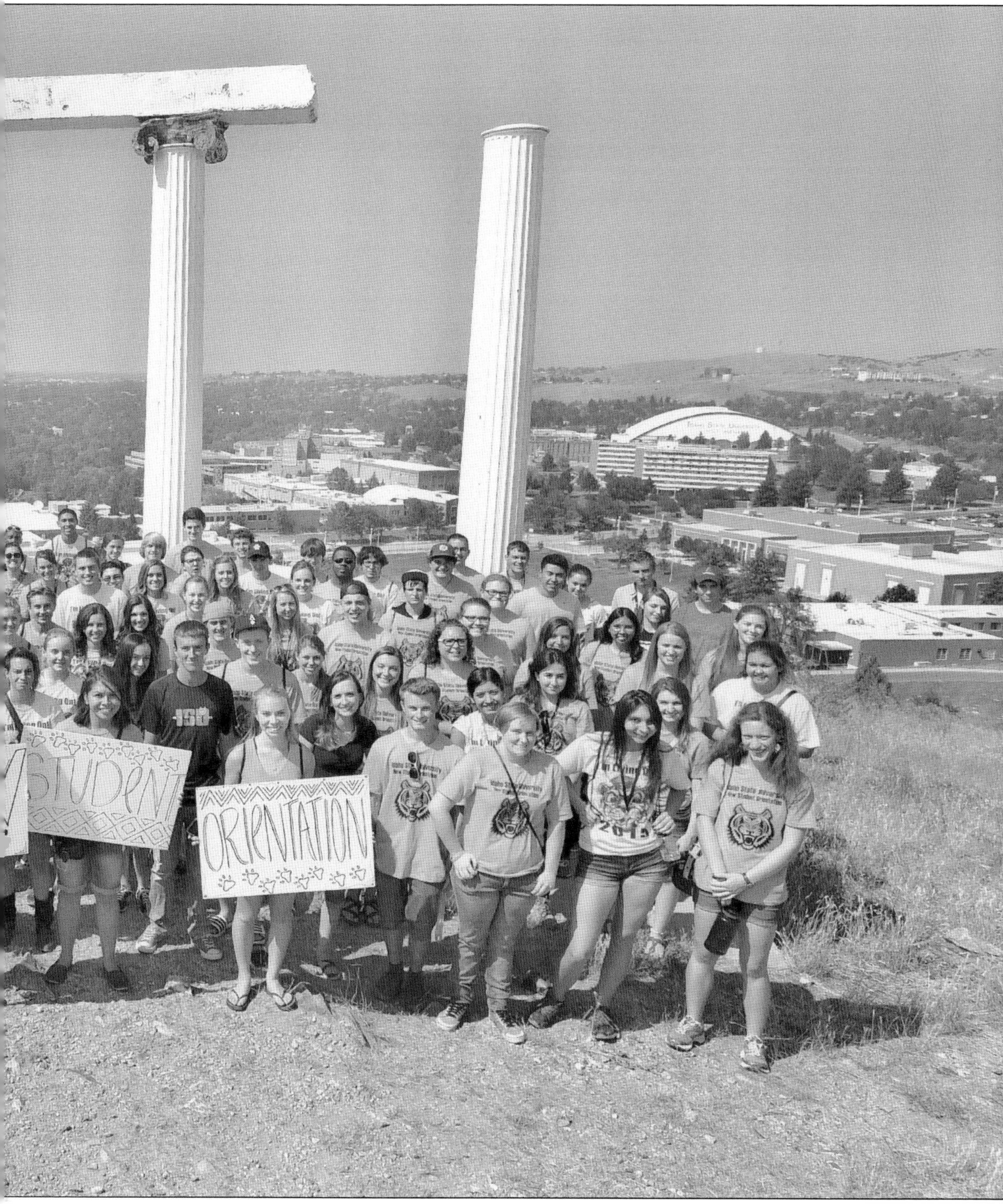

traditions. Over the past several years, NSO has grown to a multi-day event with all manner of activities designed to truly welcome new Bengals into the ISU family. Here, a group of incoming students poses in front of the iconic pillars on Red Hill. (Courtesy of Idaho State University.)

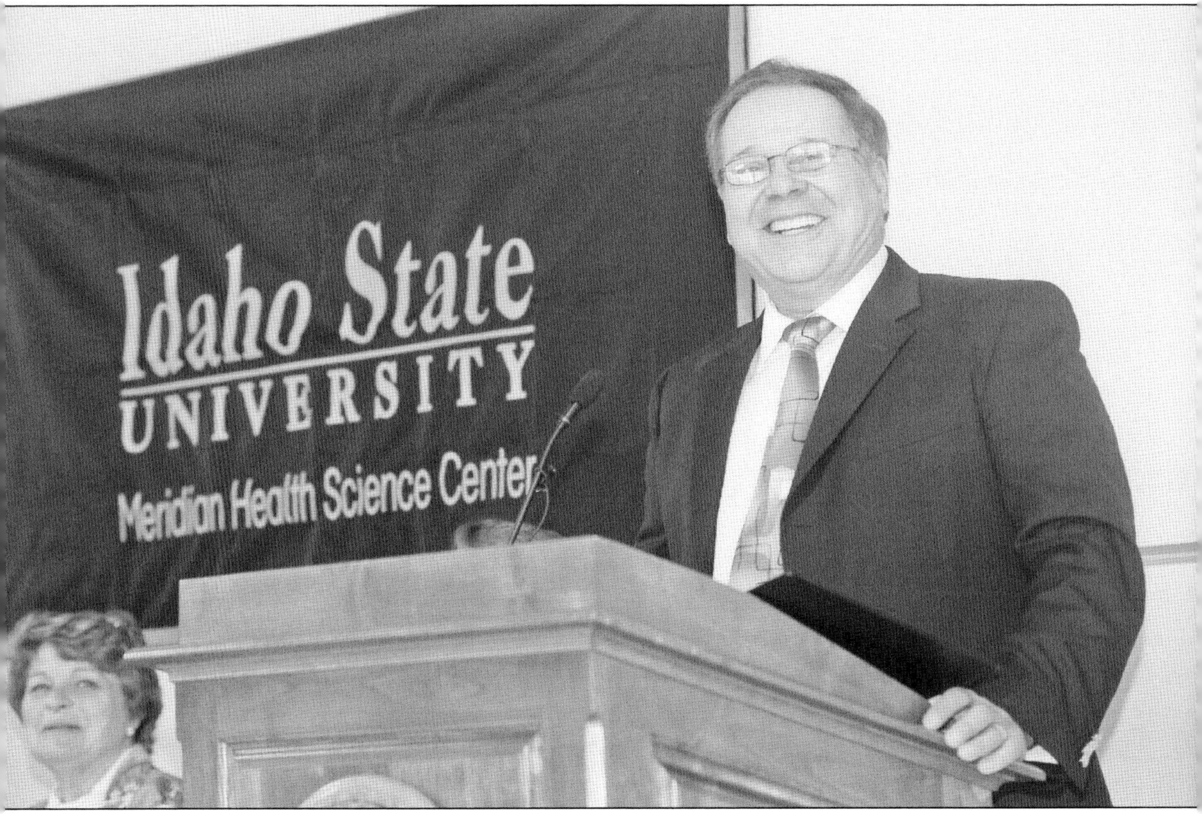

Idaho State University has the healthcare mission for the state of Idaho, and ISU is the leader in health-related programs statewide. Pictured here is Pres. Arthur Vailas speaking at the grand opening of the new L.S. and Aline W. Skaggs Treasure Valley Anatomy and Physiology Laboratories in 2014. After decades of pushing for a medical school in Idaho, in 2016, approval was granted by the Idaho State Board of Education for the Idaho College of Osteopathic Medicine located at the ISU Health Science Center in Meridian. Classes are anticipated to begin in the fall 2018 semester. (Courtesy of Idaho State University.)

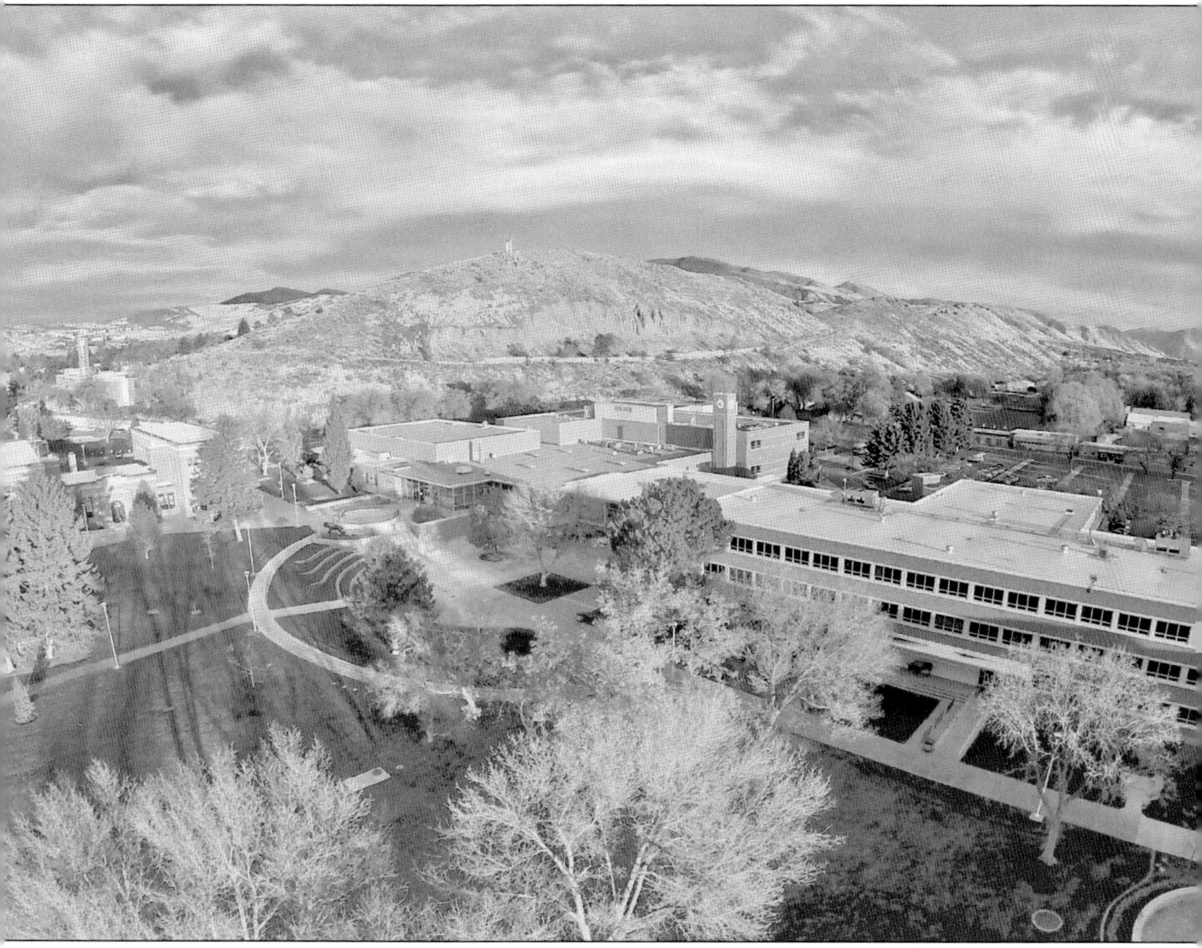

Shown here is an aerial view of present-day Idaho State University. Throughout its 115-year journey, ISU has experienced struggle, triumph, perseverance, and achievement. ISU could not be what it is today without the commitment and dedication of its students, staff, and faculty. This book celebrates those who have triumphed before us and will hopefully serve as a reminder that at ISU, anything is possible. (Courtesy of Ryan Byers.)

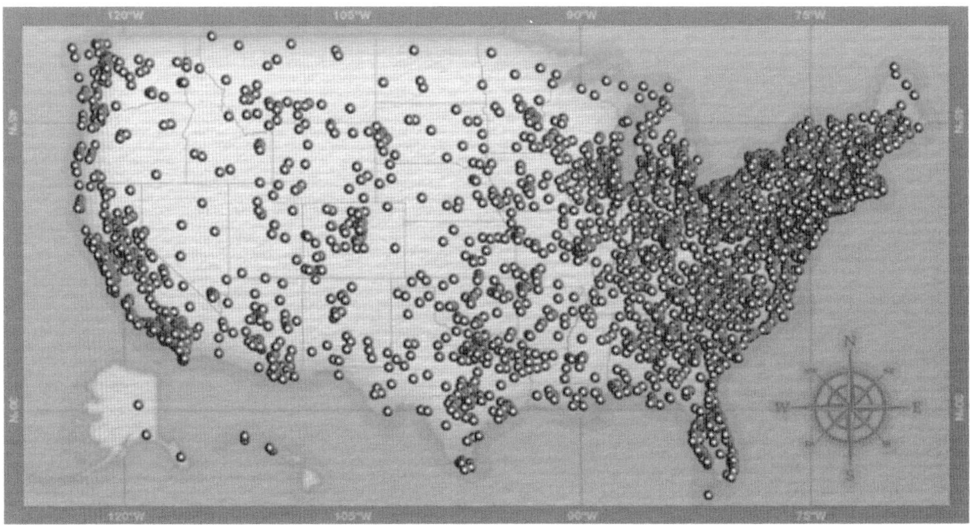